# Informal coalitions

## Mastering the hidden dynamics of organizational change

Chris Rodgers

First published 2007 by
PALGRAVE MACMILLAN
Houndmills, Basingstoke, Hampshire RG21 6XS and
175 Fifth Avenue, New York, N.Y. 10010
Companies and representatives throughout the world

PALGRAVE MACMILLAN is the global academic imprint of the Palgrave Macmillan division of St. Martin's Press, LLC and of Palgrave Macmillan Ltd. Macmillan® is a registered trademark in the United States, United Kingdom and other countries. Palgrave is a registered trademark in the European Union and other countries.

ISBN-13: 978–0–230–01991–1
ISBN-10: 0–230–01991–9

This book is printed on paper suitable for recycling and made from fully managed and sustained forest sources.

A catalogue record for this book is available from the British Library.

A catalog record for this book is available from the Library of Congress.

10   9   8   7   6   5   4   3   2   1
16   15   14   13   12   11   10   09   08   07

Printed in Great Britain by
Creative Print & Design (Wales), Ebbw Vale

*For Vera and Suzie*

# CONTENTS

## The challenge

The ability of leaders to deal effectively with organizational change is critical to business success. And yet, research shows that only around one in every three change programs deliver the sought-after improvements in business performance.[1] *Informal Coalitions* suggests that, by failing to address the underlying dynamics of organizations, many of these formal change programs inevitably contain the seeds of their own downfall. Against this background, the book offers a fresh perspective on organizational change, and takes thinking and practice beyond its conventional boundaries. In doing so, it aims to increase leaders' chances of achieving success, by exploring a new change-leadership agenda and introducing a number of practical tools to support it.

## Background

This book has its roots in my background as a practicing manager in UK industry, and as a management consultant to both public- and private-sector organizations. During that time, I have come to a view that something vital is missing from most of the models of organizational change and performance that are currently on offer. These are usually well articulated and, on the surface at least, offer some practical ways forward. However, they consistently fail to address crucially important aspects of the "real world" organizations that managers experience day to day. Almost invariably, the prescriptions put forward place most emphasis on changing the *formal* and *structured* elements of the organization – its processes, systems and structures – and on getting these "right" through rational analysis, project management techniques and detailed implementation programs. This approach is then carried over into the less tangible aspects of organizational change, such as the underlying cultural dynamics of the organization or the challenge of building commitment to the changes. These are also treated as separate work streams in a formal project plan. Other, ever-present features of organizational life – such as the impact of power and politics, the importance of informal processes and the implications of paradox – tend to be dealt with superficially or ignored altogether.

As someone who was originally trained as an engineer, I value rational analysis and project management disciplines; but only when these are used in their proper place. For the most part, organizations do not conform to the same rules as inanimate structures, systems and machines. Instead, they comprise networks of *people* interacting with each other. And people have a habit of not conforming to the mechanistic assumptions that still channel much of the conventional management thinking about organizational change and performance. When reflecting on my own, everyday experiences in organizations, I recognize that many of the most significant decisions and actions are the outcome of much messier processes than allowed for by the wholly rational school of change management. These precedent-setting shifts in thinking and behavior rarely arise from formal, rational analysis of "the facts" and step-by-step decision-making by people whose agendas are fully aligned. More often than not, they are the result of informal interactions, joint sensemaking and political accommodations made by people who are trying to make a difference in a complex, uncertain and ambiguous environment.

I was presented with the opportunity to explore these issues in more depth when I embarked on a part-time master's degree in organizational change in the late 1990s. My research focused, in particular, on three things that I felt were critical to the ways in which I experienced organizations on a day-to-day basis. First, I was interested in the impact that the everyday conversational life of the organization had on performance delivery and on development of the change agenda. This work helped to confirm and refine my roughly formed view that everyday conversations and informal interactions are central to the way that change happens in organizations. Secondly, I wanted to consider more fully the influence of shadow-side dynamics (such as informal organizational practices, and social and political processes) on behavior patterns and organizational outcomes. This proved to be another fruitful area of inquiry, which reinforced my emerging ideas about the leader's role in the change process. Thirdly, I was fascinated by the paradoxical nature of much of what takes place in organizations. In particular, I was interested in the inability of conventional, either–or thinking to deal with the challenges that this brings. Having set out to explore paradox, it was difficult to find *any* aspect of organizational dynamics that was not touched by it. Despite this, our ingrained patterns of perception, language and behavior ordinarily blind us to paradox's existence, impact and potential power. The above three factors – the centrality of conversation, the impact of shadow-side dynamics and the importance of embracing paradox – underpin much of what follows in this book.

Whilst studying for the degree, I left my long-standing career as an in-company manager to become an independent management consultant. The different perspectives that I have gained from this move have further strengthened my conviction that leaders and organizational specialists need to enlarge their perception of organizational dynamics beyond its formal, rational and structured conventions. *Informal Coalitions* aims to help managers and others to meet this challenge in two ways. First, it gives them an original framework through which they can *make sense of what's actually going on* in their organizations. This enables them to understand the leadership implications and potential issues that arise from their adoption of particular approaches to change. Beyond this, though, it explores in more depth the informal, hidden and messier aspects of change, which most conventional, so-called "common sense" approaches ignore. Armed with these insights and an intuitive feel for their own situation, managers will be better placed to understand how change happens in their organizations and to engage with it more effectively.

## Approach

*Informal Coalitions* brings informal talk and interactions, power and politics, and paradox out of the shadows and places them at the forefront of change-leadership practice. It aims to increase the chances of success, by setting out an alternative change-leadership agenda and introducing a number of frameworks to support it. Using straightforward language throughout, *Informal Coalitions* presents a provocative but compelling argument for change leaders and other practitioners to embrace this new agenda and master its challenges.

*Informal Coalitions* is aimed primarily at line managers in all types of organization. It will also enhance the understanding and practice of external consultants and internal specialists in change and organizational development, by expanding their view of organizational dynamics beyond its traditional limits. Many strategic HR practitioners will also find the book a useful stimulus to their thinking. It constructively challenges important aspects of current HR practice and offers alternative ways of engaging people to achieve organizational success. For line managers, OD specialists and HR strategists alike, it provides a number of practical tools through which they can more readily get to grips with the hidden, messy and informal side of organizational life. The book is applicable to managers in all sectors of the economy, both within the UK and internationally. Importantly too, it is relevant to managers in leadership positions throughout an organization, not simply those operating at Board level.

Successive chapters of the book aim to bridge the gap between the highly credible but often inaccessible research-based texts, and the superficially appealing but often overly simplistic and faddish books that appear to offer managers a ten-easy-steps solution to their most critical leadership task. Unlike many of the other books aimed at the practicing manager, *Informal Coalitions*:

- charts a range of explanations about how change happens in organizations, and the strategies that arise from these, rather than focusing on "the one best way;"
- recognizes and explores the critical role that conversation, power relationships and politics play in the overall process;
- discusses why and how these and other shadow-side dynamics of the organization have such a critical impact upon the processes and outcomes of change;
- highlights the paradoxical nature of organizations, and challenges managers to view this as a potential source of creative energy, rather than as a problem to be avoided or conflict to be resolved in an either–or, win–lose way;
- makes clear that managers are *not* objective observers and remote controllers of other people's actions – "sitting in the stands," so to speak – but that they are "on the pitch, playing;"
- explains why talk and action should be seen as team mates, not rivals, in the quest for improved organizational performance.

The book resists the temptation of offering readers the outwardly attractive, "quick fix" prescriptions that have contributed significantly to the high rate of failure reported above. At the same time, it avoids the use of the overly technical language and academic conventions that make many research-based texts unattractive to practicing managers. The focus of *Informal Coalitions* therefore differs significantly from the single-company success stories, best-practice guides and academic texts that currently inform management practice. Rather than offering managers a model of "heroic leadership," a series of prescriptions to follow or a detailed academic treatise, it sets out to help them and others make sense of organizational change *within the context of their own organizations*. In particular, it draws attention to the *a*-rational dynamics of change, which are often ignored in other texts. In doing so, it provides readers with a sounder basis on which to engage more successfully in the organizational changes – big and small – that they lead and participate in on a daily basis.

The apparent shift in emphasis from "taking action" to thinking and talking is an important one to address. Although the approach might seem to buck the trend toward more "hands on," action-oriented leadership, the shift is illusory. The *primary action tool* of all managers is *talk* – in the broadest sense of the word – whether this is used to interact with others, or as part of the inner dialogue that informs their own managerial judgment. This book will help them to use that tool more insightfully and effectively, to influence the content, dynamics and outcome of change within their organizations.

## Structure of the book

*Informal Coalitions* begins by developing a sensemaking framework, the Change Map, which captures the main views on how change happens in organizations (Chapter 1). This chapter also identifies the outcomes that might be expected in pursuing the various approaches, describes the generic leadership and facilitation roles relevant to each, and introduces four key aspects of organizational dynamics that are fundamental to the change process.

In Chapter 2, the focus shifts to the hidden, messy and informal dynamics that characterize day-to-day life in organizations. It is these dynamics that ultimately determine the effectiveness of organizational change and performance. Some of the insights and propositions put forward here don't sit comfortably with conventional views of leadership. In some cases, they run counter to them. Despite this, managers who have been exposed to them during various workshops and consultancy projects invariably recognize that these play a significant part in shaping their everyday experience of organizational life. What is more, they also acknowledge the power that these dynamics have to affect the nature, direction and ultimate outcomes of planned organizational changes. Interestingly, several managers have expressed their relief that many of their well-established but unacknowledged practices have been "legitimized" by the ideas expressed here.

Chapters 3–8 take the ideas introduced in Chapter 2 and explore the implications of these for leadership principles and practice. *Reframing Communication* (Chapter 3) argues that the focus of leadership communication needs to move beyond formal, structured message passing to one that emphasizes relationship building and sensemaking through informal conversations and everyday interactions. Chapter 4, *Thinking Culturally*, explores the role-modeling implications of viewing organizational "culture" as the *active process* of shared sensemaking, rather than as a static "thing," that can be designed, built and communicated to others by management. In Chapter 5, *Acting Politically*, the critical importance of power and political processes in effecting organizational change and transforming performance is addressed head-on. In particular, this chapter explains how managers can act politically with integrity, and in organizationally enhancing ways. Chapter 6, *Building Coalitions*, adds to this, by identifying and exploring the key task of building informal coalitions of support for new ideas and specific change interventions. In doing so, it addresses the psychological and emotional impact of change on people, as well as dealing with its intellectual and physical dimensions. Chapter 7, *Embracing Paradox*, discusses ways of dealing with the inherently paradoxical nature of organizations, both strategically and as part of day-to-day organizational practice. To complete this distinctive change-leadership agenda, Chapter 8, looks at the part that organizational vision has to play in what is essentially an "inside–out" approach to organizational change and performance. *Providing Vision* therefore seeks to shift managers' attention away from developing *a Vision* (with a capital "V") and communicating it *to the organization*. It argues instead that they need to concentrate on providing vision through their everyday conversations and interactions with staff. In contrast to the conventional, step-wise approaches to change, "providing vision" is also included as one element of the ongoing change-leadership agenda rather than as the first step in a regimented change process. Finally, a short *Postscript* briefly serves to underline the point that this new change-leadership agenda is not about leaders doing *more* things. It is about them doing things *differently*.

The opening two chapters of the book introduce the nature and philosophy of informal coalitions, to anchor the change-leadership agenda in a sound understanding of its underlying principles. However, if preferred, Chapters 3–8 can be read independently and in any order. These offer new, thought-provoking perspectives and practical tools on a range of important issues relating to organizational change, including leadership communication, organizational culture, political action, commitment building, organizational paradox and "the vision thing."

## Walking case studies

In introducing the notion of informal coalitions to managers, it has been interesting to see how readily they have connected with the idea and its implications for their leadership practice. Leaders at all levels – from Board members to first-line supervisors – never fail to "get it." Some people initially feel uncomfortable with the challenges that the dynamics of informal coalitions make to their established views on what constitutes "good leadership," and to the rational assumptions on which these are based. Nevertheless, they all accept that these dynamics will happen anyway – with or without their active involvement in them as leaders. They know this to be the case not least because, when they are not wearing their formal leadership "hats," they take part in informal coalitional activity themselves. In this sense, they are all "walking case studies" of informal coalitions in action. Readers can therefore gain the most from this book if they similarly reflect on their own experiences of organizational life, when interacting with the ideas contained in it.

In the end, the only meaningful choice that leaders have is whether or not to engage with informal coalitions in an informed and deliberate way. For those that choose to do so, the following pages offer new insights and practical ways of addressing these powerful influencers of organizational change and performance.

## Thanks

As suggested above, *Informal Coalitions* is the product of many years spent in and around the world of organizations. During that time, I have had the privilege of working alongside a multitude of people whose words and actions have enriched my understanding of how organizations work *in practice*. All of those interactions have, in some way or other, influenced the ideas and perspectives that are reflected in this book. I'm therefore grateful to all past colleagues, and to current and past clients, for helping me to make better sense of the dynamics of organizational change than I might otherwise have done.

There are, though, a few people whose contributions over the years deserve particular mention. First, looking back on the early days of my career in the mid-1970s, I should like to thank John Reid for providing me with the opportunity to make my initial forays into management and sparking my interest in leadership and change. He could have stopped all of this!

Next, I owe a special debt to David Bramley and Guy Eccles who have provided unstinting support and enthusiasm for the ideas and practices expressed in *Informal Coalitions*, first as colleagues and latterly as clients. They have each been the source of much needed encouragement, at times when it didn't look as though I would ever finish the book!

The two years of part-time study for my MSc undoubtedly reinforced some of my developing views about how change happens, as well as shifting my perspective significantly on others. The conversations that I had with fellow participants, presenters and tutors during that period were immensely helpful. The bulk of those conversations were held with other members of my learning set who provided support – and challenge – as I began to formulate my views on organizational dynamics that have since found their way into this book. My thanks go to Andy Smith, Ella Yeshin, Mike McKeon, John Sidnell and Nic Brown.

Over the latter months of the book's "writing," Dominic Mahony generously took time out from his busy schedule to offer his comments on the developing text – as it emerged somewhat haphazardly from my laptop and in random chapter order. Our ensuing conversations were invaluable in helping me to finalize the structure of the book and decide how best to put forward the concepts and practical tools contained in it.

Despite the help and encouragement of the many people referred to above, a book is not a book unless someone is willing to publish it. For that, I am particularly indebted to Palgrave Macmillan's Publishing Director Stephen Rutt, who showed great enthusiasm for the project from the outset. Assistant Editor Alexandra Dawe also provided invaluable guidance and support along the route from contract negotiation to publication. I thank her and the rest of the team at Palgrave and Integra for the excellent work they have done in getting *Informal Coalitions* onto the bookshelves.

Chris Rodgers
Bibury, Gloucestershire
October 2006

# ACKNOWLEDGMENTS

The author and publishers gratefully acknowledge the permission granted by copyright holders to reproduce the various extracts included within the text. Source publications are fully referenced in the Bibliography. In addition, specific acknowledgments are made in relation to excerpts from the following.

"The Exploits of the Incomparable Mulla Nasrudin" by Idries Shah, on page 1, reproduced by permission of Octagon Press Ltd, London.

"Strategies for Cultural Change" by Paul Bate, on page 13, reprinted by permission of Elsevier.

"Beautiful Boy (Darling Boy)" by John Lennon, on page 36, © 1980 Lenono Music. Used by permission. All rights reserved.

"Cultures in Organisations" by Joanne Martin, on page 39, reprinted by permission of Oxford University Press Inc.

"Strategic Management and Organisational Dynamics, 2 Ed." by Ralph Stacey, on page 42, reprinted by permission of Pearson Education Ltd.

"Mind-Set Management" by Samuel Culbert, on pages 43 and 114, reprinted by permission of Oxford University Press Inc.

"Lateral Thinking" by Edward de Bono, on pages 45 and 262, © MICA Management Resources (UK) Inc. 1970. Reprinted by permission. All rights reserved. No photocopying or reproducing permitted.

"Strategic Management and Organisational Dynamics, 3 Ed." by Ralph Stacey, on pages 48 and 74, reprinted by permission of Pearson Education Ltd.

"Fuzzy Management" by Keith Grint, on page 51, reprinted by permission of Oxford University Press.

"Technology, Management and Society" by Peter Drucker, on page 62, reproduced from Management Today magazine by permission of the copyright owner, Haymarket Business Publication Ltd.

"Strategic Management and Organisational Dynamics, 4 Ed." by Ralph Stacey, on pages 82 and 195, reprinted by permission of Pearson Education Ltd.

"Organization Theory" by Jo Hatch, on page 103, reprinted by permission of Oxford University Press.

"Confronting Company Politics" by Barbara Stone, on page 114, reprinted by permission of Palgrave Macmillan.

"Mintzberg on Management" by Henry Mintzberg, on pages 115 and 226, originally published in the "Structuring of Organization" (1979) and "Power In and Around Organizations" (1983), reprinted by permission of Pearson Education.

"Understanding Organizations 4 Ed." by Charles Handy, on page 135, reprinted by permission of Penguin Books Ltd.

"On Becoming a Leader" © by Warren Bennis, on page 198, reprinted by permission of William Morris Agency Inc. on behalf of the Author.

"Paradoxical Thinking" © by Jerry Fletcher and Kelle Olwyler, on page 219, reprinted by permission of Berrett-Koehler Publishers, Inc. San Francisco, CA. All rights reserved.

"The David Solution" by Valerie Stewart, on page 231, reprinted by permission of Ashgate Publishing Ltd.

"Your Signature Path" © by Geoffrey Bellman, on page 232, reprinted by permission of Berrett-Koehler Publishers, Inc. San Francisco, CA. All rights reserved.

"The Art of Framing" by Gail Fairhurst and Robert Sarr, on page 235, reprinted by permission of John Wiley and Sons Inc.

"Ethical Ambition" by Derrick Bell, on page 255, reprinted by permission of Bloomsbury Publishing Ltd.

# CHAPTER 1

# Mapping the territory

Someone saw Nasrudin searching for something on the ground.
"What have you lost, Mulla?" he asked.
"My key," said the Mulla.
So they both went down on their knees and looked for it.
After a time, the other man asked: "Where exactly did you drop it?"
"In my own house."
"Then why are you looking here?"
"There is more light here than in my own house."

– Idries Shah

## Introduction

Over the past 40 years or more, much light has been cast on the nature and management of organizational change. Several useful concepts, tools and techniques have been introduced during this period, which have helped managers to lead and facilitate change more effectively. At the same time, research consistently suggests that upwards of two-thirds of all structured change efforts fail to deliver what they set out to achieve. As further evidence of this high failure rate, I constantly meet and work with managers who are exasperated by the inability of quick-fix prescriptions and seductively packaged change methodologies to make a real and lasting impact on the challenges they face. And yet, confronted by ever-increasing demands for performance improvement, they continue to search in these same areas for the keys to organizational change and performance improvement.

Given the pressures that today's managers face to deliver short-term results, it is understandable that most prefer to look for answers where there appears to be "more light." Despite their regular disappointments, there is some comfort in continuing to look "out there" – at the familiar, well-documented areas of formal structures, systems and processes, and the *n*-step change methodologies that promise to transform these painlessly into high-performing organizations. Unfortunately, as research evidence and our own experience shows, an exclusive focus on these well-lit areas of the organizational landscape is unlikely to deliver the benefits that managers are looking for – however commonsensical this approach might appear to be.

Against this background, Chapter 1 progressively introduces the elements of a sensemaking framework – the Change Map – that blends together the formal, rational and conventional approaches to change with insights into its hidden, messier and more informal dynamics. In doing so, it offers a means through which leaders and change specialists can make sense of change as it unfolds in their organizations and help to shape its outcome. Many managers have found that this approach has enabled them to get to grips with the underlying dynamics of change and to find pathways through the challenges that these bring. Whilst recognizing the value that many of the established approaches can offer, the Change Map invites managers to look for the "lost keys" of change leadership and organizational performance within the *in*formal, *un*structured and *a*-rational dynamics of their organizations, rather than being seduced by the superficially attractive, but ultimately misleading, "light" provided by many of the keep-it-simple fads and fashions. In particular, it calls upon them to look "inside their own houses" – at the ways in which they, as leaders and organizational specialists, understand and engage with the everyday dynamics of change and performance.

## Rational views on how change happens

Figure 1.1 identifies three basic views on how change happens in organizations, which I call *management edict*, *education and training* and *joint problem solving*. These represent the conventional perspective on how change is achieved in organizations.

*Management edict* sees change as being imposed by management to achieve decisiveness and control. The focus of *education and training* is on explaining the required changes and modifying the behaviors of staff to achieve alignment between people's values and ensure consistent behaviors across the organization. The third view, *joint problem solving*, argues in favor of involving a wide constituency of people to achieve consensus in decision-making and to create a sense of ownership for

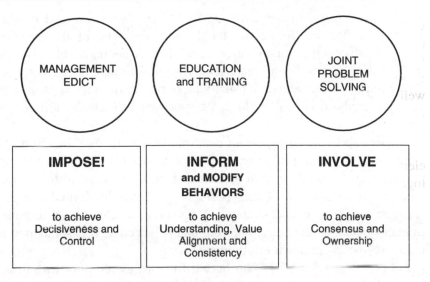

**Figure 1.1** Rational approaches to change

the changes. Each of these is described in turn below, before their interrelationships are discussed and the implications of these for understanding the dynamics of change explored more fully.

## Management edict

This represents the classic, top–down view of organizational change. It is often presented as the primary route to organization-wide transformation; and, for many managers, it is what change leadership is all about. As its title suggests, it is imposed on the organization by management. Bate (1994) calls this general approach "aggressive." It presents an attractive view of the world to many managers because it takes for granted management's ability to exert its will on the organization. Most high-profile stories of organizational change start from this perspective. Its main appeal is that it can achieve some highly visible "quick wins," in terms of shifts in strategic direction, physical re-structuring, systems redesign, organizational re-sizing and so on. It can also appear radical and innovative; which matches the expectations of some key stakeholders (such as City analysts) for a "bold and decisive" style of leadership. It is usually built around a simple message and therefore reduces the feeling of ambiguity – for managers and staff alike – by setting out a clear vision of the way ahead and appearing to offer a certainty of outcome. On the downside, it can lead to high levels of resistance from those on the receiving end of the imposed changes. Managers, though, often view this as an inevitable price to pay for the felt need – and management right – to take decisive action. Being imposed from above, it usually lacks buy-in from the organization at large, tends to be inflexible in its approach and can be difficult to sustain.

Leadership in the *management edict* mode sometimes flows from the personality of a high profile leader, who imposes his/her vision through new strategies, structures and systems. More often, it is vested in one who uses the legitimacy of their position to enforce the desired changes. Resistance is seen as undesirable and, by some, an illegitimate response to management's intentions; and from this perspective, it is something to be overcome, worn down or eliminated.

*Management edict* will often be put forward as the *only* way to act where there is a perceived crisis to be addressed. In such circumstances, it is argued that there is little time for structured participation or an incremental approach to change. Similarly, even where a more participative approach is planned, it is often preceded by a "dose" of management edict, to overcome any initial inertia. In these cases, the "burning platform"[1] metaphor is frequently invoked to motivate change. According to Conner (1993: 93), "The urgency of burning-platform situations motivates us to sustain major change. Two types of situation can generate this urgency: the high price of unresolved problems or the high cost of missed opportunities."

The principles and practices embodied in the *management edict* view of change leadership can clearly make a significant impact on organizational performance and capability, as evidenced by the large number of company biographies that line management bookshelves. In challenging the status quo, the approach can create energy and revitalize a flagging business. It can also help to reinvigorate individuals who are lacking in challenge and motivation. But it can easily degenerate into confrontation and destructive conflict, if not handled well or if used as the sole tool for managing change. Crucially, it is also built on the false premise that the manager is an objective observer and controller of the change process. But more of that later. *Management edict's* dominant position in conventional management thinking and practice inevitably means that any consideration of organizational change must take account of the impact of this approach on the overall dynamics of the process.

The core assumptions of the *management edict* approach can be summarized as follows:

- Change occurs in episodes that are initiated by formal management action.
- Effective change requires decisive and integrated organization-wide programs.
- Management has the right *and ability* to impose change.
- Successful change depends on rational, emotion-free analysis and a design-and-build approach.
- The whole organization is improved by improving its parts.
- Outcomes can be predicted and controlled.

The pros and cons of the approach are summarized in Table 1.1.

**Table 1.1** Management edict – strengths and weaknesses

| Strengths | Weaknesses |
|---|---|
| ✓ Can achieve some quick wins | ✗ Generates high levels of resistance |
| ✓ Appears radical | ✗ Lacks "ownership" by those affected |
| ✓ Can be idealistic and seemingly offers a clear vision of management's intent | ✗ Often rigid and inflexible |
| ✓ Appears to offer certainty of outcome | ✗ Difficult to sustain |
| ✓ Can create energy to revitalize a flagging business | ✗ Usually underestimates the complexity of change dynamics |
| ✓ Can reinvigorate individuals | ✗ Underplays social and psychological dimensions |
| ✓ Provides focus in a *genuine* crisis | ✗ Can easily degenerate into confrontation and destructive conflict |
| ✓ Can help to overcome initial inertia | ✗ Assumes management knows best |
| ✓ Matches expectations of some key stakeholders (such as City analysts) for "bold and decisive leadership" | ✗ Places immediate results ahead of capability development |

## Education and training

For those who view *education and training* (including *formal* communication strategies and practices) as the primary means of achieving organizational change, their aim is to immerse staff fully in a core message, and/or to instil a widely shared and aligned set of values, attitudes and behaviors. Bate's (1994) use of the term "indoctrinaire" to describe this broad approach reflects the emphasis that it places, overtly or by implication, on themes such as compliance, consistency and control. Disney and McDonalds provide high profile examples of this strategy in action. But it also features prominently in most organizations' "toolkits," under the guise of such things as internal communications programs ("to get the message across"), competency frameworks (to develop the "right" behaviors) and disembodied cultural change programs. I have used the term "disembodied" to reflect the tendency of most conventional change strategies to treat culture as a separate building block of performance, which can be attended to independently of the structural aspects of the change process and everyday management action.

*Education and training* is a less pejorative way of describing this mode of thinking about change than Bate's indoctrinaire label. In essence, it sees change as being achieved through such things as developing shared understanding, modifying behaviors, redefining and supporting changed roles and responsibilities, and so on. It also points to the importance of continuously renewing organizational capability, although this lesson is not always learnt. From an *education and training* viewpoint, rational analysis, logical argument and behavioral conformity tend to be seen as the foundation stones of organizational leadership and performance; with adherence to a formally defined best way of doing things as the hallmark of success.

Education- and training-based change strategies and practices can provide structured learning opportunities, through which new knowledge, attitudes and behaviors can be developed. They can also reinforce the changes introduced through *management edict*; enabling these to penetrate more deeply into the organization than would otherwise be possible. In the extreme, though, no deviants are allowed; and this can lead to rigidity or "cloning," with a consequential lack of creativity and experimentation. It can also be difficult to sustain the initial momentum, as the intensity of structured communications and change-related training gives way to the messier and amorphous realities of business as usual.

As with *management edict*, the *education and training* approach is usually applied in ways that perpetuate the myth of management control; and it often adopts the modern-day equivalent of scientific-management assumptions about organizational dynamics. The term "McDonaldization" has even entered the language, to describe the extreme expression of this view of the dynamics of change and organizational performance.

The core assumptions of the *education and training* approach can be summarized as follows:

- Organizations work best by achieving consistency and predictability:
  - ensuring compliance with management's intentions
  - developing and adopting a set of shared values and behaviors
  - adhering to formal roles, systems and procedures.
- Effective change requires a structured, programmed, design-build- and-communicate approach.
- Cultural change is best managed as a separate stream of the overall change process.

The benefits and drawbacks of the approach are summarized in Table 1.2.

**Table 1.2** Education and training – strengths and weaknesses

| Strengths | Weaknesses |
| --- | --- |
| ✓ Emphasizes the critical importance of communication | ✗ Communication is often limited to top–down message passing |
| ✓ Provides structured learning | ✗ In the extreme, no "deviants" are allowed |
| ✓ Can help to reinforce changed behaviors | ✗ Can result in excessive rigidity |
| ✓ Can achieve greater penetration into the organization than *management edict* alone | ✗ Paradoxically, can stifle learning and creativity by emphasizing conformity |
| ✓ Can improve consistency of behavior and outcomes | ✗ "Macdonaldization" can result in machine-like approach to people and relationships |
| ✓ Can support longer-term capability development | ✗ Difficult to sustain momentum when high profile programs fade |

## Joint problem solving

*Joint problem solving* reflects a more inclusive view of the dynamics of organizational change. It argues for a more collaborative approach to organizational leadership than those identified earlier. Proponents of this view therefore seek to tap into a wider pool of talent and ideas than do those who adopt the earlier perspectives. By working to achieve buy-in to the specific changes being adopted, its advocates feel that it can help to build mutual trust and generate greater commitment. Using participation as a key organizing principle, its approach is inevitably less dogmatic and more flexible than those discussed above. As a result, it is argued that its outcomes are likely to be more durable. This view of organizational dynamics is characteristic of that advocated by the culture-excellence school, which grew in popularity and prominence during the 1980s and 1990s (see, for example, Peters and Waterman, 1982), and of the Human Resource Management movement in general. Here again, though, change is seen as a design-and-build activity, with the emphasis often placed on the "culture change" element of the overall program. This perspective usually sees team working and empowerment as critical elements of an organization's working practices.

Managers who are reluctant to accept *joint problem solving* as the primary means of achieving change will usually support their position by arguing that it takes longer to arrive at decisions and can dilute management's message or intent. Some would also claim that the approach shows a lack of leadership, vision and decisiveness; although, having the courage and insight to tap into the wealth of under-utilized talent that often exists in organizations would be seen by many others to be visionary in itself. It is generally agreed that, if this approach is to flourish, people need to be willing, able and allowed to collaborate. Effective group dynamics and an enabling work climate are therefore important factors in its success.

Action flows from this mode when shared acceptance of a way ahead is reached. At its best, this might reflect the creative integration of diverse views into a new approach, through open dialogue. More usually, though, it will be the result of compromise or, worse still, consensus around some lowest-common-denominator points of agreement. Management control of *joint problem solving* is often achieved through the framing of terms of reference, retention of the right to decide, or the imposition of resource limits on the implementation of any actions that might result.

Conventionally, *joint problem solving* groups are used at the "back end" of top–down change programs. Typically, these involve staff in the detailed implementation of already decided upon changes; and they may also be used to symbolize the principles of delegation and empowerment, where these form part of management's "grand design." More recently, though, several large-group change methodologies have been introduced, which place *joint problem solving* at the center of the change process. These include such approaches as Real-Time Strategic Change, Whole-Scale Change, Preferred Futuring, Open Space Technology and Participative Design (see Holman and Devane, 1999, for example).

The use of *joint problem solving* opens up the possibility of engaging a wider range of talent than is available through the earlier routes. Creating conditions in which such groups are *genuinely* unconstrained can be difficult, though. This is especially so for managers schooled in the established view of management prerogative and "heroic" forms of leadership. Often, therefore, these participative sessions are still framed within a strategic context set by management (i.e. bounded by a *management edict* philosophy). As a result, the underlying assumptions about the nature of management control and the validity of the design-and-build notion of cultural change typically remain intact.

In summary, the core assumptions of the *joint problem solving* approach are that:

- Organizations work best by adopting people-based assumptions.
- Change can be facilitated and potentially improved by involvement.
- Results are achieved by analysis and a participative, design-and-build approach.

The benefits and drawbacks of the approach are summarized in Table 1.3.

**Table 1.3** Joint problem solving – strengths and weaknesses

| Strengths | Weaknesses |
|---|---|
| ✓ More inclusive than *Edict* and *E&T* | ✗ Takes time |
| ✓ Taps into a wider pool of talent and ideas | ✗ Can dilute management's message |
| ✓ Can create greater trust, commitment and buy-in | ✗ Some argue that it lacks vision (compared to the "heroic leadership" model) |
| ✓ Less dogmatic and more flexible | ✗ People need to be willing, able *and allowed* to participate effectively |
| ✓ Outcomes likely to be more durable | ✗ Requires effective group dynamics to gain full benefits |
| ✓ Cross-functional working can improve understanding and foster collaboration | ✗ Often overly constrained by Terms of Reference |
| ✓ Provides evidence of "walking the talk" when the plan advocates a more participative style | ✗ Can create cynicism if seen as paying lip service to participation |

## Mixing the colors

The three approaches discussed so far are rarely – if ever – used in isolation. It is more likely to be the mix of approaches used and their practical application that will differ from situation to situation and user to user. As illustrated in Figure 1.2, the perspectives discussed so far cover a broad spectrum of approaches, from "tight" (imposed, directed and programmed) to "flexible" (more involving than imposed, facilitated

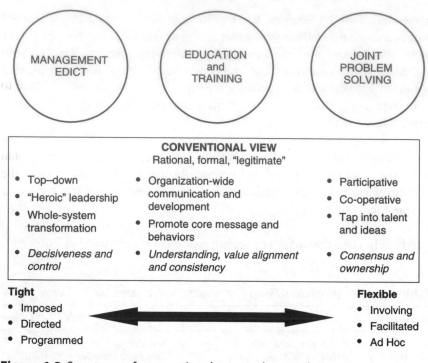

**Figure 1.2** Spectrum of conventional approaches to change

rather than directed and with a degree of adhocracy as opposed to being overly programmed).

## What's missing?

Although these approaches embrace the full range of conventional views on how change happens in organizations, something is missing from the discussion so far. What this something might be is best addressed *initially* by considering what happens in an organization when management announces a specific change – whether organization-wide or more locally.

Invariably, people get together informally and talk to each other about it. They share their perceptions, interpretations and evaluations of what's going on; and they decide – individually and collectively – what to make of what they've heard, and how they will react. This response is universal. When introducing this "What's missing?" question into discussions on organizational change, everyone recognizes that this happens. This is not least because they initiate and/or participate in it themselves on a continuing basis. It is a basic human need to make sense of the world in which we live. And these informal conversations with people in our personal networks and incidental encounters are the way in which we satisfy this need. Importantly too, people also agree that this activity *unavoidably* impacts significantly upon (i.e. *changes*) the nature, time to implement, and ultimate effectiveness of management's original proposition, whether overtly or covertly.

This leads to a fourth view of how change happens in organizations, which is critical to a full understanding of change and organizational dynamics. Amongst other things, it is an approach that recognizes the impact that these informal conversations, power and politics have on organizational outcomes, whether or not these are seen as legitimate in the formal arenas of the organization. I call this fourth perspective *informal coalitions*.

## Informal coalitions

Figure 1.3 adds *informal coalitions* to our earlier three views on how change happens in organizations: *management edict, education and training* and *joint problem solving*.

The dotted line signifies that the *informal coalitions* mode of change is qualitatively different from the other three. It differs fundamentally, for example, in terms of its assumptions about the dynamics of organizations and its view of the nature and role of leadership in the change process.

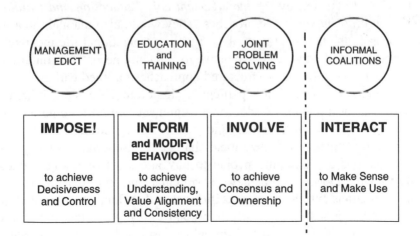

**Figure 1.3** How change happens in organizations

The *informal coalitions* view of organizational dynamics stresses the complex, developing and unpredictable nature of the process. It therefore rejects the ability of managers to plan and control change in the ways that the other perspectives imply. Instead, it sees outcomes arising from the coalescing of people around particular "themes" that emerge from the informal networks of conversations that take place spontaneously around the organization – and beyond. These themes may either support or oppose the organization's officially stated positions. Change in line with management's intentions occurs where the informal conversations reinforce the official line. Other, unplanned changes occur where the informal conversations run counter to the formally stated position and themes emerge around which a sufficiently powerful coalition of support forms to make these other things happen.

Informal coalitional activity is present in all change, although it is usually only recognized in terms of so-called "resistance" to management-imposed initiatives. When viewed as a conscious approach to "managing" change, it is deliberately informal. It seeks to influence outcomes through everyday conversations and interactions – working with these natural dynamics to build support for the desired changes. Its disadvantages – from the perspective of a management world wedded to "keep it simple" mantras and quick-fix solutions – are that it appears "messy," indecisive and lacking in structure. Change arising from this mode appears slow to build and unfocused. At first sight, therefore, it does not appear able to deal with crises or generate rapid step change. Its outcomes are also necessarily unpredictable. However, those who adopt an *informal coalitions* perspective would argue that this is no less so that in the *seemingly* more certain world created by the *management edict, education and training* and *joint problem solving* approaches. They would also maintain that its emphasis on the here-and-now of everyday organizational life inevitably makes it more adaptive and responsive to changing needs and conditions than are the more formally structured approaches outlined earlier.

The notion of a coalition is particularly important here, since it breaks away from the accepted wisdom that alignment behind a common and enduring set of values, beliefs and behaviors (a "strong culture") is essential for effective organizational change. It's important to recognize that coalitions don't require people to buy into a set of shared values, only to agree the need to achieve a particular outcome. Coalitions also tend to be transient and issue-specific, rather than long-standing and all embracing. It is also particularly important to recognize that those who decide the intention, nature and timing of particular management edicts (ordinarily members of senior management), themselves participate in informal coalitions. And these coalitions will often owe more to political accommodations and social networking than to the "unity of purpose" implied by the popular conception of a unified top team.

*Informal coalitional* activity is therefore unavoidably political. It is political in the sense that it recognizes the *inevitability* of differences of view and motivation within *all* organizations; and it also uses a wide range of informal power sources to influence the nature and direction of the change process. Bate (1994: 186) views this type of activity primarily as negative and uses the term "corrosive" to describe a politically based approach: ". . . corrosives tend to be covert and devious, skillfully manipulating relationships in order to achieve their ends. Theirs is a zero-sum game conception of life in which gains are made only at other people's expense." Clearly, the informality and potentially covert nature of this change strategy could lead to it being driven more by self-interest than organizational need. If abused, it could fuel suspicion and mistrust. Equally, if it is used by managers – or perceived and interpreted by others – as simply a more subtle form of top–down control (i.e. *management edict* in disguise), it is unlikely to add much to our understanding of organizational dynamics.

However, whilst recognizing the potential for these more negative characteristics to arise, I see coalition building both as an essential aspect of leadership *and* as a natural process of organizational dynamics, which *everyone* engages in. Furthermore, the *informal coalitional* mode is the only one of the four perspectives that overtly engages with the shadow-side dynamics of the organization. These are the characteristics of the "hidden organization," as embodied in its informal networks, social and political processes, underlying patterns of taken-for-granted cultural assumptions, and so on. It is here that much of the real business takes place, even though what goes on is not discussed in the organization's formal arenas. Those wishing to influence the outcome of change in organizations must therefore become aware of these dynamics, *including the impact of their own talk and actions on the emerging pattern of relationships, assumptions and outcomes*.

From this perspective, *constructive* engagement with the political nature of organizations is seen as the very essence of leadership. For the dynamics of *informal coalitions* to be properly understood, though, some of the cherished assumptions of management need to be set aside; and we will explore this aspect of the model later. For now, it is sufficient to note that leadership in the *informal coalitional* mode, like the strategies and changes that result from it, is emergent. It is not based upon formal position or even expert technical knowledge. Instead, it arises from an ability to get people willingly to engage in things that matter. It is about helping them to make sense of the events that are going on around them, and to act in ways that advance the change agenda. In short, it is about interaction, sensemaking and coalition building.

In summary, the core assumptions of the *informal coalitions* approach are that:

- Change is continuous and outcomes are uncontrollable by any one individual or group.
- Power and political processes are central to effective performance.
- Organizations do not behave in line with conventional wisdom:
  - mess is inevitable and can be productive
  - small changes can have large, unpredictable effects
  - outcomes are jointly created ("co-created") by participants through their everyday interactions and conversations
  - managers are active participants in this process, not detached, objective observers
  - leadership is informal and often invisible.

The benefits and potential drawbacks of this as an approach to change are summarized in Table 1.4.

**Table 1.4** Informal coalitions – strengths and weaknesses

| Strengths | Weaknesses |
| --- | --- |
| ✓ In tune with the natural, everyday dynamics of organizations | ✗ Initially invisible – could be seen as covert and devious |
| ✓ People "sign up" voluntarily | ✗ Potentially subversive – could be used to promote own self-interest at organization's expense |
| ✓ More adaptive and responsive to changing needs and conditions | |
| ✓ Overtly engages with the political dimensions of organizations | ✗ Ordinarily slow to build |
| ✓ Uses a wide range of power sources | ✗ Outcomes unpredictable |
| ✓ Welcomes ambiguity, paradox and contention as sources of energy and creativity | ✗ Relinquishes management's (apparent) control |
| | ✗ Diffuse rather than focused |
| ✓ Values diversity | ✗ Out of step with "heroic," visibly decisive model of leadership |
| ✓ Adopts a relationship-building and sensemaking view of communication | |

In reviewing this, it is critical to recognize and act upon the following point: Managers cannot prevent informal coalitional activity from happening. The only choice they have is whether or not they wish to engage with it in an informed and deliberate way.

We can now complete the picture of how change happens in organizations, as shown in Figure 1.4.

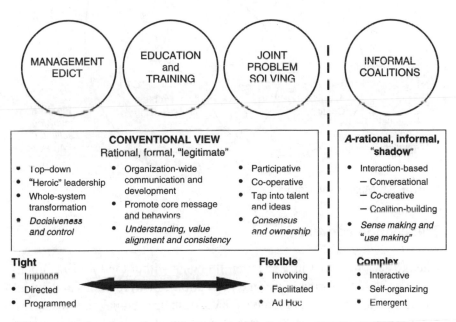

**Figure 1.4** The dynamics of organizational change

## Interrelationship of the four views of change

The four basic views of the dynamics of change, outlined above, do not occur in isolation. They each exert their influence, to a greater or lesser extent, in all organizational change. This is illustrated in Figure 1.5, the core of the Change Map, which shows the four perspectives overlapping. Moving in a clockwise direction, the diagram arranges the earlier "continuum" of rational change modes, from imposed and so on (top left) through to involving and so on (bottom right). The *a*-rational dynamics of the *informal coalitions* mode occupies the bottom left zone of the resulting Map.

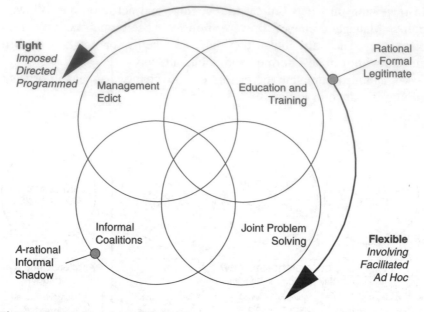

**Figure 1.5** Mixing the colors

## The change context

Change does not exist in a vacuum. It occurs within (and impacts upon) a change context, formed from the perceptions, interpretations and evaluations that organizational members make of their personal circumstances, organizational factors and external environment. A full appreciation of the dynamics of change therefore needs to reflect its contextual nature, as suggested in Figure 1.6.

Conventional views of managing change recognize the importance of an organization's external environment to the nature, direction and success of change; but less attention is usually paid to its internal context when seeking to import ideas and concepts from elsewhere. Appreciation of this aspect of change dynamics is critical because of the *unavoidably* complex nature of organizations. Complexity here does not mean complicated. Organizations are complex because they comprise an intricate and ever-changing web of interdependencies and interrelationships.

As a result of this, it is important to recognize that initiatives that have been successful elsewhere have been so within the context of specific *local* circumstances and the *unique* network of relationships that

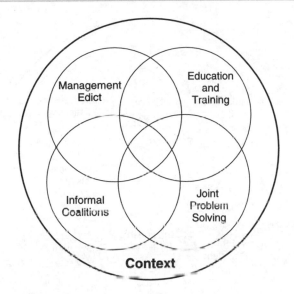

**Figure 1.6** The change context

comprises that organization. This has important implications for such things as:

- the blind application of fads and fashions, however successful these appear to have been in other circumstances;
- the notion, interpretation and application of so-called "best practice;" and
- the way that external benchmarking is used as an improvement tool.

## Key aspects of organizational dynamics

The interplay of the four primary views of the change process, as illustrated in the Change Map, highlights four key aspects of organizational dynamics that are central to an understanding of organizational change. These are identified in Figure 1.7 and described briefly below.

### Overt management philosophy

The development, formal communication and adoption of a core management philosophy are key elements of all strategies that rely primarily on *management edict* and *education and training* as the prime movers

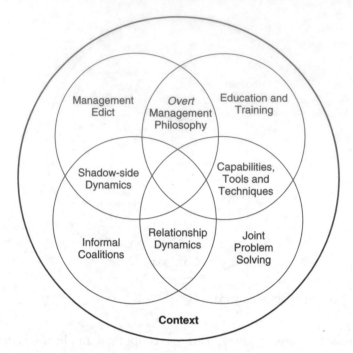

**Figure 1.7** Key aspects of organizational dynamics

of organizational change. This statement of philosophy typically covers aspects of organizational "hardware," such as strategy, structures and systems; but it is also likely to refer to the publicly stated beliefs and values that the organization sees as the desired "recipe for success." Purpose, mission and vision statements, brand promises, annual reports, organizational manuals, press briefings and formal presentations are the most likely places to find this philosophy articulated. This segment of the Change Map is labeled *overt* management philosophy to recognize that, more often than not, there is a gap between the *formally stated* position and that which people experience in practice.

## Capabilities, tools and techniques

As the emphasis shifts toward a more participative view of the change process, *education and training* interventions aim to enrich the *joint problem solving* approach by introducing new capabilities, tools and techniques through which organizations can function more effectively.

The range of change enablers is unlimited, but these might typically include:

- access to relevant organizational, team and individual assessment frameworks, including psychometric instruments, diagnostic questionnaires and so on;
- a practical understanding of the concepts and techniques of group dynamics and situational leadership techniques;
- a compendium of performance- and capability-enhancing models, concepts and interventions;
- a toolkit of problem solving and opportunity-search tools and techniques;
- new behavioral competency frameworks to support more empowered and participative working.

Similarly, besides addressing issue-related tasks, *joint problem solving* groups may be used to create and develop new capabilities, tools and techniques for wider dissemination through various *education and training* interventions. The latter distribution routes might include communication programs, leadership development initiatives, competency frameworks, focused training courses and so on. Sustaining and developing the capability to deliver *both* the desired changes *and* the continuing demands of current business commitments are central to this aspect of the change process.

## Relationship dynamics

Since organizations are nothing more than people interrelating with each other for a purpose, the dynamics of these relationships are of critical importance to an organization's capability and performance.

Relationship dynamics are positioned within the *joint problem solving* mode to emphasize that the effectiveness of (formal) problem-solving groups as agents of change depends heavily upon the quality of interpersonal relationships that exist within and beyond the business. Building a context of collaboration and promoting the active networking of knowledge, ideas and resources across the organization are therefore usually seen as being crucial to the effective delivery of these more empowered approaches to change. This is reflected in the emphasis that many organizations place on team building, team working and related issues, as part of their planned organizational change programs.

At the same time, the positioning of relationship dynamics within the *informal coalitions* mode recognizes that all organizational relationships are power relationships. And these will not necessarily embody the ethos of trust, collaboration and mutual support implied by the *joint problem solving* ideals set out above. Whilst the existence of informal coalitions *may* lead to increased trust within them, this is not the issue. The notion of *informal coalitions* recognizes that it is the fluid network of power relationships that will govern the dynamics of the change process. And this will be the case *irrespective of* the "quality" of those relationships. Key influences on the dynamics of relationships from an *informal coalitions* perspective include:

- the relative power of participants;
- their personal motivations;
- the opportunities that present themselves for them to interact; and
- their sense of identity that may be threatened, reinforced or transformed by the relationship.

During a workshop, a group of senior managers suggested that relationships within a *joint problem solving* mode are essentially relationships of the "head." That is, the functional needs of the task and a rational assessment of group members' capabilities primarily determine these role-based relationships. In contrast, they suggested that *informal coalitions* are relationships of the "heart." These are driven primarily by an emotional commitment or attraction to a particular cause. This insight will be important later, when we consider in more depth how managers can engage effectively with the complex, messy and self-organizing dynamics of *informal coalitions*.

## Shadow-side dynamics

I first came across the notion of the shadow side of organizations in the work of Egan, and later in the complexity-based writings of Stacey. Egan (1993: 91) describes the shadow side of an organization as:

> ... [those] realities that often disrupt, and sometimes benefit, the business but are not dealt with in the formal settings of the organization.

The shadow-side dynamics of an organization have a powerful impact on all aspects of its performance and capability. However, *by definition*, such issues are rarely raised in open, formal meetings and publications, where these ordinarily remain undiscussable.

Egan identifies five components of the shadow side of organizations. These are:

1 the impact of real-life *messiness and informality* on business strategy, organization and management, which doesn't sit easily with the way that orthodox, "rational" theories of management suggest things should work;
2 the *problems and idiosyncrasies of individuals*, which run counter to the "universalist" assumptions and approaches that tend to dominate conventional management thinking and practice;
3 the operation of the *organization as a social system*, with its in-groups and out-groups, social routines and rituals, all of which "distort" the interrelationships and decision-making processes implied by the "legitimate" organization;
4 the *organization as a political system*, which recognizes that *all* organizations reflect a diverse range of viewpoints, motivations and self-interests, leading to competing coalitions of people, each seeking to define the organization's agenda and to shape its course of action;
5 the *cultural assumptions* of the organization, through which many of the above characteristics become embedded and taken-for-granted ways of operating – whether these are outside people's immediate awareness or known but undiscussable.

In later chapters we will further explore and extend the themes that organize shadow-side activity and the dynamics that these generate. For now, it is sufficient to recognize two things. First that shadow-side dynamics are a powerful and unavoidable characteristic of organizational activity, even though these are not formally acknowledged. Secondly that shadow-side behaviors are not necessarily negative or destructive, despite the sinister sounding name. Indeed, a central proposition of this book is that active engagement with these dynamics is a key leadership task.

*Why "shadow-side dynamics?"*

I have been asked on a number of occasions why, given these potentially negative connotations, I continue to use the term "shadow-side dynamics." My answer is twofold. First, the term has gained some currency in recent years through the writings of Egan, Stacey and others. And, secondly, the idea of a shadow conveys the sense that any action by management will *necessarily* generate shadow-side activity, in the same way that shining a light on an object will *always* cast a shadow. You can't have the light without the shadow. Nor can you have a management action without its shadow-side effects.

In the Change Map, therefore, shadow-side dynamics sit on the cusp between the formal, top-driven, decide-and-impose, *management edict* view of change and the *informal coalitions* that significantly influence change in the "real world." Its positioning in the model also serves to emphasize the inherently paradoxical nature of organizational dynamics, which belies the simplistic, either–or choices that many managers equate with decisive leadership.

## Organizational outcomes

Figure 1.8 suggests the outcomes that might be expected to occur, if the different views of change dynamics outlined above were translated into specific change strategies. Over recent years, most change programs have sought to design and build the characteristics of a so-called "strong culture." The five shown in the model are:

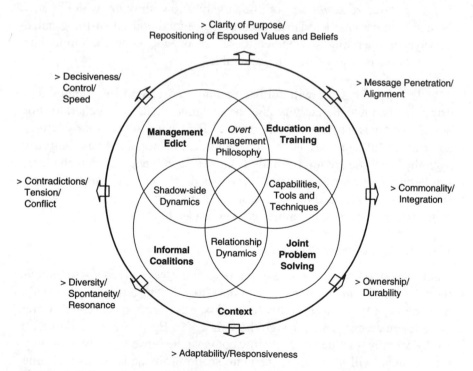

**Figure 1.8** Organizational outcomes

- strong leadership, characterized by *decisiveness, control and speed*;
- greater *clarity* of purpose and *repositioning* of values and beliefs;
- *penetration* of key messages into the depths of the organization and *alignment* of organizational members behind a new set of behavioral norms;
- greater *commonality* of approach and *integration* of effort across the organization; and
- high *durability* of the changes over time, through generating a widespread sense of *ownership* of the changes.

More recently, the rapidly changing demands of the business environment and recognition of the complexity of the internal dynamics of organizations have pointed to the need for greater *adaptability* and *responsiveness* to change. The greater *diversity, spontaneity* and *resonance* that can be achieved and/or exploited through less formal and seemingly less rational approaches are also increasingly being recognized.

The juxtaposition of these attributes of what has ordinarily been viewed as a "weak culture" with those that have historically been pursued, adds to the *tension and conflict* identified alongside the shadow-side segment of the model. The task for organizations is to work to ensure that these *inevitable* tensions are managed creatively and that any conflict is handled insightfully. It means seeking to move the organization away from divisive and adversarial "either–or" thinking towards a paradoxical, "both–and" approach that will be discussed later.

## Roles within the change process

Three roles are of particular interest when considering the dynamics of change. These are change leader, change "specialist" (sometimes referred to as the "change agent"), and change participant. In the language of the *management edict* and *education and training* approaches, the term "change target" is sometimes used to describe the last of these (see Conner, 1993, for example). However, this label misrepresents the position on three counts:

- First, it focuses solely upon those participants *within* the business and ignores the critical impact that *external* stakeholders have on the dynamics and outcome of change.

- Secondly, it implies that those "on the receiving end" of change are *passive* participants in the process, rather than active, co-creators of its outcomes.
- Thirdly, its use sets apart those in the change leadership and change agent roles (the "doers") from those who are "done to" – preserving the myth that the first two roles exist outside the process, as objective observers and controllers of the actions of others.

Leaders and change agents are participants too – "on the pitch playing," so to speak, not objectively observing and commanding events "from the stands"! This should be borne in mind when looking at Figure 1.9, which illustrates six elements of the change leader's role (R1–R6); each of which relates to a particular area of the Change Map. Similarly, there are six corresponding aspects to the change specialist's role that can be mapped onto the diagram.

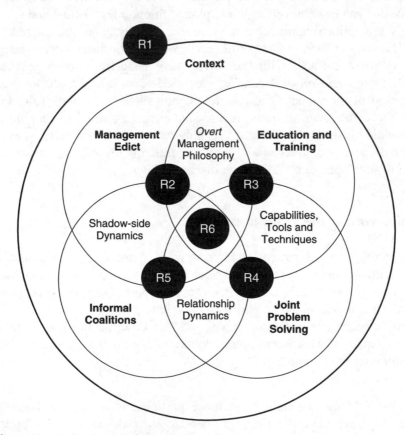

**Figure 1.9** Roles in the change process

## Change leadership

Clearly, the role that a leader carries out when operating from a *management edict* perspective is different in approach and content from that which he or she carries out to support, for example, *joint problem solving*. The ability of the leader to recognize this, and to adapt to different role requirements according to their intentions and the prevailing circumstances, is therefore essential, if the rational approaches to change are to make a meaningful contribution to organizational outcomes. Specific aspects of the change leader's role, as embodied in the Change Map, are summarized in Table 1.5.

**Table 1.5** Summary of change-leadership roles

| Change mode | Role | Change leader (Line manager) | |
| --- | --- | --- | --- |
| | | Description | Explanation |
| | **Mode-specific** | | |
| MANAGEMENT EDICT Impose the change on the organization. *Aims:* decisiveness, control and compliance. | R2 | Dictator/Driver | • Imposing changes in strategy, structure, systems and philosophy. • Driving major, centrally managed change programs "from the front". |
| EDUCATION and TRAINING Inform and persuade people about the change. *Aims:* alignment, consistency and willing acceptance. | R3 | Advocate/Teacher | • Formally selling the need for change and explaining its intended outcomes. • Articulating the new management philosophy and its practical implications. • Teaching others, through formal, structured processes. |
| JOINT PROBLEM SOLVING Involve people in developing the changes. *Aims:* active participation, joint agreement and ownership. | R4 | In-line Coach/ Boundary Manager | • Observing and reflecting • Challenging, guiding and supporting team members. • Clarifying and managing boundaries, such as: – required contributions – interdependencies – constraints, etc. |

**Table 1.5** (Continued)

| Change mode | Role | Change leader (Line manager) | |
|---|---|---|---|
| | | **Description** | **Explanation** |
| **INFORMAL COALITIONS** Interact with people to engage them in the changes. *Aims*: joint sensemaking, engagement and personal resonance. | R5 | Coalition Builder/ Sensemaker | • Working with the hidden, messy and informal dynamics of the organization.<br>• Building informal coalitions of support for desired changes.<br>• Dynamically managing in-built structural and political tensions.<br>• Stimulating and engaging in ongoing sensemaking and relationship building.<br>• Role-modeling the desired values and behaviors during everyday interactions. |
| | **General** | | |
| *Note*: The adjacent roles support all four of the change modes. These roles will be expressed in different ways, according to the primary focus of the intervention. | R1 | Context Setter/ Visionary | • Understanding the context.<br>• Setting the strategic and conceptual framework for the changes.<br>• Providing vision. |
| | R6 | Sponsor/Enabler | • Demonstrating consistent, sustained and *active* support for the changes throughout the program.<br>• Providing relevant inputs and removing barriers, to underpin other roles and enable the effective and efficient implementation of the changes. |

Roles R2–R4 comprise the conventional view of change leadership. An appropriate mix of these would be performed as part of the formal change-management process. These would be designed to suit the specific demands of the change task and preferred leadership style, from directive (R2), through informative (R3) to participative (R4).

Role R5 relates to the leader's ability to engage with the underlying dynamics of organizations, as reflected in the *informal coalitions* view of change. This "below the line" capability differentiates the practiced change leader from those whose knowledge is limited to the textbook, project- and program-management elements of the process. Successful change leadership requires the leader to engage effectively with these dynamics, irrespective of other aspects of the role that they might decide to carry out.

Roles R1 and R6 support all four of the change modes. These will be expressed in different ways, according to the primary focus of the intervention. Many initiatives under-deliver because managers fail to *actively* sponsor the changes throughout the *line* organization (Role R6). Too often, senior managers see their sponsorship role as having been fulfilled when they sign the authorization to commit resources to a particular change effort. Or when they endorse it as part of a formal communication plan. Others feel that they can satisfy this role by turning up when asked to "lend their weight" to specific structured events in the change program. However, *active and sustainable* sponsorship requires much more of a commitment than this. Additional guidance on this critical aspect of a leader's role is therefore set out in Box 1.1.

---

**Box 1.1 – The need for *active* sponsorship**

Line managers have a pivotal role to play in legitimizing specific strategies, initiatives and activities, by providing *active* sponsorship throughout the implementation process. It is not sufficient simply to "roll out" these changes to staff in a matter-of-fact way. Or to believe that sponsorship is complete when the decision has been taken to proceed and a senior, project-specific "sponsor" appointed. Active sponsorship, *throughout the line*, demonstrates commitment to the changes; and it also validates any actions that staff need to take to bring these about. Equally, its absence severely reduces the likelihood of success. For sponsorship to be effective, leaders need to:

- help staff to make sense of what needs to change and why, in ways that connect with their intellectual and emotional needs;
- provide active and visible support for the changes throughout the program – including the provision of any necessary time, information and resources;

- reinforce their formally stated commitment to the changes through their informal interactions;
- recognize and empathize with the inevitable disruptions that individuals will face, as the personal impacts of the changes become clear;
- continue to show genuine interest in the progress of the changes, even when other demands put pressure on available time and resources;
- talk regularly with staff about the changes, to ensure that any issues of concern are adequately addressed;
- ensure that sponsorship is carried out equally effectively throughout their own line organization.

See also Conner (1993).

## Change facilitation

As with the change-leadership roles outlined above, distinct facilitation roles are required to support different leadership interventions. For example, if change leaders are operating from a *management edict* perspective (i.e. dictating what is required and seeking to drive these changes through "from the front"), they might decide that they require support in two areas. First, they may need expert input to develop the detailed design for the changes that they intend to impose ("Architect"); and, secondly, they may need support to orchestrate the implementation of these changes on their behalf ("Engineer"). Traditionally, large, strategy-based consultancies have offered to fulfill these two roles. In contrast, where a more participative leadership style is adopted, such as when operating in a *joint problem solving* mode, the leader's in-line coaching and boundary setting might need to be supported by the more directly facilitative role of "Team Coach/Facilitator." Each of the change-leadership roles set out above is therefore supported by a corresponding change-facilitation role. These pairings are set out in Table 1.6.

These corresponding aspects of the change facilitator's role are also embodied in the Change Map, as summarized in Table 1.7. Dependent upon the nature of the challenges faced and the capabilities of participants, these roles might either be combined with those of change leader or separately resourced.

**Table 1.6** Links between change-leadership and change-facilitation roles

| Change leadership | Role | Change facilitation |
|---|---|---|
| Context Setter/Visionary | R1 | Envisioner/Diagnostician |
| Dictator/Driver | R2 | Architect/Engineer |
| Advocate/Teacher | R3 | Modeler/Developer |
| In-line Coach/Boundary Manager | R4 | Team Coach/Facilitator |
| Coalition Builder/Sensemaker | R5 | Process Consultant/Catalyst |
| Sponsor/Enabler | R6 | Enabler/Implementer |

**Table 1.7** Summary of change facilitation roles

| Change mode | Role | Change facilitator (External/Internal consultant) | |
|---|---|---|---|
| | | **Description** | **Explanation** |
| | **Mode-specific** | | |
| MANAGEMENT EDICT Impose the change on the organization. *Aims*: decisiveness, control and compliance. | R2 | Architect/ Engineer | • Prescribing approaches to strategy development and implementation. • Designing structures, processes and systems. • Planning and orchestrating integrated change programs. |
| EDUCATION and TRAINING Inform and persuade people about the change. *Aims*: alignment, consistency and willing acceptance. | R3 | Modeler/ Developer | • Supporting formal, structured communication processes. • Introducing frameworks, maps and models to guide and support the changes. • Developing new capabilities and behaviors through structured training and development programs, competency-based development schemes, etc. |
| JOINT PROBLEM SOLVING Involve people in developing the changes. *Aims*: active participation, joint agreement and ownership. | R4 | Team Coach/ Facilitator | • Facilitating participative, group-based problem solving processes and issue-based workshops. • Designing and orchestrating large-group change methodologies. • Addressing group/team processes, relationships and performance. • Facilitating Action Learning groups. |

**Table 1.7** (Continued)

| Change mode | Role | Change facilitator (External/Internal consultant) | |
|---|---|---|---|
| | | Description | Explanation |
| INFORMAL COALITIONS Interact with people to engage them in the changes. *Aims*: joint sensemaking, engagement and personal resonance. | R5 | Process Consultant/ Catalyst | • Enabling managers to gain insights into their own processes and resolve their own issues.<br>• Helping them to understand and work with the underlying dynamics of the organization.<br>• Detecting the patterns of assumptions, beliefs and behaviors that are channeling everyday sensemaking and action.<br>• Provoking new perspectives, exploring possibilities and identifying latent potential. |
| | **General** | | |
| *Note*: The adjacent roles support all of the four of the change modes. These roles will be expressed in different ways, according to the primary focus of the intervention. | R1 | Envisioner/ Diagnostician | • Envisioning potential futures.<br>• Assessing the current situation.<br>• Diagnosing needs.<br>• Conducting appreciative-style inquiry. |
| | R6 | Enabler/ Implementer | • Supporting each of the other contributions as appropriate, to secure maximum value from the various interventions.<br>• Providing implementational support (such as additional resources) where necessary. |

As before, Roles R2–R4 comprise the conventional view of change facilitation. An appropriate mix of these might be performed as part of the formal change-management process. These would be designed to suit the specific demands of the change task and prevailing change-leadership roles, from prescriptive (R2), through informative (R3) to facilitative (R4).

Role R5 reflects the facilitator's ability to engage with the underlying dynamics of organizations, as reflected in the *informal coalitions* view of change. This "below the line" capability makes the difference between the mechanistic application of conventional change theory and the informed facilitation of "real world" change and development. Successful change facilitation requires effective engagement with these dynamics, irrespective of other aspects of the role that might be required. Roles R1 and R6 support all four of the change modes. These will be expressed in different ways, according to the primary focus of the intervention.

## The Change Map as a whole

For completeness, Figure 1.10 shows the Change Map in its entirety.

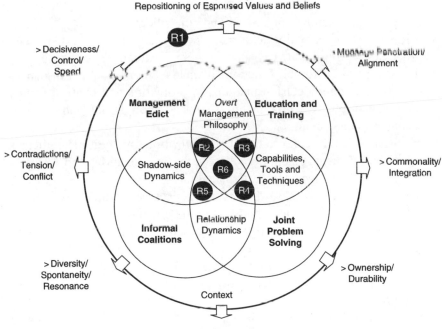

**Figure 1.10** The Change Map

## The rational view of change

*Management edict, education and training* and *joint problem solving* provide the main routes for managing change from a "rational" mindset. Those who advocate these perspectives share a common set of beliefs about organizational change, including the view that:

- change takes place in discrete episodes between periods of (relative) stability;
- change is brought about deliberately, and within the formal settings of the organization;
- the meaning of a particular change is determined by management, who are external, objective observers and controllers of other people's actions;
- change strategies and programs have predictable outcomes, if cause and effect are properly analysed and "leveraged" to achieve the desired ends (e.g. through incentives).

This viewpoint goes on to argue that *effective* change is change which:

- is thoroughly planned, organized and controlled;
- follows organizationally legitimate power structures, systems and processes, with top–down leadership being critical;
- focuses on the textbook functions of management, such as organization, planning and decision-making, co-ordination and control, formal communication, extrinsic incentives-based motivation, and detailed resource management;
- emphasizes, and seeks to instil, organizationally legitimate themes (such as top management's vision for the organization, and formally adopted policy stances on particular issues);
- views opposition to these themes as "resistance," which needs to be overcome, if organizational success is to be achieved;
- values analysis and being right, in the sense of finding and adopting the "one best way" to proceed;
- suppresses emotions, politics, "mess" and informality, which are seen as illegitimate aspects of organizational life and signs of poor management;
- uses as its reference point "the real world," where reality is seen as a universally recognized given, which is already known or that can be discovered through experience and/or expert analysis.

Theories such as these underpin the stories of corporate transformation and inform the best-practice guides that populate management bookshelves. They also provide the principal rationale behind the change-management offerings of the mainstream consultancy firms. At best, these provide a partial view of how change happens. At worst, the failure of these to address the hidden, messy and informal aspects of organizations means that they provide seriously flawed prescriptions for moving forward.

## Integrating the rational and *a*-rational dynamics of change

Acknowledging the impact of shadow-side issues and power relationships on organizations is the missing ingredient in the many approaches to change that embrace the rational assumptions set out above. Dealing with the effects that these have upon organizational dynamics must therefore provide a central focus for managers who wish to take change seriously.

The Change Map brings the issues of power relations and shadow-side dynamics into the open. It reveals why change strategies that ignore the underlying dynamics of organizations are doomed to under-achieve. At the same time, it integrates the rational and *a*-rational aspects of organizational change into one sensemaking framework. Managers and organizational specialists can use this to help them make sense of what's going on in their organizations and to intervene more effectively.

However, managers who have thrived under the assumptions – and privileges – of the well-established and rational concept of management may not welcome this challenge to their relatively comfortable worldview. Nor will the need to manage paradox and to deal with the shadow-side realities of organizations appeal to those who crave certainty, are uncomfortable with complexity or see the world in win–lose, either–or terms. Sadly, managers' thinking in these areas is rarely challenged at a fundamental level. Instead, their felt need for control and predictability continue to be fed by "ten easy steps"-type recipes, and the change-management equivalent of satellite navigation that is promised by a plethora of scorecards, dashboards and IT-steered project plans.

In contrast, the Change Map argues for a "stripped down" version of the rational, formal and "legitimate" approaches to change to be melded with its *a*-rational, informal and messy dynamics. This then enables managers:

- to gain the benefits that can accrue through the use of a structured approach to the management of certain "structural" aspects of organizational change; and, at the same time,
- to engage with the messy, informal and uncontrollable dynamics of "real world" organizational change, as embodied in the *informal coalitions* element of the Change Map.

In Chapter 2, we will examine in more detail the underlying aspects of organizations that are typically ignored by the conventional views of leadership, change and organizational dynamics. As for the rational, structured elements of the change-management task, there is already a surfeit of books that provide recipes, tools and techniques in these areas. I therefore don't intend to labor these here.

## Any map will do

Finally, in his book on organizational sensemaking, Weick (1995) tells the story of a small group of Hungarian soldiers who had lost their way in the icy wilderness of the Alps. Having been missing for over two days, they eventually found their way back to base camp, weary but alive. They said that they had almost given up hope of survival, when one of their number had discovered a map in his pocket. This had enabled them to gain their bearings and make their way to safety. When the senior officer asked to see it, he was astonished to find that it was not a map of the Alps at all, but of the Pyrenees. Weick uses this story to suggest that, when sensemaking takes hold, "any map will do." The fact that the map was not the right map was irrelevant. It was good enough. It spurred them into action, and gave them confidence that they could make progress. In particular, it enabled them to ask useful questions of themselves. They were then able to make sense of where they were, and make use of that understanding to get to where they needed to be.

Similarly, the issue here is not whether the Change Map is "right" in an academic sense – although it is based on sound principles. More important is whether or not it is useful to those whose job is to lead their organizations through the often "icy wilderness" of organizational change.

# CHAPTER 2

# Underlying dynamics of change

Life is what happens to you while you're busy making other plans.

– John Lennon

## Introduction

The Change Map identifies relationship and shadow-side dynamics as keys to the emergence and operation of *informal coalitions*. It is therefore important to explore these in more depth, if we are to understand the underlying dynamics of change and to gain some insights into how leaders might engage with these more effectively.

## Relationship dynamics

Each of us operates within a constantly shifting network of relationships in every sphere of our lives. Some of these relationships are formal, others informal. Some are overt and some covert. Some occur deliberately and others arise incidentally. As individuals, we try to operate effectively in all of these relationships at the same time. That is, we try to handle all of the competing demands in ways that preserve our sense of integrity, self-worth and identity; and which, at the same time, sustain each of the relationships in a desired state.

### The art of organizational "plate spinning"

At a basic level, this situation is analogous to the plate-spinning act that is popular in variety shows and circuses. There, the performer attempts to keep several plates spinning simultaneously, as these are balanced on the tops of long, thin poles. As they stimulate each of the poles in turn, to keep the plate spinning, others teeter precariously. Their attention shifts constantly from plate to plate, as they strive to prevent them falling.

In a similar fashion, we each try to keep all of our relationship "plates" spinning, by stimulating them through talk and other forms of interaction. As with the plates in the variety act, not all of these relationships will be "spinning" perfectly all of the time. Misunderstandings will exist, people will feel let down or neglected from time to time, competing agendas will surface and subside, new influences will emerge to upset the dynamic stability of particular relationships and so on.

The plates in the variety act spin independently of each other. The gravitational pull on each plate is constant and its effects predictable to the trained eye. That is, the performer can anticipate precisely when each plate is likely to fall and take steps to prevent it. In contrast, our relationship networks interact with each other in complex and unpredictable ways. The "gravitational field" at work here comprises the conversational patterns[1] that emerge through the everyday interactions of people within our networks. It is affected by the relative power that these people have to command our attention, the personal importance of these relationships, and the ways that we each perceive, interpret and evaluate these interactions. The simultaneous "inner conversations" (or thinking and feeling) that precede, accompany and follow on from our interactions with others are channeled by our unique perceptual patterns and assumptions about "how the world works."[2] And these patterns of assumptions are themselves shaped over time by the nature of our everyday interactions.

Through this continuous process of everyday feeling, thinking and acting, we each try to manage our relationships in ways that sustain those that we wish to (or need to) preserve. We do this both consciously and subconsciously, with the aim of maintaining our sense of personal and organizational competence and self-worth. If we ask ourselves who is spinning these metaphorical "plates," the answer is clear. We are each spinning our own. In doing this, though, we also each affect – to a greater or lesser extent – the dynamics of the "plates" that are being spun by everyone else in our own relationship networks. This process is self organizing. Nobody is sitting outside of these networks and orchestrating what is going on. There is no "Great Plate Spinner in the Sky" – or in the Boardroom!

## Organizational implications

The above dynamics of relationship networks have a number of implications for our understanding and management of organizations, which the *informal coalitions* perspective seeks to raise awareness of and address.

First, we need to recognize that managers are themselves members of many such networks, both within and beyond the organization. These have a major impact upon their behavior and effectiveness as leaders. Managers therefore cannot credibly claim to be external, objective observers and controllers of the interactions within their organization, or of the performance that flows from these, in the way that conventional wisdom requires. They are, unavoidably, influential participants in those networks. In their roles as formal leaders, they are key contributors – for better or worse – to the performance of everyone else in their work-based relationship networks.

Secondly, no single individual or group of individuals can control, in any meaningful sense, the directions or outcomes of the interactions that emerge from these networks. This is not to say, of course, that some people (such as managers) are not more influential than others in these exchanges. But the power relationships that determine the potential that people have to influence interactions and outcomes will vary over time. These will also differ from relationship to relationship, and from situation to situation.

Thirdly, the above insights bring into question the notion that "all for one and one for all" teamwork and team play are essential for effective performance. This is usually reflected in the pursuit of such things as shared values and beliefs, consensual decision-making or the suppression of individuality and personal agendas for the "common good." Instead, the *informal coalitions* perspective sees the existence of competing personal and organizational agendas as endemic. This applies equally to the behavior of the "top team" as it does to those of any other group. Managers (including members of the Board) are just as likely to be achieving results through their participation in a number of *informal coalitions*, as they are through textbook team-working behaviors. These coalitions form and grow around "shadow" conversational themes that relate, for example, to underlying assumptions about how the organization should operate (cultural), differing personal and organizational agendas (political), issues of social inclusion and exclusion (identity) and so on. It follows that not all members of a particular management group will coalesce around the same themes. Tensions (and potentially conflicts) are therefore inevitable. Importantly, as we shall explore in Chapter 5, these differences can be the source of originality and creativity as well as destructive conflict and "machiavellian" political behavior.

Fourthly, it recognizes that managers apply their *unique* combinations of strengths and weaknesses within a context of *constant flux* and *specific* relationships. These cannot therefore be generalized into a set of pre-ordained and universally applicable "recipes for success" or behavioral competencies. This suggests that it is probably more useful to build on the strengths that exist rather than focusing too much on overcoming weakness, as many of the "paragon of virtue" competency frameworks tend to do. In terms of leadership and organizational development, this points to a strategy of working with the warts-and-all of the here-and-now rather than imagining some idealized state or waiting in vain for managerial self-sacrifice to take place for the greater good. For example, a manager who has a recognized track record of getting the task done and delivering results, but who seemingly has no qualms about trampling on others to do so, may have great difficulty in embracing the idea of becoming more "relationship oriented." They might genuinely feel that their approach is nothing more that a robust way of making sure that the job gets done. However, accepting their robust approach as a given, doesn't mean that this needs to be expressed in negative and destructive ways. For example, in its most negative expression, others might perceive robust as crude, insensitive and divisive. However, when expressed in its most positive terms, robust might be seen, say, as straightforward, consistent and determined. We will look at this further in Chapter 7.

Fifthly, this perspective understands organizational culture as an *ongoing process* of meaning making, not a static "thing." This stands in stark contrast to the "design, build and communicate" approaches to cultural change. A *sense* of shared understanding might well emerge through these networks of relationships; but it is the active *process* of meaning making that is shared, not the outcome itself. This perspective has much in common with the fragmentation perspective of organizational culture, which ". . . sees issues as connecting individuals in temporary, issue-specific coalitions. Other individuals and other issues are linked in different, overlapping, temporary patterns of connection" (Martin, 1992: 153). We will say more about this in Chapter 4.

Overall, the relationship dynamics described above point to informal coalitional activity as being the underlying source of progress within organizations – as well as the engine of opposition to that progress! This is inevitable from a view of organizational dynamics that sees the desire to maintain a personal sense of worth and identity as being a key motivator of individual and group behavior. Against this background of differing perceptions, motivations and levels of power, one person's progress will inevitably be seen as another person's change for the worse. People will coalesce around these differing perspectives, energized and sustained by their personal networks of interactions. Eventually, one coalition or another will prevail. Alternatively, circumstances will cause other perspectives and propositions to emerge through these same sense-making and use-making processes.

When shadow themes surface and become formalized through these conversations, various structural changes that result will serve to rein-force the new position. These formal aspects of the change (such as new structures, new procedures, new language and new behavioral patterns) are not neutral in their effects. They vest power in some people and dis-empower others. New coalitions will emerge and others will re-form, as these newly established "legitimate" themes seek to guide the organ-ization's formal interactions and new, shadow-side conversations emerge in reaction to them.

## Shadow-side dynamics

As mentioned in Chapter 1, the shadow-side dynamics of an organization relate to those below-the-surface aspects of organizational life. Argyris (1992) points out that organizational defense routines often prevent such issues being raised in the formal arenas of organizations. He refers to their "undiscussability" and the fact that this undiscussability is itself often undiscussible. This makes resolution of shadow-side issues particularly challenging!

Although shadow themes are undiscussable in formal arenas, Stacey (2003) emphasizes that these organize the shadow-side conversations that significantly influence people's sensemaking activity. A number of these themes are identified in Table 2.1. These echo and build upon Egan's five categories. Each of these organizing themes suggests a particular aspect of organizational dynamics with which leaders need to engage. The nature and impact of these shadow-side themes are discussed more fully below.

## Messiness and informality

This idea that organizations are unavoidably messy doesn't sit comfort-ably with the deeply ingrained ideas of mainstream, rational-management thinking. Nor is it in tune with the leadership models and change strategies that flow from these. Conventional wisdom seeks to impose order on chaos. It sets out to eliminate "mess," and to apply rational methodo-logies to the issues that managers face. Mess is seen as synonymous with inefficiency, lack of control, inadequate thinking and so on. This

**Table 2.1** Shadow-side dynamics

| Interwoven Themes that organize the shadow-side behaviors | Organizational Dynamic with which leaders need to engage |
|---|---|
| The hidden, messy and informal dynamics of "real world" organizations | Organizations are much messier and less well structured than implied by statements in formal documents, presentations and publications. Less-than-solid links *unavoidably* exist between management's formally stated position and people's day-to-day experience of organizational life "on the ground." As a result, much of the activity that is most influential in determining organizational performance and change takes place through informal processes and relationships; and in unstructured, emergent ways. |
| Individual differences and idiosyncrasies | On the one hand, characteristic patterns of response to change and other aspects of organizational dynamics can be identified. On the other, people differ in terms of the specific personal circumstances, needs, perspectives, values, reasoning, behaviors and so on that they bring to bear on issues. |
| Social networks and processes | Social networks, like informal task-based relationships above, can facilitate information exchange and task delivery. At the same time, these have a tendency to lead to differentiation and polarization of views, generalization of attributes between the various in-groups ("good") and out-groups ("bad"), preferential treatment for those in particular in-groups, and exclusion of those that find themselves in one or more of the out-groups. |
| Organizational politics | Differing power relationships, competing interests and ideologies, and limited resources make contention and conflict inevitable in organizations. The resulting political processes might be entirely self-serving and organizationally dysfunctional. Alternatively, these same dynamics might be other-directed and organizationally enhancing. Organizational politics is concerned with how these *unavoidable* differences are managed – and for whose benefit. |
| Paradox and contradiction | Paradox and contradiction are endemic in organizations. Rather than seeing these as either–or "problems" to be solved, the *informal coalitions* perspective argues that paradox and contradiction need to be actively engaged with. This means that both sides of the paradox need to be embraced simultaneously and the resulting tensions managed dynamically. |
| The cultural patterning process | The ongoing process of shared sensemaking creates patterns of taken-for-granted assumptions. These both enable and constrain organizational sensemaking and behavior. The dynamics of interaction will mean that some elements of these patterns will be common across the organization, whereas others will be more fragmented. Understanding these patterns, and shifting the conversational dynamics that both generate and flow from them, is the essence of cultural change. |

perspective remains firmly embedded, despite the fact that its seemingly unarguable logic rarely seems to translate into practice in the ways
envisaged. Detailed plans and programs, precisely defined organizational
roles and relationships, so-called SMART target setting and other related
approaches dominate much of this well-ordered world of management
orthodoxy. This taken-for-granted response to the challenges of leadership and organizational change is now as prevalent in the public sector
as it is in commercial organizations. For example, when there was a
sudden increase in the occurrence of the MRSA virus in a number of UK
hospitals, the immediate reaction of the relevant Government minister
was not to focus on the standards of basic hygiene. Instead, he sought
to assure the public by promising that further targets would be set in
relation to the level of infection recorded in each hospital.

Interestingly, this desire for order might also reflect the pattern-making
tendency of human thinking in general and meaning-making in particular.
Contexts, events and behaviors that fail to make sense to us are often
felt to be threatening. In contrast, if we discover an apparent pattern of
meaning and order, which we can name and make sense of, this can
give us a feeling of mastery and being "in control." Formal systems of
measurement and target setting similarly help to provide managers with
this felt sense of control and being in command of events – however
illusory this might be.

Egan (1993) uses the term "messiness" to refer to two things. First,
he argues that organizations in practice are loosely coupled, not neat and
tightly knit as described in formal publications and standard management
texts. Secondly, organizations are awash with informal systems and relationships, which frequently contravene and take precedence over formal
policies, rules and procedures. The fact that this is the case in a particular
organization is widely known by its members, even though it is rarely if
ever acknowledged in formal forums and documents.

In a later book Egan (1994) replaces the term "messiness" with
"hidden organization." This captures the sense of the informal systems
but is less descriptive of the "loosely coupled" characteristics of
organizations. It also loses the connection with the point Stacey
(1996: 337) makes about the *importance* of mess to organizational
dynamics:

> Contrary to some of our most deep-seated beliefs, mess is the material
> from which life and creativity are built and it turns out that they are
> built, not according to some prior design, but through a process of
> spontaneous self-organisation that produces emergent outcomes.

I, therefore, prefer to stick with the word "mess." Also, arguing that mess is a valid characteristic of organizational dynamics provides another important jolt to the grip that conventional management theory has on many managers' thinking!

## Individual differences and idiosyncrasies

When we talk about idiosyncratic individuals, we mean the *normal*, complex individuals who people all organizations. People's behavior rarely conforms to the "rational-economic man" assumptions (Schein, 1970) that frequently govern management thinking, rhetoric and actions. Each of us has a unique set of perspectives, attitudes and motivations. Some aspects of these are deeply embedded and hard to change. Others are more pliable or ephemeral.

Schein (1970) introduced the term "complex man" to describe the multivariate nature of individuals' characteristics and motivations. Treating individuals according to simplistic, universal assumptions, as rational management strategies often tend to do, not only ignores the rich diversity of talent but can also blind managers to the dysfunctional, shadow-side effects of this approach.

To talk of individual behaviors as idiosyncratic and the overall shadow-side dynamics as *a*-rational is not meant to imply that people engaged in them are unintelligent or acting illogically. Some years ago, de Bono introduced the useful idea of a "logic bubble" (de Bono, 1982). This describes the specific perceptual pattern within which a person is acting at any given time. It includes such things as their perceptions of the particular circumstances, relationships and context. De Bono acknowledges, of course, that people *will* often act illogically – even from within the perspective of their own logic bubble. However, the concept reflects the view that, in interaction with others, we each construct our own sense of reality (our own logic bubbles). And we use these as the basis of our ongoing interactions and behaviors.

In a similar vein, Culbert (1996: 14) argues that "Organization Is an Artifact of The Mind That Views It." A corollary he draws from this (p. 30) is that:

> Self-interests and personal, work-related effectiveness agendas significantly impact – even wholly determine – how people see events at work, and ultimately how they think to operate given these perceptions.

He goes on to say that everything that a person perceives, and every comment that they make, has a self-interested dimension that is specific to the individual involved. Two relevant conclusions arise from Culbert's work, which run counter to conventional management thinking and practice. First, the personal biases that channel people's perceptions down well-trodden, self-centered pathways cannot be bypassed – however indoctrinaire an approach might be pursued by management. Secondly, however clearly management might state their intentions in relation to particular aspects of organizational performance, it is impossible to conceive of a situation in which everyone will perceive and interpret these in the way intended.

This suggests that leaders need to recognize and take account of the *subjective* personal and work-related agendas that govern what individuals (*including themselves*) see as sensible and appropriate behavior in any given set of circumstances. Seeking to encourage and enable coalitions of co-operative effort to emerge around particular themes is therefore likely to be more effective than attempting to get people to subordinate their personal values and agendas to some impersonal mission statement or CEO-imposed vision. From this perspective, effective leadership is more about helping people to reframe the *context* within which they are operating. That is, enabling them to see this in more organizationally insightful *and* personally meaningful ways. They can then *both* serve their own interests *and, at the same time*, further the organization's overall purpose. It also suggests that managers should add psychosocial skills to their leadership "toolkit."

## Social networks and processes

The social structures and processes that exist within all organizations have a powerful impact upon how decisions are made and work actually gets done "on the ground." Social routines, rites and rituals reinforce and sustain these patterns of interaction and delineate group membership. And these also strongly influence which ideas and viewpoints take center stage, and which get sidelined. In their most positive expression, these informal relationships can lubricate organizations, cut through "red tape" and improve commitment to organizational decisions. Too often, though, membership of the various social groupings has no connection with individual capability and contribution. Talent that is potentially available to the organization can then be under-utilized or lost for good. These processes can also corrupt organizations by fostering narcissistic behavior

(Downs, 1997). Or they can put its very survival at risk by undervaluing diversity and leading to the appointment of "identikit" people in key positions. Social relationships and processes therefore have a marked effect on how organizations function – whether beneficially or otherwise. Egan (1994) cautions that viewing these issues as optional extras and failing to address them effectively adds cost to the business. In contrast, leaders who remain sensitive to the impact that these social dynamics have on organizational performance and deal with them constructively can add value.

As a result of these dynamics, "in-groups" and "out-groups" form and influence the way work gets done in all organizations. However, the tendency toward polarization and exclusion is a particular effect of this process. As described in some detail by Stacey (2001), differences that exist between members *within* a group tend to be glossed over, whereas similarities are exaggerated. At the same time, similarities that exist *between* groups are ignored and differences magnified. This marked tendency to polarize means that, even though the differences between groups – and the ideas that they espouse – may be minimal, extreme positions are likely to be maintained and the potentially value-enhancing middle ground ignored. This dynamic is also reflected in de Bono's comments about the self-organizing behavior of the mind (1990: 35–36):

> Patterns can be created by divisions which are more or less arbit rary. What is continuous may be divided into distinct units, which then grow further apart. Once such units are formed they become self-perpetuating. . . . Even though the choice between two competing patterns may be very fine, one of them will be chosen and the other one completely ignored. . . . There is a marked tendency to "polarise". This means moving to either extreme instead of maintaining some balanced point between them.

By definition, *informal coalitions* reflect this natural process of group formation. People coalesce around stories that make sense to them. In particular, successful coalitions are those that capture people's imagination in relation to one particular framing of events rather than an alternative one. Working with these natural dynamics, to attempt to build bridges between potentially competing positions rather than accepting the tendency for these to polarize, is an important aspect of the *informal coalitions* approach to change leadership.

## Organizational politics

Diverse agendas, perspectives and motivations affect the ways in which events are viewed, power is exercised and results are achieved in organizations. Some of these differences arise from the very nature of organizations, which are deliberately designed to divide up tasks between different groups and individuals. Other differences result from the personal differences that we outlined earlier. As a result of these natural organizational and psychosocial dynamics, people continually vie for power to achieve their work agendas and/or to satisfy their personal interests.

Amongst others, Eccles and Nohria (1992) contend that, at all times, organizations consist of competing political coalitions of people. This is the essence of the *informal coalitions* view of organizational dynamics. Coalitions form and re-form continually around different interests; each with the aim of defining aspects of the organization's agenda and shaping its outcomes. Politics – in organizations as in life – is about the management of these differences. Although organizational politics are most often viewed in negative terms, the ways in which difference and contention are managed can enhance as well as undermine the organization's capability and performance.

Stacey (2003, for example) also takes up this legitimate $v$ illegitimate theme. In some instances, he argues, politics will be used to reinforce the themes that are organizing legitimate (openly expressed) conversations and behavior. That is, they will be used to strengthen the organization's formally adopted policies and accepted wisdom. In other cases, political strategies and actions will be used to advance the illegitimate or shadow themes, which are not part of the organization's formally acknowledged patterns. In both cases, the effects of political behavior may be either functional or dysfunctional. The need to address issues such as power, territorial game-playing and conflict management is therefore essential in dealing with organizational strategy, change and performance.

It follows from the above that organizations are networks of shifting power relationships, through which influence is exerted and results achieved. So-called "legitimate" power is overtly recognized and/or reinforced through an organization's formal authority networks. However, there are many more sources of power in organizations than formal authority; and we will look at these in some depth in Chapter 5. There, we will explore four interrelated aspects of power that impact upon the dynamics of change and performance in organizations. These are summarized in Table 2.2.

**Table 2.2** Characteristics of power in organizations

| Characteristic | Summary description |
| --- | --- |
| Instrumental | Certain attributes of an individual's capability and behavior can be directly used to modify the knowledge, attitudes and behaviors of others. |
| Inner | An individual's internal power bases enable them to use power instrumentally with more potency. |
| Relational | Power exists, and can only be exercised, *in relationship with* other people. |
| Embedded | Power is also embedded in the structures, processes, language and other aspects of the organization that serve to define its formal rules and norms of behavior. |

## Paradox and contradiction

Paradox is endemic in organizations. Besides the inherent ambiguity and contradictions that organizational paradox brings, it can also be the source of peak performance and creativity (see, for example, Quinn, 1988 and Stacey, 2003). Despite this latter possibility, the tensions inherent in paradox are ordinarily seen as disruptive to the normal flow of management. Attempts are usually made to design them out through seemingly decisive, either–or type thinking. Or alternative viewpoints are viewed as divisive and efforts made to eliminate them. Indeed, conventional wisdom would often see the removal of these tensions as a key aim of management. From this perspective, failure to remove the ambiguities and to achieve clarity would be seen as a sign of poor leadership. However, as implied by the above, such paradoxes and tensions do not disappear. Instead, they simply re-emerge in the shadow-side conversations, and in the behaviors that these evoke.

I see the omnipresence of paradox in organizations as a shadow-side issue because paradoxes exist and exert their influence whether or not their existence is openly acknowledged. Even though these paradoxes are often subtly communicated to staff in the form of mixed messages (such as the call to increase innovation *and* avoid mistakes), it is rare for the underlying contradictions to be openly acknowledged.

Too often managers seek to deal with paradoxes such as these by making either–or choices. This presupposes two things. First, it implies that such a choice is possible; that is, that organizations could choose to pursue one side of the paradox and reject the other. Secondly, even if they could choose, the approach suggests that there is a right and a wrong answer to "the problem." This is clearly not the case. Evans (in Chowdhury, 2000), for example, comments that organizational paradoxes cannot be made to disappear. They can't be resolved or solved in any meaningful way.

Stacey (2000: 13) argues that ". . . paradoxes require both–and choices at the same time; either–or choices are not possible, nor is a sequential switching between them." As Johnson (1999) also suggests, these need to be seen as tensions to be managed, not problems to be solved. And these tensions need to be managed *dynamically*, rather than in a once-and-for-all way. We shall explore this dynamic of organizations further in Chapter 7.

## Cultural patterning process

One of the key insights that arise from the *informal coalitions* perspective is that culture is not an object that can be designed and built by managers. This is in stark contrast to the way that cultural change is dealt with in the various n-step change models;[3] or in approaches that see leaders as all-powerful "drivers" of cultural change. Instead, organizational culture is understood as the *ongoing process* of shared meaning making, which happens continuously in organizations, as people perceive, interpret, evaluate and share what's going on. Culture then exists not so much "outside" people as "inside and between" them – within their internal dialogues and through the conversations that they have with each other.

Over time, these interpretations enter the folklore and mythology of the organization, as they are passed on and reinterpreted through further conversations. In turn, these stories and myths help to embed the patterns of assumptions that influence people's ongoing thinking and behavior. The existing assumptions provide the background (unspoken) "cultural conversation" (Gallwey, 2000) that tends to route further sensemaking and use-making conversations along established channels. Organizational culture cannot be properly understood and "worked with" effectively until these underlying assumptions have been surfaced and deciphered. In many respects, this all-pervasive view of culture is the embodiment of shadow-side dynamics. The social, political and "hidden" aspects of the shadow side, outlined above, all become embedded and taken-for-granted ways of operating, through their conversational patterning into an organization's cultural assumptions. In turn, these underlying patterns affect the ways in which the social, political and informal landscape of the organization continues to develop.

This patterning process has the positive benefit of simplifying the organizational learning and socialization process. In particular, it enables people to function effectively within the everyday rituals, routines and expectations of organizational life. At the same time, it has the negative effect of tending to make organizations (or parts of them) become stuck in familiar patterns. Cultural change is therefore about influencing these everyday sensemaking conversations in ways that enable them to become "unstuck." To the extent that an intervention helps to change the overall pattern of conversations within the organization, the organization itself will change – whether in the ways intended or otherwise!

One important factor in all of this, which we touched upon briefly above, is that multiple perceptions, interpretations and evaluations are inevitable. This complicating feature of organizational behavior means that there is never likely to be one universally applicable pattern of interpretations and assumptions channeling this sensemaking behavior. The conventional view of organizational culture suggests that a clear, consistent and commonly held set of shared values and beliefs should exist, which binds the organization together. In contrast, recalling the "spinning plates" metaphor, the *informal coalitions* perspective acknowledges the existence of overlapping patterns of relationships. Each of these gives rise to different (and also overlapping) patterns of assumptions.

Surfacing the underlying assumptions of an organization, sub-group or coalition is difficult because of their taken-for-granted nature. However, clues to them can be found in informal, everyday conversations and interactions. Deeply held assumptions about what is "right" in relation to organizational life hold the key to why many well-intentioned initiatives fail to have any lasting impact. This is despite the fact that support for them is professed in the formal arenas of the organization. In relation to cultural dynamics, the *informal coalitions* perspective recognizes that it is these underlying assumptions that actually channel behavior in an organization. The beliefs, values and norms that are espoused as part of its overt management philosophy are far less influential factors in shaping an organization's emerging cultural patterns; unless, that is, these reflect people's everyday experiences of the organization in practice, as interpreted and shared through their conversations and interactions with others.

Finally here, this perspective also leads to the conclusion that decisions and actions cannot be taken (or left untaken) in any aspect of organizational performance without these having cultural implications. Everything that managers do, and the way that they do it, has symbolic significance. Managers therefore need to "think culturally" (Bate, 1994).[4] That is they need to understand the cultural impacts that their decisions and actions have on people's everyday sensemaking and use-making conversations. We will discuss this role-modeling aspect of the change-leadership agenda extensively in Chapter 4.

## The leadership paradox

The *management edict, education and training* and *joint problem solving* perspectives combine to provide leaders with a felt sense of control of the change process. This control might be exercised through a tight "command and control" regime (*management edict*) or a more flexible and empowered approach (*joint problem solving*). For example, provided that they have the necessary formal authority, managers can impose physical and directional changes on the organization (such as plant closures and strategic shifts). They can also, if they wish, choose not to invest time and resources in *education and training* initiatives or *joint problem solving* groups. Even if they do incorporate aspects of these last two approaches into their change strategy, they can still control the nature and content of the messages that are sent or the composition and terms of reference of any working groups that might be set up. Being formally in charge places managers "in control" of the formal agenda. It gives them the position power to command others within relevant parts of the organization, even if they choose not to exercise that right. However, as we have seen from our discussions of relationship and shadow-side dynamics above, leaders are *not* in control of *informal coalitional* activity; or of its impact on organizational capability and performance.

If, for example, managers decide to close a factory, make people redundant or restructure the organization, they have the power to do so. They are in control of the decision. And, subject to any statutory requirements or local agreements that might exist on the implementation process, they can ensure that these decisions are put into effect. What managers are not in control of, though, is how people perceive, interpret, evaluate and react to the actions that they take. Nor can they control the impact that these underlying dynamics have on the continuing performance and capability of the organization as a whole. Whilst the visible, surface-level changes (such as the headcount reduction and immediate savings in salaries costs) may be achieved to plan, the informal, hidden and messier dynamics of change may have a much more significant impact on the organization's wider and longer-term prospects. This paradox of being both "in control" and "not in control" at the same time is illustrated in Figure 2.1.

This situation causes difficulty for those managers who equate leadership with being in control. Conventional, common-sense thinking looks to resolve the tension. It aims to reduce – or, better still, eliminate – the sense of not being in control and to strive for certainty. Seeking to do things better and get them right becomes the guiding philosophy (Streatfield, 2001).

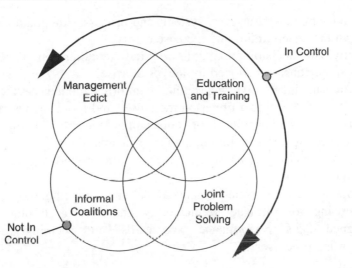

**Figure 2.1** Leadership paradox

This accounts, in part, for the popularity of management fads, "one-minute"-type solutions and linear, $n$-step approaches to organizational success. These appear to offer managers an escape from the anxieties of an uncertain and ambiguous organizational world. Instead, they tempt them with the promise of control and predictability. Unfortunately, as suggested by Grint (1997: 2) below, the seemingly common-sense solutions that these approaches offer consistently fail to deliver:

> Much of what is taught in management or business schools, or written about in management or business books, is a banal paradox. It is banal in that it appears to regurgitate what everyone already takes for granted and knows to be true. It is a paradox because, despite being full of common sense, it doesn't seem to work.

## Rejecting the paradox – striving for certainty and control

The anxiety of not being "in control" can lead managers to adopt a range of control-seeking strategies, such as:

- intervening increasingly in day-to-day decision-making, in an effort to "lead from the front" and impose their will on the outcomes;
- increasing efforts to get the message across and reduce ambiguity through more intensive, formal and structured communication programs;

- introducing new structures, systems and processes in an attempt to tie down the uncertainties and increase clarity;
- centralizing decision-making, to limit individual discretion and reduce the scope for unsanctioned initiatives to arise;
- introducing increased target setting, monitoring and measurement, with the aim of "keeping a finger on the pulse" and reducing surprises;
- introducing the latest batch of "outstanding leadership" competencies, and selecting and developing managers against them;
- signing up to the latest excellence formula and "best practice" methodologies;
- adopting the latest n-step organizational change methodology;
- searching for ultimate predictability and control, through tightly aligned plans, performance "scorecards" and seemingly rigorous reporting processes.

In summary, the belief is that by "doing things better and getting them right" they will be able to close the gap between their stated intentions and the organizational outcomes that arise in practice.

## Injecting some "uncommon sense" – embracing the paradox

Informed by the Change Map, the challenge for leaders who adopt an *informal coalitions* perspective is somewhat different. No longer is there a need to reject the idea of not being in control. Instead, the aim is to overcome the anxiety of being *both* in control *and* not in control *at the same time*. This means understanding, and actively engaging with, the informal coalitional activity that is generating and sustaining these *inevitable* dynamics of change. To understand what this might mean in practical terms, we first need to look at what managers actually *do* when they are wearing their leadership "hats."

## The nature of the leadership task

When I ask managers to describe what leadership (and/or management[5]) is about, they usually compile a list that includes such functions as strategic thinking, planning, organizing, controlling, motivating, inspiring, deciding, recruiting, evaluating performance and so on. I then ask them to boil these things down to *what they – as managers – actually do on a day-to-day basis*. They invariably come to the conclusion – if sometimes uneasily – that "talking" is at the heart of their leadership role!

I use the word "talk" here rather than communication because, in organizations, the latter has taken on a rather limited meaning. Organizational communication has largely come to be associated with the formal communication programs and structured presentations that reflect an *education and training* view of the communication task. In contrast, much of the most valuable communication occurs through the informal talk and interaction that takes place during everyday conversations and interactions. Stacey (2001, for example) would refer to this as communicative interaction in the living present, which better describes the full scope of the relationship but is less user-friendly than "talk." In any event, for our purposes, talk involves all aspects of interaction, including listening, gesturing, involuntary signaling through body language and so on, as well as talking itself. It also includes self-talk (i.e. thinking). For managers, then, talk *is* action; and we will return to this theme, and its practical implications for organizational leadership, in Chapter 3.

## Socially and politically constructed reality

To understand the dynamics of *informal conditions*, we also need to think about what we mean when we say something is "real." We ordinarily talk as though we live in an objective reality – something that exists "out there" – a given. If we reflect on this, though, we can see that we take an active role in bringing our realities into being through the various ways that we perceive, interpret, evaluate and share what we see (and hear and feel, etc.). We then think of these mental constructs as "the way things are."

There is a story that Picasso was completing the portrait of a woman when her husband asked if he could see the picture. Picasso showed him the work, which was painted in his usual style. Wishing not to offend the artist, the man said that the picture was very good, but that it didn't really look like his wife. When Picasso asked the man what his wife really looked like, he took out a photograph of her from his wallet and showed it to him. Picasso thought for a minute then replied: "Small, isn't she?"

We *enact* the reality of our everyday world through our self-talk and the conversations that we have with others. That is, we bring it into being through the ways in which we perceive, interpret, evaluate and share our views of unfolding events. Echoing this view, Eccles and Nohria (1992) argue that the things we take for granted in organizations and "know to be true" (such as facts, procedures and strategies) are socially and politically constructed. To put it another way, when people get together they literally "make things up" through their everyday conversations and interactions. Bate (1994) similarly reflects this view, when he describes managers – in a positive, not deprecating way – as "fiction writers." The talk and language we use is powerful. It is through the way that we talk with others about everyday experiences and happenings – rather than the happenings and experiences themselves – that ultimately shapes the way we see things and the way we act.

## Organizations as networks of self-organizing conversations

From an *informal coalitions* perspective, organizations can be thought of as networks of ongoing, self-organizing conversations. These conversations take place continually. They occur any time, any place, anywhere; not just in the formal structures, processes and confines of the organization. Many of the conversations occur incidentally and spontaneously, as a result of random interactions. These are frequently emotion-laden; and they often take place covertly and in private. The themes that the conversations reflect, embellish or create may be unconsciously held; and they may even be based on pure fantasy. But this makes them no less powerful in shaping the dynamics of particular organizations and influencing the outcomes that emerge (Stacey, 2001). Many of these conversations provide the means through which individuals and groups perceive, interpret and evaluate the meaning of organizational symbols.[6] This enables them to develop a sense of what the organization (and/or parts of it) is about, what is going on and how they should think and behave in the light of the interpretations that they have made. Other conversations provide the means for agenda-shifting proposals to be seeded and support for them to be garnered before they are raised and exposed in official forums.

Stacey (2003) distinguishes between "legitimate themes," which he sees as organizing the official conversations, and the "shadow themes," which are banished by the official themes to the shadow side. Informal conversations therefore "stitch together" the legitimate (formally acknowledged) and shadow-side aspects of organizations. They also generate their own shadow-side effects. The shadow-side aspects of organizational conversations are most evident in the ways that these generate and transmit organizational folklore, mythology, humor and rumor. The most "subversive" of these rarely surface in the formal organizational settings. However, these are rife when protected by the informality of casual chat, private peer-group meetings and one-to-ones. The anonymity of the grapevine provides another safe route for these to surface and be discussed. Shadow themes also frequently provide the sub-text of formal meetings, even where the overt conversations appear to reflect the official line. This occurs through collusion during meetings to promote or subvert a particular proposition. We have all been aware, for example, of how informal, pre-meeting discussions and agreements have been played out during the meetings themselves through covert glances, nods and winks.

The patterns of meaning that shape the organization's objectives, activities and outcomes emerge through this everyday conversational process. Some of these become part of the formal missions, strategies and policies of the organization whilst others remain in the organization's shadows. People continuously coalesce around the hidden or emerging themes, either to further particular causes or to frustrate them. This is illustrated in Figure 2.2.

In this way, through current conversations and interactions, the past is continually reinterpreted and made sense of and the future perpetually constructed, *in the present*. It is therefore important for leaders to pay attention to the conversational patterns that are taking place in the "here

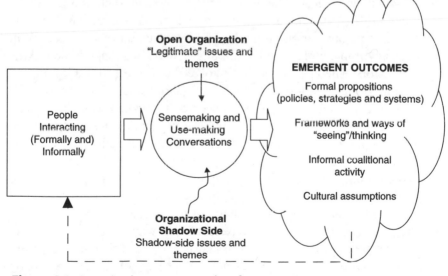

**Figure 2.2** Organizations as networks of conversations

and now," if they are to help to shape the outcomes that emerge. This process is not mandated or controlled in any formal way. Nor can it be. However, this is not to imply that all participants within the process have equal power to influence the nature, direction and outcome of the conversations. As suggested earlier, the dynamics of the process are affected by the power relationships that exist between participants. And this power balance will change from time to time, and from situation to situation. Managers are *active* participants in this everyday process, not external objective observers of other people's actions. Leadership, in the context of *informal coalitions*, arises from having sufficient *power* (in the eyes of relevant others) and a compelling enough *story* to cause people to see things differently and to "sign up."

## The origins of organizational change

What inferences can we draw, from our discussions to date, about how change *originates* in organizations? As we saw in Chapter 1, change is commonly thought of as originating through some form of management decree, with other strategies being brought into play as appropriate. From the perspective of those on the receiving end, most change programs reflect, in large degree, the assumptions underlying the *management edict* view of change. It is also the case that a range of *education and training* initiatives and *joint problem solving* interventions usually accompany these top–down edicts. The former often include such things as the publication of statements of desired organizational values; an emphasis on formal communication programs; the introduction of new leadership competency frameworks; and the training of staff in a range of new skills and behaviors. The latter typically involve the use of task forces, implementation groups, team development workshops and so on. These *joint problem solving* initiatives are often seen as things that can be engaged further down the road, once the structural aspects of the changes have been put in place. Occasionally, though, a group will be brought together at the outset (often "in secret") to provide expert inputs at the idea-formulation stage. The adoption of one or other of the large-group change methodologies referred to earlier might also lead to the more widespread involvement of staff at an earlier stage of the formal change process.

   The above pattern of events reflects the way that staff typically become aware of and experience formal organizational changes. However, our discussion of organizations as networks of ongoing, self-organizing conversations suggests that this is not the way that change *originates* in organizations. Stacey (2000) suggests that change occurs when major shifts in power relationships lead to conversations through which important, informal shadow themes are brought to the surface and become formal, official propositions. So-called "resistance to change" is then the label given by the currently dominant coalition to the actions that others take to deal with the fears generated by changes in these power relationships.

These shadow themes are nurtured and eventually surfaced through the dynamics of *informal coalitions*. Whilst this informal coalitional activity never features in conventional descriptions of the organizational change process, I would contend that *all* significant change originates through that mode. This is illustrated in Figure 2.3, which outlines the process through a simplified version of the Change Map. The actual dynamics of the process are much messier and disjointed than described here, of course. However, managers have found this form of presentation useful in giving them an overall feel for what's going on.

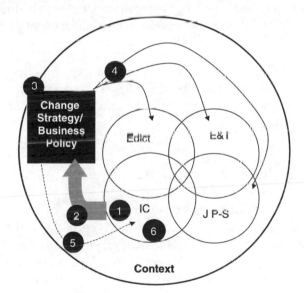

**Figure 2.3** How change originates

1 Informal conversations occur amongst influential players, to address perceived problems, to deal with emerging shadow-side issues or to advance their own agendas.
2 Eventually, when a sufficiently powerful informal coalition has been built around an emergent theme, this is raised in "legitimate" arenas, as a formal proposition.

3 Following formal processes, the proposition is incorporated into the organization's change strategy and/or business policy.

4 Proposed changes are then formally and openly implemented through a mix of *management edict*, *education and training* and *joint problem solving* approaches.

5 Powerful players use informal socio-political networks, during and after these earlier steps, to reinforce their favored aspects of the changes and to stymie or modify less favorable elements.

6 Informal coalitions re-emerge spontaneously in the organization, as a reaction to the perceived effects of the changes. These coalitions may operate either covertly or overtly; and they may be politically or socially based (as outlined earlier). Active, overt coalitions, which question the official approach or respond negatively to the imposed changes, are labeled as "resistors of change." It is important to recognize that members of the dominant coalition within the organization (ordinarily members of senior management) will also be following this pattern of behavior, whether collectively or independently.

The conversations generated within and between these new coalitions and with potential "new recruits" will trigger a repeat of the cycle, from steps 1 to 6 above; and this pattern will recur continually throughout the organization's life.

## Informal coalitions assumptions

Most competing theories of organizational change adopt a rational-management standpoint. These can usefully be thought about in terms of differing mixes of the *management edict*, *education and training* and *joint problem solving* modes of change. In sharp contrast to these is the *a*-rational view of the change process, as encapsulated in the *informal coalitions* mode of change leadership. This perspective:

- sees change as continuous and ordinary, rather than episodic and extraordinary;
- engages with the hidden, messy and informal dynamics of organizations, which have a significant – and potentially beneficial – impact on the outcomes of organizational change;
- works both with the official organizational themes and processes, *and* those that are organizing the shadow-side conversations;

- understands that power and politics are central to the dynamics of change;
- acknowledges that everyone is involved in determining the outcomes and meaning of particular organizational changes, although from differing (and shifting) power bases – these cannot be mandated by any one individual or group;
- recognizes, in particular, that managers are participants in this ongoing process, not objective observers and controllers of other people's actions[7];
- is aware that most – if not all – formally adopted propositions begin life through informal, shadow-side conversations, and that these surface only when they are perceived to be supported by a powerful enough coalition to win through;
- accepts that *informal coalitional* activity will happen whether managers want it to or not – the only choice open to them is whether or not to engage with it in a deliberate and informed way.

## Implications of the dynamics of informal coalitions

The implications of the *informal coalitions* perspective for the conventional understanding of change leadership and organizational dynamics are profound. Its emphasis on relationship and shadow-side dynamics, its use of conversation and coalition building as the main routes to change, and its rehabilitation of power and politics as legitimate aspects of leadership, raise a number of critical issues for leaders and change specialists to embrace. Amongst these are the following propositions:

- "Managing change," as this phrase is usually understood, is not possible in the ways that the *management edict, education and training* and *joint problem solving* perspectives imply that it is.
- Instead, change occurs as shifts take place in the patterns of conversation through which people make sense of organizational life and coalesce with others around themes that reflect mutually beneficial outcomes. This process is self-organizing and its outcomes emergent.
- Although managers are formally empowered to initiate changes within their authority, they cannot control the resulting conversations or coalitional activity in any meaningful sense. They cannot, therefore, predetermine the results of any changes that they or others instigate.
- Shadow-side dynamics and power relationships are critical to how change happens – these won't go away simply by ignoring them.

*Constructive* politics – defined here as the organizationally beneficial management of differences – therefore becomes a central plank of change leadership, not something to be denied, wished away or seen as necessarily destructive and divisive.

- "Culture" is not a separate component of organization that can be designed, built and communicated by managers. It is the *ongoing process of shared meaning making*. This process is fragmentary and gives rise to multiple interpretations and patterns of taken-for-granted assumptions, rather than to a single, homogeneous set of "shared values."

- Those in leadership positions throughout an organization are *both* "in control" *and* "not in control" at the same time – "doing things better and getting them right" helps with the former but won't overcome the latter.

- Leadership is not about being "right" but about being able to influence others to see, interpret, evaluate and do things differently. That is, its aim is to help people to make sense of what's happening in terms of one particular interpretation of events rather than an alternative one, and to integrate these new ways of feeling, thinking and acting into their everyday behavior.

- The ultimate aim of this change-leadership activity is to build active coalitions of support for desired changes.

- "Talk" (in the broad sense of the word used earlier) is the primary *action* tool that leaders have to achieve this.

- Effective leadership will often be invisible and the antithesis of the outstanding, heroic form of leadership that is often equated with leadership *per se*.

The above characteristics of *informal coalitional* activity do not sit comfortably with the rational view of change leadership and organizational dynamics that dominates conventional management thinking. Making the required shift in perspective can therefore be challenging and uncomfortable. But it opens up the possibility of engaging with the natural dynamics of change and offers a way of embracing the leadership paradox of being both *in control* and *not in control* at the same time.

## Change-leadership agenda

From an *informal coalitions* perspective of change, leaders are "on the pitch, playing," rather than "in the stands" observing and controlling other people's actions. This means that they are unavoidably involved as participants in whatever emerges. It also provides them with a significantly different leadership agenda from that which is usually associated with organizational change:

- First, leaders need to *reframe communication*. This means valuing everyday talk and interaction as their primary *action* tool and seeing its main purpose as sensemaking and relationship building rather than message passing. In doing this, they need to exploit opportunities that arise from official statements and emerging events to help people make sense of what's going on and to make value-adding use of the sense that they've made.
- Secondly, they need to *think culturally*. That is, they need to recognize that cultural patterns emerge from the *active process* of shared sensemaking, and that their own words and actions (including silence and inaction) provide powerful culture building symbols for this sensemaking process.
- Thirdly, they need to *act politically*. This involves *actively* engaging with the shadow-side dynamics of their organization and using their power with integrity in organizationally enhancing ways.
- The next challenge provides the central focus of the *informal coalitions* approach to change, by calling on leaders to work with the natural dynamics of their organizations to *build coalitions* of support for desired changes.
- Also, since paradox is ever present in organizations, effective leaders look to *embrace paradox* and work to make the *inevitable* contradictions livable for their staff.
- Finally, leaders recognize that *providing vision* through their everyday interactions with staff is more useful than providing *a* vision; that is, an end-state view of some aspired-to future position.

The following chapters explore in more detail these six key aspects of leading change from an *informal coalitions* perspective.

# CHAPTER 3

# Reframing communication

> Communication communicates better the more levels of meaning
> it has and the less possible it is, therefore, to quantify it.
>
> – Peter Drucker

## Introduction

One of the widely accepted "truths" of management is that however much leaders communicate with their staff it's never enough. This is especially the case during periods of significant change, where people's thirst for information appears unquenchable. Whenever those issues of most concern to staff are identified, communication invariably features high on the list. To argue that organizations need to communicate more effectively with staff is therefore unlikely to be contentious. However, to question the purpose of leadership communication and challenge the long established ways in which it is typically carried out may well be.

Conventionally, leadership communication is thought of primarily in terms of the linear, sender–receiver model. From this perspective, management determines and transmits the meaning of a particular event, change or policy *to* staff. The emphasis of this conventional approach is therefore on how best to "get the message across." Its success is judged in terms of the extent to which "the *right* facts are transmitted to the *right* people at the *right* time." This notion sits at the heart of most communication programs that accompany formal change events. In contrast, an *informal coalitions* view of the leadership task argues that outcomes emerge spontaneously from the *local* perceptions and interpretations of issues and events, including the process and content of formal statements made by management. We therefore need to reframe the limited understanding of leadership communication that the established view reflects. In particular, we need to bring the role of the leader's everyday interactions with staff into the foreground. The more conventional, structured elements of organizational communication then provide an informational backcloth to this dynamic and ongoing process of shared sensemaking and relationship building.

## Leadership communication grid

Seeing organizations as dynamic networks of ongoing, self-organizing conversations puts communication at the heart of organizational change and performance. As we have seen, outcomes flow out of these conversational networks *in the moment*, as people make sense of what is going on and decide how to make best use of the sense that they've made. As we've also recognized, these *self-organizing* conversations occur with or without the leader's active involvement. The only choice that a leader has in this is whether or not to engage with these natural conversational dynamics in an informed, meaningful and organizationally beneficial way.

Our focus here, therefore, is on the critically important communication role of those in formal leadership positions. It is not on organizational communication in the round. That having been said, much of what follows will have relevance for others who wish to make a difference to their organization's performance and the delivery (or direction) of its change agenda. We will use the sensemaking framework in Figure 3.1, the Leadership Communication Grid, to facilitate this discussion. This categorizes different facets of the leader's communication role in relation to organizational change and performance. The framework suggests that the conventional view of communication forms only one part of a much wider – *and more powerful* – range of communication approaches available to leaders within organizations.

The Grid identifies four separate aspects of leadership communication. These are distinguished by the *degree of structure* and the *degree of formality* that each of them involves. Structured communication is planned in advance; and efforts are made to contain outcomes within management-controlled boundaries. In contrast, unstructured forms happen spontaneously ("in the moment"); and whatever emerges, emerges. Formal communication focuses on the passing of messages *from* managers *to* staff; whereas informal communication is about managers and staff *jointly* making sense of issues and events, deciding *together* how best to proceed, and building value-adding relationships *with* each other.

Quadrant C1 (structured–formal) includes the established forums, processes and techniques that are most readily associated with the conventional notion of leadership communication. These reflect an

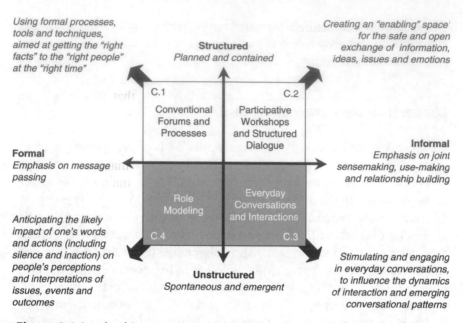

Using formal processes, tools and techniques, aimed at getting the "right facts" to the "right people" at the "right time"

**Structured**
*Planned and contained*

Creating an "enabling" space for the safe and open exchange of information, ideas, issues and emotions

C.1
Conventional Forums and Processes

C.2
Participative Workshops and Structured Dialogue

**Formal**
*Emphasis on message passing*

**Informal**
*Emphasis on joint sensemaking, use-making and relationship building*

Role Modeling

Everyday Conversations and Interactions

C.4

C.3

Anticipating the likely impact of one's words and actions (including silence and inaction) on people's perceptions and interpretations of issues, events and outcomes

**Unstructured**
*Spontaneous and emergent*

Stimulating and engaging in everyday conversations, to influence the dynamics of interaction and emerging conversational patterns

**Figure 3.1** Leadership communication grid

*education and training* view of the communication task. Quadrant C2 (structured–informal) seeks to introduce a degree of informality and openness into what is still a structured approach to the communication process. Examples of this would include participative workshops, pre-planned coaching sessions, and similar structured methods. All of these approaches adopt a *joint problem solving* stance in relation to communication, change and performance management. Quadrants C1 and C2 house the "classic" approaches to leadership communication, as described in most books on the subject. Internal communication strategies that are devised to support planned organizational change rarely step out of this structured environment. Indeed, the degree of structure and formality often increases at these times.

However, the Leadership Communication Grid introduces two further modes of leadership communication. These incorporate the *a*-rational, messy and unstructured forms of communication that are embodied in the *informal coalitions* view of organizational dynamics. In the diagram, these are included "below-the-line," in Quadrants C3 and C4. Quadrant C3 (unstructured–informal) recognizes the pervasiveness and power of everyday, self-organizing conversations in shaping the change agenda and delivering specific outcomes. It therefore calls on leaders to become actively involved in this critical conversational space. Finally,

Quadrant C4 (unstructured–formal) highlights the communication impact of a leader's everyday behaviors – *as observed by others*. This is a *formal* means of communication because it is about one-way message passing and comes into play the instant that anyone is formally appointed to a leadership role. From that point onward, anything that they say or do (including everything that they don't say and don't do) sends "messages" to staff. Crucially though, it is these staff – not the leader – who decide what these words and actions mean. It is also therefore an *unstructured* form of communication because the sense that staff make of a leader's behavior emerges spontaneously, as they perceive, interpret and share their observations with others.

Although all four approaches can apply equally well to internal and external communication, our main interest here is on leaders' interactions with their teams. What follows is therefore crafted in terms of *internal communication*.

## Conventional forums and processes – Mode C1

In the language of the Change Map, mode C1 reflects an *education and training* view of organizational change. This sees communication as a tool for talking *about* the change – in terms of its "whys, whats, wheres, whens and hows." This is where most thinking about management communication begins – and often ends! It is about using formal and structured processes, tools and techniques to satisfy the felt need to "get the right facts to the right people at the right time." Formal, structured communication is a taken-for-granted element of all planned programs of organizational change. It is therefore important to deal with this first, before moving on to explore the leadership implications of the other perspectives.

The aims of the formal, structured approach to internal communication are, typically, one or more of the following:

- to inform people of management's intentions – with or without any attempt to sell these changes;
- to achieve compliance, acceptance or, preferably, buy-in to management's view of the future and/or intended course of action;
- to reposition the organization's espoused values, if changes in these form part of the overall strategy;
- to specify required ways of working, as a step toward realigning people's attitudes and behaviors with the demands of the new strategy;

- to "roll out" new systems, processes and procedures;
- to obtain a limited level of feedback from staff – *primarily to gauge whether or not the intended message has got through to people*, rather than to seek others' inputs to decision-making.

## Formal communication programs to support organizational change

The internal communications and/or HR departments of organizations usually put much thought into the design of these programs. Despite this, any initially positive effects that these might generate often tend to wear off relatively quickly. It can be particularly difficult to sustain the early momentum if these programs are only used to reinforce the intellectual and physical aspects of the process, such as changes to strategy, structure and systems. An exclusive emphasis on providing information in these areas can overlook the continuing need for managers to address the psychological and emotional impact of the changes on people. Communication in this *education and training* mode is also usually couched in terms of carefully crafted, strategically framed messages. These can hit a barrier when they come face to face with the day-to-day realities of people's ongoing activities, personal concerns and everyday experiences of organizational life.

As an example of this, I remember carrying out a series of formal presentations to groups of staff in the late 1980s. These related to the impending privatization of the Central Electricity Generating Board (CEGB) and the launch of one of its commercial offshoots, National Power. Along with managers from other locations, I had been briefed on the forthcoming changes, at a management conference held in central London. Armed with carefully prepared scripts, a set of presentation slides in the new corporate livery, and a video of the forthcoming television advertisement for the new company, our task was to engender enthusiasm for the venture amongst local staff. The materials had been expertly prepared, potential questions anticipated and answers provided. No stone had been left unturned in the desire to give managers the support that they needed to help them launch the company successfully.

The video was particularly stirring. It began by introducing images of various of the country's national institutions to the background strains of "I vow to Thee, My Country." National Power, it claimed, was "The National that Makes the Other Nationals Tick." However, each time that the video was played to successive audiences, at its assigned slot within the thoughtfully crafted presentation, muffled conversations spread around the room. At the end of its third showing, I thought that I had better refer openly to the image that seemed to be causing this reaction, so that we could deal with it and move on. It turned out that the National Youth Theatre was one of the "nationals" featured; and the scene being acted out was of Brutus stabbing Julius Caesar in the back! Being "stabbed in the back" was how many of the CEGB's employees felt at that time about the privatization process. So, far from igniting their passion for the new company, the abiding emotion of many attending these carefully orchestrated events was precisely the opposite. Here, as in all other attempts at top–down message passing, the *de facto* meaning of the communication is determined locally, through the conversational exchanges that flow from it.

The perceived authenticity of local managers is another important aspect of leadership that can suffer when centrally orchestrated communication programs require the dissemination of common messages by line managers. Shadow-side comments along the lines of "that was not 'X' speaking," only serve to undermine the local leader's credibility. These also reduce the likelihood that the intended changes will be readily bought into by staff, who often view these set-piece communications with cynicism.

Formal communication methods are also often hamstrung by managers' felt need to control the message tightly and to maintain an image of management as "all knowing." Allied to this is the common practice of avoiding the sharing of bad news. This results in the sanitizing of communications to eliminate any acknowledgement of their likely emotional impact. Whilst formal communications can be honed to address some of these deficiencies, the impersonality of communication in a message-passing mode still leaves a big sensemaking and relationship-building task to be done.

## Written materials

Ekman (in Sjöstrand et al., 2001) also draws attention to the limited power of formal, *written* communication as a tool of management. He acknowledges that local, conversational interpretation will always be required to make sense of such documents. These conversations will necessarily distort or embellish the official text, since this can never provide definitive guidance on all possible interpretations. When making sense of such material, people explore the limits that these impose on their freedom to act and the nature and likelihood of any sanctions that might apply if they were to overstep the mark. As a result, Ekman argues that policies and directives are embellished or even "disqualified" through this everyday small talk.

Despite these (often unacknowledged) limitations, reams of written communications, and the structured talk and action that goes with them, typically punctuate formal change-management programs. These conventional forums and processes ordinarily include a selection of the following:

- cascaded ("rolled-out") presentations
- team leader–led briefings
- specially commissioned videos
- posting of messages and responses to anticipated questions on the organization's intranet
- e-mail notices
- in-house newspapers and newsletters
- information on notice boards
- use of employees' representatives to disseminate information.

## A linear model of communication

The linear, sender–receiver model sits at the heart of these conventional communication methods and programs. From this perspective, good communication occurs when the messages are packaged (encoded) effectively and the barriers to reception (or "noise") overcome, so that the recipients will receive (decode) the information in the way intended by management. Management's attention therefore focuses on such things as:

- honing the content and structure of the message, to ensure clarity;
- getting the timing "right" – that is, synchronizing the messages with relevant events and milestones in the wider change program;
- deciding the format(s) and media that are best suited to conveying the message;
- attending to the physical barriers that might get in the way of reception (e.g. location); and
- making sure that negative emotions don't get in the way of "the facts."

A number of myths about managerial communication have emerged alongside the adoption of this message-passing model. These have led to taken-for-granted assumptions about how best to communicate with staff, which continue to distort much of management's thinking in this area. Amongst the limiting assumptions are that it is best for managers to:

- wait until they know the whole story, so as not to "set hares running" as people speculate about the "not sure yets;"
- avoid any suggestion that they don't know all of the answers, as this will undermine people's confidence in them as leaders;
- share information only on a need-to-know basis;
- make sure that formal communications deal with facts, and don't get bogged down in feelings and emotions that might interfere with people's reception of the intended message;
- ensure that information is rolled out in a tightly scripted way, to ensure consistency of the message;
- avoid sharing bad news;
- just get on with the substance of the change and pick up the pieces later.

Many managers defend these assumptions by maintaining that staff need to be shielded from unnecessary distress at times of significant change. They argue that most employees can't handle difficult information or understand the complexities of organizational management. As an example of this, I was consulting with one client at a time when they were planning to outsource their customer-service call centers. Managers expected that this would lead to the closure of one or more of their current locations; but they were reluctant to share this with the staff that might be affected. They argued that the speculation would cause undue anxiety and distract them from their everyday work. Interestingly – though not surprisingly – when I asked the managers if *they* would want to know about the possibility of closure if it were to affect them personally, they all agreed that they would!

Where formal, structured communication is unencumbered by these assumptions, and approached on an adult–adult (rather than parent–child) basis, it can add value to the change process. It does this by providing much sought-after information *about* the change. However, it still fails to engage in any meaningful way with the active processes of shared sensemaking that are taking place continuously and disparately throughout the organization at large. Formal communications – good or bad – provide a significant input to these sensemaking processes. The processes themselves, though, take place locally and, primarily, in informal settings (around the coffee machines, in private offices, changing rooms and restaurants, and outside the "factory fence" altogether).

Significantly, any emotions and complexities that have been studiously designed out of the formal texts and presentations are factored back in through these many and diverse sensemaking conversations. Also, if staff perceive that they are not being told the whole story (as this is currently understood), they will fill in the blanks for themselves. This will happen whether this gap filling is based upon genuine information gleaned from elsewhere or simply the product of people's collective imaginations.

I recall a conversation that I once had with an executive director of a FTSE 100 company. I was sharing with him the ideas and concerns expressed by a large tranche of senior managers one year on from a substantial change in organizational structure and processes. One of the consistent themes that had emerged was that these managers claimed not to know what the company's strategy was. The director was livid. "What do they mean, they don't know what the strategy is?" he challenged, "We've told them dozens of times!" "Yes," I replied. "And, if you were to put any one of them against that wall and threaten to shoot them if they couldn't tell you what the strategy was, they'd have no difficulty at all in telling you what it is. The issue is not that they don't know what the strategy *is*; it's that they don't feel that they've been involved in developing it. They don't own it." Which point brings us on to quadrant C2 of the Leadership Communication Grid.

## Workshops and structured dialogue sessions – Mode C2

To overcome some of the limitations that arise from the exclusive use of conventional forums and approaches to communication (C1), several other structured methods have been introduced. These include issue-based workshops, and other ways of injecting greater participation and two-way interaction into the process. At the core of these methodologies are the ethos and practice of dialogue. Ellinor and Gerard (1998), for example, talk about the "conversation continuum," which exists between, at one end, dialogue and, at the other, discussion and debate. The characteristics of dialogue that they identify are particularly relevant to the concepts, tools and techniques that facilitate the C2 mode of communication. These are

- seeing the *whole* among the parts
- seeing the *connections* between parts
- *inquiring* into assumptions
- *learning* through inquiry and disclosure
- creating *shared* meaning among many.

Dialogue sessions can be run and facilitated by anyone with the relevant knowledge and skills. Here, though, we are considering structured dialogue as a mode of *leadership* communication. The perspective set out below therefore explores this approach from the perspective of the formal leader.

Communication sessions that adopt this approach are designed to enable leaders to introduce more informal dynamics into their exchanges with staff, whilst still setting and maintaining the boundaries of the interactions. The formal leader in these circumstances takes on the role of in-line coach and boundary manager, rather than acting in the advocate/teacher role that applies in the *education and training* mode of communication (C1). In the best of these dialogue-based, *joint problem solving* approaches to communication (C2), leadership *of the process* is more widely distributed, as everyone involved is personally responsible for the quality of conversation that takes place.

The value of embracing this dialogue-based methodology is that it can deepen conversation and expose taken-for-granted assumptions that are channeling existing behaviors and causing misunderstandings. It also highlights and encourages the development of interactive skills that serve everyday relationships and on-the-job problem solving. Structured dialogue sessions have their own "rules of engagement," to encourage and enable the required degree of openness and exchange to occur. However, the more widespread use, effective leadership and skilled facilitation of less rigid, issue-based workshops can help to shift communication in this general direction.

The sought-after benefits are unlikely to be delivered, though, simply by bringing people together and expecting them to participate fully as a matter of course. Some years ago, I was due to attend a workshop-style conference with other senior managers, at which the CEO was about to share his vision of the future. This was intended to stimulate dialogue and creative thinking amongst this wider management team. The night before the workshop, a colleague privately voiced the thoughts that govern many people's actions at such events. Even though he was a senior manager, he said that there was no way that he would be asking any questions of the CEO or others on the Executive at the next day's workshop. He summed up his position by saying, "It is more than your job's worth to ask a question, because you become a marked man." He was not alone in this view; and evidence from working with many organizations suggests that this stance is commonplace – whatever the organization or management levels involved.

## An enabling space for leadership communication

Where staff have grown used to being on the receiving end of top–down message passing (mode C1), leaders need to make special efforts to foster the trust required for C2 communication methods to bear fruit. This is especially the case where the former has accompanied a largely *management edict* approach to organizational change. Large-group change advocate, Kathleen Dannemiller, argues in favor of a technique that I have found very useful in creating the space necessary for more open and trusting communication to develop.[1] This is deliberately designed to overcome the reticence that many people have to asking leaders the questions that really matter to them. The method is quite straightforward; and it has proven to be very effective, both in terms of surfacing people's issues and concerns, and in climbing the first rung of the trust-building ladder. It works roughly as follows.

First, the leader sets out his or her vision, strategy, situational assessment or whatever they consider appropriate, without interruption. They then leave the room for an agreed period, to allow the other participants to reflect and comment upon what has been said without being inhibited by the leader's presence. Having been briefed before the session that they would be asked to do this, the group are requested to identify the *key themes* that came across to them during the presentation; and to capture their *reactions* to what the leader said (positive and/or negative, rational and/or emotional, form or content, etc.). Dependent upon the size of the group, participants may work in sub-groups to carry this out. This facilitates sensemaking conversations; and it increases the likelihood that everyone's views will be reflected in the group's output.

At the agreed time, the leader returns to review the outputs from the session and to address those issues of most concern to participants. Within this, the first task is quickly to review the key themes that have been identified. This ensures that the leader and team are "on the same page," so to speak, before the in-depth discussion of people's reactions begins. The main onus here is on the leader to assess quickly whether or not the main points that they intended to convey have been adequately and accurately reflected in the group's output. If not, this can be addressed, to prevent misunderstandings distorting the more potent review of people' reactions to what has been said.

In one such session, involving the entire workforce of a small business unit, I forewarned the managing director that one of the sub-groups appeared to be particularly agitated by what he had said. On his return to the room, the review of key themes made it clear that this sub-group had "misinterpreted" something in his initial presentation, and he was then able to clear up the misunderstanding very quickly. Without that preliminary session, their misperception of his intentions would have adversely colored their views of everything else that followed. When the leader is satisfied that the key themes have been sufficiently well identified, and when any misinterpretations have been dealt with, the group's reactions are explored in open forum, in the order that participants consider most important.

This approach provides the leader with a much sharper challenge to their thinking than is usual from a more conventional question-and-answer session. At the same time, it engages people much more meaningfully in the substance of the leader's words and the emotional impact of the interaction. It provides an opportunity for people to clarify and explore the leader's vision and stance on key issues and so on with their peers, before exposing their perceptions to the wider group. The open-forum review then provides a safe environment in which to challenge the leader's thinking, remove misunderstandings and (re-)build relationships. From the leader's perspective, it provides an opportunity for them to test and confirm, refine or reshape their thinking.

Two aspects of this process are critical to its effectiveness. These are the requirement for the leader to leave the room during the group's review of their input; and the fact that questions on the leader's return are asked on behalf of a particular sub-group, rather than by a specific individual. On one occasion, a director of a major retail organization challenged this first step in the process. He argued that it did not make sense for the new COO to leave the room, given that she had just said that she wanted to foster greater openness and trust within the leadership team. I suggested that he and his colleagues should trust the process, and that we would review this aspect later. After some persuasion he agreed; and the session continued as planned. On her return, the COO was subjected to some very pointed questions and open challenges to her new vision for the organization. As expected, she dealt with these very well. At the end of the meeting, though, the dissenting director acknowledged that the depth and quality of the exchanges would have been much lower if the COO had remained in the room during the team's identification of the main themes and their reactions to them.

The process outlined above is designed to encourage and enable more open dialogue to take place between leaders and their staff. It is one of many that can be used in the C2 mode of communication to promote more meaningful and genuine dialogue. However, whilst a shift in this direction facilitates greater participation and informal exchanges, it still involves only *structured* communication events, as in mode C1. Although offering an alternative, more participative way of approaching these, it does not address what happens *in the spaces in between these events*, or in the conversations held by people who are not themselves involved in the dialogue sessions or workshops. To the extent that it influences the perceptions and subsequent actions of those involved, it can help to shift the patterns of local conversations that they become involved in. However, it does not – and cannot – attend to these everyday conversations directly. The informal talk embodied in the *informal coalitions* view of organizational dynamics sets out to fill this hole.

## Everyday conversations and interactions – Mode C3

The *informal coalitions* view of change recognizes that sensemaking and use-making conversations go on throughout an organization, with or without leaders' involvement in them. It also accepts that these will be fueled both by formal statements from management *and, at the same time*, by rumor, the grapevine, casual conversation and personal fantasy. However well the structured communication events are carried out, this self-organizing patchwork of conversations will not go away. The only choice that leaders have, therefore, is whether or not they wish to engage with this process *in a deliberate and informed way*. If so, the aim is to help people make different sense of things than they might otherwise have made; and to make value-adding use of the sense that they've made. This is the essence of communication – *and leadership* – in an *informal coalitions* mode.

In contrast to seeing communication as being *about* change, this perspective argues that communication *is* change. That is, it sees change as taking place *through the everyday conversations* that people have with each other, both within the formally defined boundaries of the organization and beyond them. From an *informal coalitions* perspective, "talk" (embracing all aspects of "communicative interaction," as earlier described) is a leader's primary action tool. Stacey (2000: 413) emphasizes the strategic nature of this role:

> Strategic management is the process of actively participating in the conversations around important emerging issues.

Conversations are therefore central to effective leadership and successful organizational change.

## How we talk about talk

Unfortunately, in Western management circles, action is almost universally seen as being superior to talk. "Action orientation" is the stuff of leadership; whereas talk is more likely to be equated with indecision and dismissed as the antithesis of doing. So our first task is to challenge the negative perception of talk that currently distorts people's view of what organizational leadership and value-adding performance is all about. Talk needs to be reclaimed as a vital component of leadership. It needs to be seen as the "master key" that leaders can use to unlock the hidden dynamics of organizational change and performance.

When I have asked managers to give examples of how we talk about talk in organizations, one or more of the following phrases have typically been offered:

- "All talk and no action"
- "Action speaks louder than words"
- "Cut the talk and get to the action"
- "Talk is cheap"
- "Empty words"
- "Idle talk"
- "Action not words"
- "Silence is golden"
- "Verbal diarrhoea"
- "Delivery is everything"
- "Where is the action list?"
- "Ready, Fire, Aim!"
- "A bias for action"
- "Just Do It!"
- "Cut the crap"
- "Those who can, do; those who can't just talk about it"
- "It doesn't matter what you do, so long as you *do* something!"

This negative view of talk is pervasive in organizations. Despite this, when asked to deconstruct their leadership task, managers invariably agree that "talk" – in the broadest sense of the word – sits at the core of *everything* they do. "Talk" is indeed a leader's *primary action tool*. It is not something that needs to be gotten out of the way so that leaders can get on with the all-important action-taking task.

## The role of talk

For leaders, talk *is* action. Amongst other things:

- Talk sets the context within which action takes place. Failure to understand the critical link between context and action is, perhaps, one of the main causes of poor "follow through" and failed initiatives.
- Talk is central to sensemaking and the creation of meaning.
- Talk articulates the local visions and themes that inspire and energize action.
- Talk helps to mobilize and sustain people's commitment to action.
- Talk is essential to the effective implementation of action by aligning effort, solving unforeseen problems and charting progress.
- Talk validates action, by defining what constitutes "success" and "failure;" and, as a result, determining which results deserve recognition and comment – and which don't!
- Talk builds the relationships and creates the mutual understandings that facilitate future action.
- Talk extracts the learning from action – enriching the organization's knowledge and increasing the ability of its members to decide and act more effectively in the future.
- Talk can avoid the damaging – and potentially fatal – actions (such as the premature launch of the Challenger space shuttle), which occur when the political or cultural pressure for action suppresses vital information and limits understanding.
- Talk helps to build the coalitions and new mindsets that are the key to effective organizational change. As Bate (1994) points out, if managers want to change the way people think, they need to do it by changing the way they talk.
- Talk about purpose, values and objectives enables people to anticipate and respond effectively to actual events, rather than those that might have occurred if the "real world" had actually turned out in the ways assumed in formal plans, programs and budgets!

Talk, therefore, is not simply a ritual precursor to action, even where action taking is its intended outcome. Organizations that fail to follow through on management edicts, or on action lists agreed during joint problem solving sessions, do not lapse into some form of suspended animation. They continue to act – and to talk! But they do so in ways that sustain the status quo, rather than carrying out the supposedly agreed actions.

Each of the roles that talk fulfills, as set out in the above list, embodies a sense of purpose and organizational relevance. It might reasonably be assumed therefore that these can be adequately dealt with through the structured forms of communication outlined earlier. However, the dynamics of *informal coalitions* highlight the powerful impact that informal talk has upon people's perceptions and interpretations of organizational life, and on the actions that they take as a result of them. The seemingly incidental conversations and small talk that are interwoven with the delivery of work agendas play a crucial role in helping to shape organizational outcomes and in embedding cultural assumptions. These conversations are often much richer, in terms of emotional content and motivational quality, than formal workplace communications. Also, people often express themselves more openly and authentically through their informal talk and interactions than they do during more formally bounded interactions.

Most importantly, the outcomes associated with the above roles are always enacted through *local* networks of talk and interaction. These include those apparently peripheral conversations that are limited to chitchat, gossip and other social exchanges. What seems to be marginal and unimportant from a conventional, rational view of management is therefore central to leadership, change and organizational dynamics from an *informal coalitions* perspective. In essence, the conversations that are dismissed as small talk often contribute significantly to the ways in which people frame the issues and situations that they face (Sjöstrand and Tyrstrup, in Sjöstrand et al., 2001). And it is through these and other local interactions that people make most sense of what's going on, shape their personal relationships, clarify local behavioral norms and choose how to behave. Even though these conversations are random and fragmented, they help to embed – and potentially change – the patterns of cultural assumptions that channel ongoing sensemaking. What is more, the spontaneous, voluntary and emotionally flavored nature of everyday informal conversations means that these are ordinarily more influential in framing issues and constructing people's view of reality than are formal attempts by management at framing these *for* them.

In our discussion about the way in which change emerges through the shadow-side dynamics of the organization, we saw how informal conversations and interactions cause *informal coalitions* to form. These coalitions might challenge the existing, formally adopted position or else align with it. Where a challenge to the current orthodoxy attracts sufficient support, the potential exists for the status quo to be changed or formally proposed changes to be thwarted. Similarly, where a sufficiently strong coalition of active support can be built around the organization's formal agenda, the likelihood of this being delivered successfully is significantly increased. Leading change from an *informal coalitions* standpoint is therefore about working with these natural dynamics to build coalitions of support for organizationally beneficial changes.

## Sensemaking, use making and relationship building

The *informal coalitions* approach to change places talk at the center of its philosophy and practice. As outlined above, it also recognizes that much of the talk that takes place in organizations occurs informally and incidentally, outside its formal arenas and agendas. Since many issues that impact significantly upon organizational performance are undiscussable in formal forums, this adds to the relevance of these informal conversations to the successful delivery of organizational change. It is here that much of the real sensemaking takes place, ways of moving forward emerge and new patterns of cultural assumptions become embedded (or not!).

This approach shifts the balance of leadership communication away from passing messages toward joint sensemaking and relationship building. This means helping people to make sense of what is going on, to make effective use of the sense that they've made, and to build relationships as the basis for ongoing communication and commitment. Effective leadership here is about continually seeking to exploit sensemaking opportunities as events unfold; as well as deliberately creating openings to shift the existing conversational patterns. Its purpose is to stimulate and engage in everyday conversations, to influence the dynamics of interaction and the patterns of conversation that emerge. Every interaction that a leader has with their staff – however brief – is therefore critical to the way that change happens. It provides an opportunity for them to make a difference to people's understanding, contribution and commitment, and to stimulate change in the desired direction. The important point to recognize here is that the aim is to influence the overall *network* of conversations. In some instances this will be achieved through the cumulative effects of diverse conversations with a range of individuals. In other cases, a shift in the pattern of conversations might occur as the result of a leader tapping into the natural "influence hierarchies" within these informal networks.

In all cases, the need is for leaders to engage *purposefully* with the informal, diverse and incidental conversations and interactions that constitute the bulk of everyday organizational life. This includes:

- sharing perceptions and interpretations of what's happening, to help people (*including themselves*[2]) to make sense of what is going on and to make effective use of the sense that they've made;
- seeking to understand people's socially constructed "personal frames of reference" through which they perceive and interpret events (as discussed further in Chapter 5);
- becoming aware of people's psychological and emotional reactions to the changes that are taking place, and helping them to move to more positive and constructive states, by managing the transition process effectively;
- detecting and surfacing underlying themes and assumptions that are patterning shadow-side conversations, channeling interpretations and stimulating or inhibiting movement;
- becoming aware of emerging themes that are finding resonance with staff *or*, *alternatively*, *causing dissonance* – seeking to build on the former and address the latter;
- helping to unblock conversations that have become "stuck" through lack of perspective, premature closure or ritualistic position-taking;
- identifying and addressing any disconnections that exist between people's perceptions and interpretations of what's actually happening (including perceptions of the leader's own behavior) and expectations raised by the organization's stated values and beliefs;
- challenging unhelpful language and metaphors that sustain existing power relations and prevent the organization from making progress;
- building, sustaining and encouraging the development of wide networks of relationships, to increase interaction and improve "connectivity;"
- helping people to reconstruct their own "reality" when conflicts arise (as in Stone et al., 2000, for example):
  - exploring differing perceptions and interpretations, rather than seeking to identify what is "true" in a particular situation
  - moving from allocating blame to mapping each person's contribution to the current state of affairs, as a basis for identifying constructive ways forward
  - encouraging and enabling people to take responsibility for their own state, rather than accusing others of making them "feel bad;"
- using perceived breakdowns in communication as further sensemaking opportunities:
  - listening and questioning, to understand the underlying factors that are being perceived and interpreted as poor communication

- identifying any "*mis*interpretations" (i.e. different interpretations) that have arisen, which can be constructively challenged and potentially reframed
- addressing the underlying processes and dynamics that are causing dysfunction;
- introducing new language, concepts and stories, to challenge thinking, stimulate movement, and focus attention on areas of possibility and unfulfilled potential;
- resisting pressures to force premature closure on issues and ambiguous situations:
  - seeing ambiguity and "not knowing" as positive and creative states, rather than as signs of weakness and indecision
  - exploring the positive potential of competing (and often paradoxical) viewpoints by seeking creative "both–and" solutions that will either generate new possibilities or, where this is not possible, redirect negative energies in positive directions (see Chapter 7 for more guidance);
- working to build coalitions of support for organizationally beneficial changes (as described more fully in Chapter 6);
- encouraging and facilitating reflection on current practice, to draw out the lessons learnt and to build resilience to continuing change.

## Blending-in official communications and emerging events

Official communications disseminated through mode C1, together with ad hoc events, also provide important sensemaking opportunities. Leaders operating from an *informal coalitions* perspective can use these to:

- mark key stages in the organization's development;
- relate seemingly disparate initiatives to a coherent theme;
- help to check and (re-)frame people's perceptions and interpretations of emerging issues, events and situations;
- focus attention on emerging priorities and implications;
- highlight key interdependencies;
- address latent issues and concerns that are brought to the surface;
- explore any adverse reactions;
- detect any errors and omissions in "official" thinking;
- "take the temperature" of the organization.

Continually speaking with staff about things that are going on is a straightforward aspect of organizational communication that many mangers consistently fail to make full use of. One consequence of this failure is the feeling of "initiativitis" that reflects many people's experience of organizational change. I have sometimes used the football-v-dried-peas analogy to emphasize this point. If you ask someone to catch a handful of dried peas that are thrown toward them, they will find it almost impossible to do so. However, ask them to catch a football and they will usually succeed. In a similar way, if we ask people to "catch," or make sense of, what appear to be a succession of disparate initiatives, they are likely to fail. If, though, we can help them to see how the various initiatives fit together and relate to some overarching theme or organizing framework, then sensemaking becomes a comparatively easier task – like catching a football. Linking emerging statements and events to a unifying framework, model or theme aids sensemaking and builds confidence. This is valid even where some degree of post-event rationalization or "poetic licence" is required. The important thing is not whether the link that has been made is "technically" correct. What matters is whether or not it is *useful* in sensemaking terms for those who need to assimilate and respond to emerging events (recall the "Any Map Will Do" point about sensemaking, at the end of Chapter 1).

## Where do intention and accountability fit in?

Leaders cannot control the self-organizing interactions and emergent outcomes that are the nature of informal coalitional activity. However, they can – and should – use their power to influence the dynamics and outcomes of this process. That is, after all, how informal coalitions work. People coalesce around conversational themes that appeal to them in terms both of the sensemaking content of the story and the perceived credibility of the storyteller.

This book focuses on the dynamics of change *within organizations*. And organizations exist for a purpose. The role of leaders within an organization is to mobilize resources to further that purpose. So the notions of intent and accountability for results are central to the concept and practice of leadership. This means that, although conversations may be informal and unstructured, they should not be thought of as necessarily unintentional. On many occasions, a leader can influence when these occur and what the conversations are broadly about. For example, they might seek out specific opportunities to speak informally with particular people as part of a deliberate coalition-building strategy (see Chapter 6). They might also increase the opportunity for incidental conversations to take place between themselves and others, around issues of mutual interest and concern. In this way, existing intentions can be pursued and new ways of making progress can emerge.

Within this, it is important to recognize that intentions are themselves socially constructed. Stacey (2003: 352) makes the important point that an individual does not simply "have" an intention but that this emerges through their conversational interaction with others:

> Intention and choice are not lonely acts but themes organised by, and organising, relationships at the same time.

Recall the plate-spinning analogy that I introduced in Chapter 2. There, I suggested that we each try to manage our relationships, consciously and subconsciously, in ways that sustain those that we wish to preserve, and that maintain our sense of personal and organizational worth. Our intentions emerge from the various interactions that occur within these relationship networks. At the same time, the emerging intentions re-pattern and re-order those networks. As Stacey (2003) again says:

> ... people have the freedom to respond [to other people's gestures only] within the constraints of who they are and the relationships they are in.

Ford and Ford (in Holman and Thorpe, 2003: 146) refer to this as "...a type of structural coupling." They argue that all organizational conversations need to be seen as part of a conversational network. We have earlier seen how these dynamic networks both enable and constrain the interactions and conversations that take place within them. And so, individual conversations take place within what we described in Chapter 2 as a background cultural conversation (after Gallwey, 2000). As a result, Ford and Ford point out that existing conversational patterns hold other conversations in place; and these dynamics contribute to outcomes that are experienced (and framed by management) as resistance to change. We will discuss the nature and power of this patterning process further in Chapter 4.

Intention therefore forms an important part of the leader's sense-making role – even in informal, ad hoc situations. This suggests that, to be effective, leaders need to *think through in advance* how best to engage *spontaneously* with others! Planned spontaneity is the essence of peak performance. This is the case whether we are talking about the creative visualization used by elite athletes to prepare for competition, the rehearsed *"ad libs"* of leading comedians or other situations where performance *in the moment* is crucial. The context, specific content and actual outcome will depend upon the people involved in the conversations and the situational factors that exist at the time. However other aspects can always be thought through in advance – even if only in part and from an incomplete perspective. These might include, for example:

- the frames that leaders might offer as sensemaking tools;
- the typical patterns of assumptions that might be blocking or stimulating progress in particular situations; or
- answers to the *"Why"* question.

## Role modeling – Mode C4

Finally, the *formal–unstructured* quadrant of the Leadership Communication Grid, C4, captures the powerful communication impact that leaders – at all levels – have as role models within their organizations. Although this mode of communication is unstructured – since it occurs at any time that staff perceive their leaders' actions (or inaction) – it is also formal, because it arises directly from the formally assigned role of the leader and communicates by "priming messages" to staff. This mode of communication is therefore not an optional extra for leaders. They operate in this space all of the time. Their everyday behaviors will *unavoidably* transmit influential messages to staff about the nature, intentions and priorities of the organization. As the chairman of one of my clients recently told his senior managers, "If you've decided that you don't want to be a role model, you've just decided to be a bad one."

People engage continuously in conversation with others across the organization. They do this to make sense of what is going on, to decide what to do in the light of the sense that they have made and to share their perceptions and interpretations with others. Through this process of perception, interpretation, evaluation and sharing, patterns of cultural assumptions become embedded (and, potentially, changed). Leaders' behaviors, *as perceived and interpreted by others*, provide a key input (if not *the* key input) into this ongoing sensemaking and pattern-forming process, whether they intend them to or not. Leaders therefore need to recognize their position as cultural role models, and think and act accordingly.

## In search of the "X-factor"

A client and ex-colleague used to manage a large process plant in North
Wales, at a time when the parent company was working toward Investor
in People (IiP) accreditation for its major sites and corporate offices. The
local IiP assessor for the area wrote effusively about the high standards
of people management achieved by the plant. As a result of this, she
decided that she wanted to use it as the model site for her area. I have
always found it amusing that, having assessed the plant's performance
against the multiple criteria contained in the matter-of-fact IiP standard,
her report concluded that the plant merited recognition as a model site
because of what she described as an "indefinable X-factor." She enthused
that this vibrant atmosphere was apparent as soon as she entered the site.
For those working on the site, and for many of us at the center who
knew the plant manager, this X-factor was embodied in the leadership
he provided. It flowed, in particular, from the values and beliefs that he
modeled consistently through his day-to-day words and actions.

At its best, C4 communication is X-factor communication. Where
people perceive leaders' everyday words and behaviors to be congruent
with their espoused values – and when those values resonate with their
own – they respond in more enthusiastic, energized and "turned on"
ways. Cultural patterns become embedded over time that reflect these
values and that enable progress to be achieved in mutually beneficial
ways. The opposite is equally true, of course. Where there is a lack of
congruence between a leader's formal words and their informal actions,
people's perception and interpretation of the latter will always carry more
weight. It is these that will have the greater impact on their assessment
of what's going on, what the organization *really* stands for and how
they should respond. The patterns of assumptions that become embedded
in this case are likely to inhibit, rather than enable, performance and
capability development. *Informal coalition* activity will then work to
frustrate those changes that the organization is seeking to bring about.

## Cultural symbols

In summary, leaders serve as important cultural symbols for their organizations. People view their everyday words and actions as the embodiment
of what the organization *actually* believes in, what its *true* priorities
are, and which behaviors the organization values *in practice*. Leadership
communication through role modeling has a powerful if elusive effect on

organizational performance, capability and change; and on the cultural patterns that help to shape these. Even though it comes into play as the result of the *formal* allocation of a leadership role, it influences change and other organizational processes through *informal coalition* activity. It is people's perceptions, interpretations and evaluations of leaders' behaviors, and the sharing of these with others, that affects the nature and performance outcomes of the change process, not leaders' behaviors *per se*. Because of its potency in shaping underlying patterns of assumptions, and the decisions and outcomes that flow from these, the leadership implications of role modeling are addressed further in Chapter 4. This forms a separate strand of the change-leadership agenda.

## Three things to remember

In seeking to embrace an *informal coalitions* view of communication and its implications for their everyday behavior, leaders need to remember three important points.

First, communication within the *education and training* mode (C1) reflects the organization's formal power relationships and the rational management model that dominates conventional management thinking. The proposition here is that informal "talk" is likely to be more potent in shaping people's understanding of, and engagement with, the organization. However, those who want to make sense of organizational change need to recognize the grip that the more conventional view still exerts on everyday management practice and employee behavior. The challenge is therefore to ensure that informal conversations and interactions factor-in the effects of formal communications on people's perceptions, interpretations and evaluations of what's going on and what's important to them.

Secondly, the *informal coalitions* perspective recognizes that managers are "on the pitch, playing" not "sitting in the stands" so to speak, as external, objective observers of other people's actions. When engaging with others in the ways suggested above, it is important for managers to recognize that it may be *their own perspectives and interpretations that need to change*, or *their own behavior that is blocking progress*. In this sense, whilst managers might adopt a non-directive, coaching-type stance when engaging in conversations with their staff, the relationship is not that of an independent coach encouraging, assisting and enabling change in someone else – "the coachee."

Thirdly, those in formal leadership positions need to recognize that, as with coalition forming, individual and collective sensemaking will go on *with or without their active involvement*. The only choice that they, as leaders, have in this regard is whether or not to engage with this process in a deliberate and informed way.

## In summary

The Leadership Communication Grid calls for both the introduction of new communication practices *and* the adoption of a particular mindset concerning what leadership communication is about. Leaders should therefore review their patterns of communication regularly. First of all, they need to ensure that they have "all the bases covered;" that is, that they are operating as and when appropriate in each of the four communication modes (C1–C4). Most importantly, though, an *informal coalitions* approach to change leadership means that leaders need to place particular emphasis on the unstructured modes of communication, C3 and C4.

Whilst recognizing that formal communication (C1) has an important role to play in keeping people informed of current and planned events, its ability to engage people emotionally, to build their commitment to organizational changes or to "shift the culture" of an organization is severely limited. Introducing opportunities for structured, dialogic (open, multiway) conversation (C2) can enhance these factors. However, although these approaches move beyond one-way message passing, they do not address what happens in the organization for the bulk of the time, when such structured events are not in progress. Nor do they recognize the powerful impact that everyday sensemaking and use-making conversations have on organizational outcomes. Stimulating and engaging in purposeful, informal interactions (C3) and becoming an effective role model (C4) address these critical aspects of leadership performance.

# CHAPTER 4

# Thinking culturally

> You must be the change you wish to see in the world.
>
> – Mahatma Gandhi

## Introduction

In Chapter 3, we saw that role modeling is a powerful form of leadership communication, which places leaders in the position of "cultural symbols" for their organizations. In this chapter, we will explore this relationship between everyday leadership behavior and cultural change in more depth. To do this, we need first to reflect on what we mean by organizational culture, how it forms and what relevance it has to organizational change and performance. We will then explore the implications of this for leaders and their day-to-day interactions with staff.

## The culture change industry

Each year, managers spend hundreds of thousands of pounds and many hours of effort in trying to "change the culture" of their organizations. Yet, despite the high level of intellectual, financial and emotional investment that this entails, results frequently fall short of expectations. In some cases an organization continues to perform in spite of the changes. In others, the effort generates more heat than light; and unforeseen side effects, new crises and changed priorities soon overtake any short-won gains. Despite this, the culture-change industry continues in full production.

## The popular view of culture

Whenever strategic changes are initiated, the issue of "culture" always surfaces. However, even though the idea of *organizational* culture is now well established, there is still no agreement on how it should be defined.

One of the phrases most popularly used to describe it is "the way we think and act around here;" but that doesn't usually get us very far! The notion of culture didn't begin to appear in management courses, business texts and organizational conversations until around a quarter of a century ago; so where did it come from and, more importantly, is it a useful concept for managers to understand and use?

Although some academics began to apply the idea of culture to organizations in the early 1970s, it was a further ten years or so before this entered mainstream management thinking. Its emergence is usually linked to the challenge that the US felt to its industrial and economic supremacy by the rise of Japan as a major trading nation. Japan's success was thought to have resulted from some distinctive differences that existed between the Japanese ways of working and those that were common in the West. The idea was popularized by some, now famous, McKinsey consultants, who published books on the subject in the early 1980s. These appeared to link business success to the existence of a strongly aligned corporate culture. By this they meant the existence of a set of core values that governed all of an organization's activities. Pascale and Athos (1982), for example, wrote a book called the "The Art of Japanese Management," that contrasted the Japanese and US approaches directly; whilst their colleagues Peters and Waterman (1982) produced the best-selling "In Search of Excellence." Both pairs used the 7-S Model that they had jointly developed to illustrate their arguments. In this, a set of "Superordinate Goals" (as they were originally called) or the more user-friendly "Shared Values," as they are now more commonly known, sits at the heart of this view of organizational dynamics.

From this perspective, management's task is seen as one of deciding upon a desired set of shared values and instilling them throughout the organization. The idea is that these will then act as the "glue" to bind together the other elements of organization (Strategy, Structure, Systems, Staff, Skills and Style) and enable it to excel. This early work caused many other writers and consultants to jump onto the culture bandwagon. And this has continued to roll ever since; with many consultancies offering to help managers transform their cultures in line with their own version of the "shared values" model. The bookshelves are also packed with texts on corporate culture and cultural change, as a brief log-on to the Amazon website will show.

## Design-and-build approach to cultural change

As we saw in Chapter 1, from this conventional management viewpoint, the "strength" of culture is seen to depend on a number of interrelated factors. These include the success with which values have been "repositioned" to match the defined management philosophy (strategy, structure, etc.); and the extent to which organizational members are aligned behind the behavioral norms that flow from these. The level of integration of effort across the business and the degree to which the changes are bought into by staff are also seen as indicative of cultural strength. From this perspective, cultural change is seen as a design-and-build activity – the organizational equivalent of fitting together pieces from a Lego® set to produce the desired "model" of culture. Above all, it is seen as a rational, management-driven activity, aimed at designing, installing and controlling the cultural "component" of organization to make it fit with the other parts.

Working from this notion of organizational culture, many tools are on offer for measuring the culture "as is," as the basis for plotting a culture-change course and tracking progress. These diagnostic tools usually comprise a set of questions that allow the culture of the organization to be typified in relation to particular dimensions of performance. Many of these tools are supported by databases that enable an organization's results to be compared with those obtained from other respondents. Most of the consultancies offer their own models; but the general structures of these are similar to those adopted by one or other of the established typologies of people like Deal and Kennedy (2000), Harrison and Stokes (1992), Handy (1993), Goffee and Jones (1998) and so on.

These questionnaire-based approaches to cultural analysis offer a number of attractions to practicing managers. They are relatively simple to apply and analyze; they provide a means of comparing and contrasting organizations in relation to the chosen categories of analysis; and they raise awareness by making some of the implicit aspects of organization more explicit. However, there are also important drawbacks and limitations with these methodologies. This is especially the case if the outcomes are treated as analytical "facts" rather than being used as inputs to more in-depth conversations. For a start, these models tend to oversimplify culture by shoehorning an organization into, typically, one of four descriptive categories. This creates the illusion of knowledge about organizational dynamics that is, at best, incomplete. Most importantly, perhaps, such approaches rarely offer insights into how managers might engage more effectively with the underlying dynamics through which these "cultures" are formed. How the observed criteria arose in the first place or how the desired shift to another cultural "form" might be achieved tend to be either treated superficially or ignored altogether. On this last point, I once came across a "how to do it" book on cultural change which offered the following advice: First analyze the culture as is; next decide the culture that you would like to create; and then "*all you have to do*" (my emphasis) is to move from one to the other! Finally, and most damagingly from our perspective, these approaches reinforce the view that culture can be changed at the behest of management, using their preferred mix of *management edict, education and training* and *joint problem solving* to achieve the desired outcome.

## Taking culture seriously

If we are to take culture seriously, we need to look afresh at its underlying dynamics. Rather than objectifying culture in the ways set out above, the *informal coalitions* perspective sees it as arising from – and being embodied in – the ongoing patterns of conversations and interactions that take place. Looked at in this way, cultural change occurs through shifts in the nature and content of these conversational patterns, as people make different sense of their everyday experiences and make new use of the sense that they've made.

### Patterns in the mind

We've seen above that the idea of "shared values" is often used to describe culture from the conventional, "culture as object" perspective. In contrast, I'm going to talk of it as *shared meaning making*. This makes the *active process of everyday interaction* central to the notion of organizational culture. Ideally for our purposes, the word "culture" would be a verb, to describe this dynamic (literally verbal) process. Instead, we're going to have to manage with it as a noun; and accept that, in using a "naming word," we are not suggesting that culture can be "made concrete" in any meaningful way.

To think of organizational culture as shared meaning making is to see it as a dynamic process that exists solely within and between the heads of people as they interact with each other. Patterns of meaning are formed and re-formed through these everyday conversational exchanges. As we've seen from earlier chapters, this process is *self-organizing*. It cannot be controlled or mandated by management – or anyone else for that matter. Instead, perceptions, interpretations and evaluations of what's going on, and what this means, are jointly constructed and shared between organizational members as they go about their day-to-day tasks and interact socially. A useful analogy that we can use here to enhance our understanding of cultural dynamics is de Bono's description of the brain as a self-organizing, pattern-making system (de Bono, 1971). To explain the notion of self-organization in a simple way, he contrasts what happens when ink is dropped onto as towel with what happens when hot oil is dropped onto a tray of gelatine. In the first case, each successive inkblot remains precisely in the position in which it lands on the towel. Successive inkblots might overlap but they don't interact with each other. Each one, individually, remains a faithful representation (or "memory") of the pattern that was formed at the instant that the ink made contact with the towel. In contrast, when hot oil is dropped onto the tray of gelatine it interacts with it to form a groove in the surface. As successive amounts of hot oil are dropped onto the gelatine, these tend to flow toward, and join up with, the channels that have already formed in its surface. This deepens the existing channels still further, making them increasingly attractive to subsequent drops of oil. And so on. Interestingly, the pattern that emerges is determined not by the gelatine but by the oil itself. In particular, it is determined by the pattern of grooves that has already formed on the surface as the result of what has gone before. It is important to note too that these grooves have not been designed and built by a third party but have arisen through the self-organizing behavior of successive inflows of hot oil onto the "memory surface." De Bono argues that the mind operates in this same self-selecting and self-organizing way (albeit in a more sophisticated manner than that described here!). That is, it provides the opportunity for incoming "information" to channel itself through existing patterns of "meaning." This pattern-recognizing and pattern-making ability is what makes the mind so powerful in everyday living – because we don't have to think afresh about every situation each time we come across it. At the same time, this is also the source of its greatest weakness – its difficulty in thinking creatively. This requires a pattern-shifting capability rather than a pattern-reinforcing one. Humor, chance interactions and mistakes are natural pattern-shifting processes; but these tend to occur randomly and infrequently. It was this that led de Bono to invent the concept and techniques of lateral thinking.

## Patterns of interaction

The pattern-making process of assumption formation in organizations can be thought of in similar terms. Here, though, we are talking about people in interaction with each other, rather than the workings of an individual mind alone. We talked earlier about organizations as dynamic conversational processes in which people interact to make sense of their organizational worlds and to make use of the sense that they've made. As they do so, metaphorical "grooves" form in the "cultural surfaces" of the organization, which tend to attract and channel subsequent sensemaking conversations through existing, taken-for-granted patterns of meaning. In this way, ongoing sensemaking and use-making processes are influenced by the existing patterns (*plural*) of assumptions that operate within the organization. In turn, these conversations further strengthen – *and potentially change* – these underlying patterns of assumptions. This self-organizing, patterning process helps us to cope with the situations that we encounter each day, and it also provides a basis for us to behave sensibly and meaningfully within the context of particular organizational relationships. In this way, we develop assumptions about our organizational world, together with the necessary personal and interpersonal skills to enable us navigate it successfully. These enable us to function competently as individuals within the various parts of the organization and its wider network of relationships. We introduced Gallwey's idea of a background, "cultural conversation" in Chapter 2 (Gallwey, 2000), to symbolize how these patterns of assumptions impact upon – and are, at the same time, affected by – ongoing conversations.

## All change is cultural change

So far so good. However, these same patterns of assumptions that enable us to perform competently within a given organizational setting also constrain our thinking and behavior. These define (*and therefore also limit*) the range of options available to us – and hence to the organization – both in strategic and in operational terms. In essence, people tend to perceive and interpret organizational contexts, events and experiences selectively, through existing channels of meaning. This makes these existing channels ever deeper, and even more likely to lead to similar interpretations in the future. It is the self-organizing dynamics of this pattern-reinforcing process that make cultural change so challenging. Cultural change is about escaping from existing patterns, not reinforcing them. So this requires a shift in peoples' perceptions and interpretations of events – and in the conversations through which these are formed. This shift is analogous to that which lateral thinking techniques seek to provoke in an idea-generation setting. The only choice that leaders have, therefore, is whether or not to try to influence this pattern-making and pattern-shifting process in a deliberate way or to leave it wholly to chance.

An important implication of this is that *all change is cultural change*. The idea of setting up a separate program for "changing the culture" makes no sense at all. Cultural change occurs *through the conversations* that flow from the formal and informal processes within the organization. This is the case even if the nature of this "change" is simply to reinforce the existing patterns of thought and behavior ("deepen the channels"). Cultural patterns cannot therefore be changed independently of other things that are happening within the organization. The corollary of this is that other things cannot happen within the organization without these impacting upon – and being impacted upon by – existing cultural patterns.

## A cultural "snapshot"

Adopting the above view, culture is *dynamic* and always evolving, albeit usually in subtle ways. Although at any given time it can be seen as having a discernible pattern, this pattern tends to be a snapshot – an abstraction of the intricate and dynamic patterning process that is constantly evolving. Ordinarily, the cultural patterns that emerge through this ongoing process will tend to reinforce the existing assumptions and behaviors. So, in this sense, culture is constantly developing (i.e. changing) in ways that strengthen the organization's attachment to its current ways of thinking and acting (i.e. not changing!).

If we were to freeze this dynamic process for a moment, and take a "snapshot" of the prevailing cultural patterns, what might these look like? I have found Schein's three-tier conception of organizational culture (Schein, 1993) to be a useful framework to stimulate conversations with managers about this. Although Schein has a more static and deterministic, culture-as-thing view, the skeleton of his model provides a useful way of emphasizing the critical differences between the surface-level manifestations of culture and its more deeply embedded patterns.

Schein argues that culture exists at different depths of meaning. At the surface level, he positions the visible artifacts of culture. These include material artifacts, like corporate architecture, logos and corporate designs, and formal mission statements; artifacts of language, such as common phraseology, popular metaphors and organizational folklore; and behavioral artifacts, such as rites, rituals and ceremonies, systems and procedures, power structures etc. At the middle level of Schein's model can be found the beliefs, values, attitudes and norms of behavior that are *stated explicitly* as being the organization's view of what is important, how to behave and so on. These may be incorporated into "Level 1" codes of practice, statements of values and so on, or realized in other tangible forms. Finally, at the deepest level are the underlying assumptions. These are deeply held, taken-for-granted orientations about how the organizational world functions. From an *informal coalitions* perspective, these unique patterns of assumptions emerge and become ingrained over time, through the conversational patterning process that we have described earlier.

## Underlying assumptions are key

Schein makes the important point that, although the surface-level artifacts are highly visible, they are very difficult to understand culturally. Observers tend to interpret them through their own, personal frames of reference. For example, in an organization in which people are casually dressed, one observer might interpret this as sloppy, whereas another might see it as an indication of open-mindedness and creativity. Similarly, some will see a very formal organization as expressing professional standards, whilst others might take this as a sign of excessive bureaucracy and stuffiness.

As the organization's stated values and beliefs are identified and explored, a greater level of awareness can be achieved. However, businesses tend to choose from a limited "table d'hôte" menu of values and beliefs; so, even here, interpretation can be difficult. I have yet to find a commercial organization, for example, which would not claim to be "customer oriented." How this is interpreted within a particular organization, and how it translates into practical action though, may differ greatly from its expression in another, seemingly comparable organization.

Organizational culture cannot be fully understood or "worked upon" effectively therefore until the underlying patterns of assumptions have been exposed and made sense of. This is difficult because of their taken-for-granted nature. Because cultural assumptions are ordinarily outside our immediate awareness, these are difficult to identify and get to grips with. This is one of the main reasons why so many so-called "culture change programs" don't seem to make much of a difference in practice beyond some temporary, surface-level changes. Mergers and acquisitions also often fail to deliver to their full potential for the same reason. *Neither* organization really understands the nature and impact of their own cultural patterns, let alone those of the prospective partner or target organization. In-depth organizational analysis can be used to address this, of course. However, clues to what these assumptions might be can be gained from reflecting upon everyday activities, interactions and conversations; and by looking for any underlying patterns that might exist amongst these.

As an example of this, I once used the structure of Schein's model to generate conversations about organizational culture within a "diagonal slice" of staff from the commercial department of a large organization. Having identified examples of artifacts and espoused values, we looked next at underlying assumptions. I began by asking them to identify a "villain" within their organization – past or present – which I defined as someone whose characteristics and/or behaviors had caused them to become sidelined or to leave the organization altogether. In response, they agreed that a past director of the department satisfied these criteria. When I asked them to describe him, they used terms such as "larger than life," "deal-doer" and "risk-taker." Without the above preamble, most people would associate these characteristics with those of an entrepreneur. Yet here, informal conversations had resulted in patterns of assumptions becoming embedded that attached the characteristics of entrepreneurship to the idea of "organizational villain." In simple terms, if you behaved like this, you were not likely to be around for long! At the debrief of the session, the commercial director and his direct reports were horrified at this. "Behaving entrepreneurially" was, after all, one of the department's espoused values! Without addressing this mismatch between embedded assumptions and stated values, they agreed that there would be little or no chance of people within the department behaving in a more entrepreneurial fashion.

Identifying the characteristics of "heroes and villains" is just one of a number of routes to surfacing underlying assumptions and generating conversations about the organizing patterns that these suggest. The grid shown in Figure 4.1 identifies 12 informal aspects of organization that can stimulate useful assumption-surfacing conversations – and this list is far from exhaustive. These are:

- *Heroes and villains* – "Heroes," in this context, are people whom the organization clearly values, as evidenced by their promotion, selection for high profile projects and so on. People who want to get on in the organization would typically see these people as cultural role models. Conversely, "villains" are those people who are sidelined or caused to leave the company because in some (often un-stated) way they don't "fit."

- *Secrets* – What are the things that everybody knows but which nobody talks about in formal meetings?
- *Mistakes* – What happens when people make mistakes in the organization? Is this used as a learning opportunity, or as a reason to look for someone to blame?
- *Humor* – What do the office jokes and cartoons imply about people's unspoken views of the organization or characters within it?
- *Unwritten Rules* – What "rules" do people have to comply with if they don't want to fall foul of the organization, even though these will not be found in any of the formal policies, processes or procedures.
- *Promotion Criteria* – The issue here, again, is to identify those criteria that are *observed* to govern promotion and recognition etc, not what the formal position states.
- *Stories* etc – What stories regularly get recounted and passed on? What do they say about the organization – positively, negatively and/or intriguingly?
- *Language* – Do particular words, phrases or metaphors keep being repeated? If so, which ones – and what does their use imply? Do they suggest, for example, that a dominant metaphor governs the way that the organization (or the part of it being considered) is managed? What does language say, for example, about how status is viewed, where power exists in the organization, who is and isn't "us," how collaboratively conflicts are addressed, and so on?
- *Coffee machine grumbles* – What do people talk about in informal gatherings and one-to-ones, that they would not talk about in open forums?
- *Rituals and routines* – What rituals and routines are part of the taken-for-granted ways of doing things? What is the *ritualistic* purpose of these?
- *Images and symbols* – What are the most significant ones in use? How are these interpreted within the organization?
- *Expendables* – When resources are tight (people, money, time, etc.), what are the first things to be sacrificed? What does this say about the organization's true priorities?

This list has proven useful in stimulating more in-depth conversations about the nature and impact of cultural assumptions on organizational behavior and outcomes. The important thing here is to *look for underlying patterns in the conversations that are generated by this reflection*. In one instance where I used this approach, the power of underlying assumptions to channel thinking and behavior was vividly demonstrated. The group

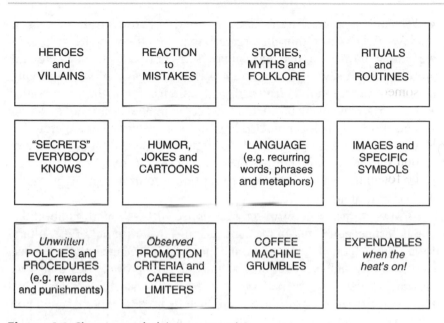

| | | | |
|---|---|---|---|
| HEROES and VILLAINS | REACTION to MISTAKES | STORIES, MYTHS and FOLKLORE | RITUALS and ROUTINES |
| "SECRETS" EVERYBODY KNOWS | HUMOR, JOKES and CARTOONS | LANGUAGE (e.g. recurring words, phrases and metaphors) | IMAGES and SPECIFIC SYMBOLS |
| *Unwritten* POLICIES and PROCEDURES (e.g. rewards and punishments) | *Observed* PROMOTION CRITERIA and CAREER LIMITERS | COFFEE MACHINE GRUMBLES | EXPENDABLES *when the heat's on!* |

**Figure 4.1** Clues to underlying assumptions

of managers of a newly formed business unit were reflecting on the underlying assumptions within their parent organization, as a preliminary to looking at their own leadership behaviors. Each of three sub-groups explored four of the above categories and, following consolidation of their outputs and further conversations, the team identified a number of recurring themes that they felt defined the pattern of the organization's prevailing cultural assumptions.

Interestingly, most of the key words and phrases that the managers used to represent these six main themes were expressed negatively. That is, they were described in terms of things to avoid rather than things to aspire to. These included a cluster of sub-themes around people's required behavior, which comprised *self-confident*, *no negatives*, *no problems just challenges* and *not saying no*. In that organization, at that time, being seen to be negative was perceived to be "career limiting." However, when the senior manager involved wrote to me with his summary of the output, he began his e-mail by commenting as follows. *"I felt it important to capture the assumptions in positive terms."* In relation to the acceptability or otherwise of negativity within the parent organization, for example, he translated the above, largely negative, descriptors as follows:

Having a confident, positive, can-do attitude.

Despite his genuine desire to expose and engage with the unspoken, shadow-side issues within the organization, he felt compelled to present the output in a culturally acceptable "self-confident, no negatives, no problems, can't say no" sort of way. It is in this way that we all become trapped – imperceptibly – in established patterns of thought, conversation and action. Few managers would argue with the desire to foster an organization in which people had a "confident, positive, can-do attitude." However, if this were perceived by staff as an organization in which they couldn't afford to say "No," express negative perceptions or raise their concerns, the effect of this would be far removed from that suggested by the positive spin.

As always, the value of using an exercise such as this rests not in the initial "data capture" but in the conversations that arise out of it. Cultural patterns are formed, embedded and potentially changed through local conversations and everyday interactions. This approach uses that same medium to uncover the patterns that currently channel organizational sensemaking. The insights gained can then be used to explore if and how these patterns might be shifted for organizational benefit.

## Organizations as networks of conversations

We have earlier described an organization as a network of ongoing, self-organizing conversations. Through their everyday conversations and interactions people *jointly* create ("co-create") characteristic ways of thinking and acting. From this perspective, new cultural patterns do not arise simply by adopting new slogans, acquiring a new leader or embarking on traditional forms of "culture change" programs; except in so far as the patterns of conversation change in response to these, and the meaning that people take from them changes. As we have seen, the patterning process is self-organizing. It is also self-reinforcing; which means that the natural tendency is for existing patterns of assumptions to be strengthened further, rather than being readily amenable to change. Whilst this same conversational process holds the potential to bring about change, the tendency is for sensemaking to be shaped imperceptibly by the dominant patterns that currently exist, and for perceptions and interpretations to follow these well-established pathways. Alternative ways of perceiving and interpreting words, actions and events will often not be seen, let alone acted upon. As we've noted earlier, this is one of the main reasons why it can be difficult to bring separate organizations together successfully, whether in some form of partnership working, or as the result of merger or acquisition. The two groups are often, quite literally, talking a different language – even if the words they are using appear to be the same!

There are some important implications to bear in mind when thinking about culture and cultural change in this way, especially at times when major organizational changes are being formally contemplated. A number of these are summarized below:

- As we began to see in Chapter 3, virtually everything that anyone in a formal leadership position says and does has potential symbolic significance. People will perceive, interpret, evaluate, talk about and act upon these symbols constantly, in their efforts to make sense of what is going on and to decide what use to make of the sense that they've made. Everyone involved in these everyday conversations helps to construct the dynamic patterns of meaning that shape organizational reality, not just those people in formal leadership positions.
- Since leadership behaviors provide a regular focus of these conversations, leaders do have a particularly significant impact on the way that these cultural patterns develop. However, this is not always in the way that they might think, as we shall see later. Often, the resulting perceptions and interpretations that help to embed particular cultural assumptions will run counter to those that leaders had intended when initiating specific changes.
- Also, many activities and practices have a greater impact on the cultural patterns that emerge than those (such as formal team-building events, development programs, empowerment projects, etc.) that are deliberately designed as cultural change interventions. If, for example, people become so preoccupied with a certain aspect of their work or working environment that it comes to dominate their everyday attention and conversations, this will significantly influence the patterning process.
- Such things as organizational structure, strategies, policies, goals, missions, job descriptions, operating procedures, rules and so on also provide indicators of the ways that people think about and make sense of the contexts within which they work. Although these are usually seen as the more objective characteristics of an organization, the meaning-making view of culture emphasizes that these are all cultural artifacts. As we saw in Figure 2.2, these are products of past conversations, which themselves have been channeled and constrained by the patterns of assumptions existing at that time. In turn, these artifacts act as cultural symbols themselves, by informing ongoing sensemaking conversations and helping to form the picture of organizational reality that emerges.

- When seeking to change the organization, therefore, managers *can't* deal with issues such as these and "leave culture until later," as many seem to believe that they can. The ways in which they talk and act when changing structures, developing systems and peopling the organization are fateful. These will be perceived, interpreted, shared with others and reinterpreted in ways that either begin to change the existing patterns of cultural assumptions or, as is more often the case, reinforce them.

In summary, organization exists within and between the heads of the people involved in it; through the ways that they perceive, interpret, evaluate and share their interpretations of everyday organizational life. As a consequence, therefore, effective change ultimately depends on *those individuals* – individually and collectively – changing the images, assumptions and values that they use to guide their actions and interactions. The way that they do this is through the conversations that they have with themselves (i.e. thinking) and with others. As suggested by Bate (1994), therefore, if managers want to change their organizations, they must start by stimulating change in the patterns and content of the conversations that people have with each other. Unfortunately, there are a number of management myths about culture that get in the way of this. We therefore need to address these first; before looking at some of the potential ways that leaders might use to help to shift the conversations.

## Management myths that obscure understanding

There are several management myths that obscure understanding of organizational culture. These are part of the taken-for-granted assumptions that govern conventional management thinking. One or two of the most damaging of these are outlined below.

### Strategy as "hard" v culture as "soft"

First, there is a frequently expressed view amongst practicing managers that strategy and structure are of prime importance – essential factors in achieving business performance – whereas culture is concerned with secondary, "nice to have" but optional ways of behaving. However, as suggested above, cultural assumptions are shaped and embedded through the everyday talk and interactions of staff. In particular, these arise through the ways in which the words and actions of managers are perceived, interpreted, evaluated and acted upon by staff *in the moment*. So culture is unavoidably being formed as the so-called "hard" aspects of organization are being put in place. The view that culture is separate from, and subsidiary to, strategy and organization leads managers to the mistaken belief that culture can safely await their attention until immediate pressures subside. Worse still, some dismiss it as the "touchy-feely" side of leadership. Culture can then justifiably be left for others (usually HR) to deal with, whilst they attend to the "real" aspects of organizational leadership.

## "Good" and "bad" cultures

A second popular myth is that culture is either good or bad in an absolute sense. For example, modern management thinking would argue that an empowered culture is good, whereas one based on "command and control" is bad. Clearly, some organizational cultures might be bad in an ethical or moral sense. Beyond this, though, the only meaningful criterion of "goodness" in organizational terms is whether or not the day-to-day process of meaning-making is enabling the organization to move from its existing set of taken-for-granted assumptions to a more useful one, or else *dis*abling its ability to do so.

By way of illustration, the following typical situations show how embedded assumptions and related conversational patterns might run counter to those implicit in management-imposed changes and prevent such initiatives taking hold:

- Structured knowledge-management initiatives (such as intranets and other IT systems) are designed to promote and facilitate the sharing of information across an organization. Regardless of how well these might be implemented in a technical sense, however, their effectiveness will be severely limited if the dominant pattern of assumptions suggests that people progress on the basis of what they know as individuals rather than by what they share with others.
- The need for innovation regularly features prominently in strategy documents, formal values statements and leadership competency frameworks. Often, these aspirations remain unfulfilled, as the well-publicized intentions fail to turn into practical action on the ground. Innovation involves people trying new things out; and this *inevitably* means that some mistakes will be made along the way, in the service of gaining new learning and ironing out unforeseen problems in the new product

or process. The crucial factor here is what people have come to take for granted and "know to be true" about how such mistakes will be handled. These assumptions will exert a powerful influence on the everyday sense-making and use-making conversations that take place around this issue. If these suggest that blaming and a search for scapegoats will follow any mistakes that do arise – however well intentioned these might have been – then it is highly unlikely that innovative practices will take hold.

- The strategic success of many businesses depends on external part-nering arrangements and other co-operative relationships. However, if internal conversations reflect deeply held win–lose assumptions, such as "we believe in partnership, provided that we always come out on top," there is little chance that the full fruits of collaboration will be harvested through the relationship.

In short, organizational performance will be undermined if those in leadership positions fail to recognize the power of cultural assumptions; or if they act as if "culture" is an independent variable of organization and a discretionary element of leadership.

## A strong culture is a uniform culture

Another well-established belief is that a strong culture is a uniform (or tightly aligned) one, based on common values, systems and behaviors. A corollary of this is that a strong culture is a guarantee of organizational success. As we have discussed earlier, the patterning process can help to reduce internal complexity and uncertainty by embedding norms of beha-vior, expectations and so on. Also, by providing *a degree* of consistency in outlook and values, it can facilitate decision-making, co-ordination and control. However, as de Bono might predict, the patterns that help organizations to create a sense of meaning, and that allow them to nego-tiate their world in an "orderly" way, can also constrain their ability to act in other ways. Characteristic ways of thinking, speaking and acting trap individuals and organizations within their own, socially constructed worlds and prevent them from engaging with – or even noticing – other latent or emerging possibilities. Miller (1990) captures this phenomenon well in what he calls the "Icarus Paradox." We have seen that this tend-ency to reinforce existing patterns, rather than search for new ones, occurs naturally. This is its greatest strength, in that it enables people to function successfully in concert with others. *At the same* time, it is its greatest weakness. It tends to block the emergence of new patterns by channeling sensemaking conversations down well-established paths and rejecting (or failing to see) other potential ways forward.

Because culture is about *shared* meaning making (or *shared* values in other conceptions), it is often presumed that everyone has to think and act in the same way. Also, that conflicting views can't be accommodated. Whilst it is true that sharing *is* a central notion of culture, Hatch (1997: 206) notes that sharing has two contrary meanings. In one sense, it conveys the idea of common experience, in which people's similarity is emphasized and strengthened through the relationship. Equally, sharing can also mean dividing something into separate pieces and sharing them out between participants. As an example, Hatch comments that sharing a meal is a *communal* activity in which each person eats their own *individual* meal: "Sharing [then] means doing something separately, together! It is a communal act achieved by splitting something up." In writings on organizational culture, sharing has been thought of almost exclusively in terms of the first of these meanings, in which the *outcomes* of the relationship are shared. However, from an *informal coalitions* perspective, it is participation in the cultural patterning *process* that is shared, not necessarily the outcomes. That is, people contribute to the ongoing patchwork of everyday conversations and interactions; but the understandings that they each gain from it, and the feelings that the interactions invoke in each of them, are not the same.

This is critical in relation to our consideration of the dynamics of *informal coalitions*. These consist of people "doing something separately, together" in the form of everyday conversations and interactions. People participate in this *joint* sensemaking process as *separate* individuals. And these individuals are each members of other relationship networks, some of which will be relatively stable and others less so. This means that any notion of consistent organization-wide patterns of assumptions and behaviors is necessarily flawed from this perspective. Although some broad assumptions are likely to be commonly held within a well-established organization, these need to be overlaid by recognition that much more fragmented and dynamic patterns will co-exist (and interact) with them. The cultural patterning processes of the organization as a whole will therefore embody both community and diversity (Hatch, 1997).

## Starting with a "blank sheet of paper"

Finally, in setting out to "change the culture," or when embarking on a new strategic direction, managers often act as if they can start with a blank sheet of paper. Their desire is to map out the organization that they wish to create, and then to set about putting it in place. From all we have said so far, it should be clear that cultural patterns are the accumulated product of an organization's past actions, interactions and transactions, and the meaning that people have taken from these in conversation with others. The idea that managers could wipe out history, impose their will upon the organization and through some top–down message passing change people's values, beliefs and attitudes is clearly nonsense therefore.

I was once faced with this challenge in a leadership-team workshop. A manager said that he was fed up about reflecting on the past and wanted the group to design the future by starting with a blank sheet of paper. To illustrate the above point, I wrote the words "THE PAST" on a writing pad. I then tore off the top sheet and threw it into the waste bin, to leave a blank sheet on top of the pad. Needless to say, an imprint of the words "THE PAST" still remained. And so it is with organizations. The past leaves its own imprint on the present (and hence the future) of the organizations within which we work. Ignoring the impact of this, or believing that it can simply be wished away, is not a credible way for leaders to proceed.

Also, as we shall explore further in Chapter 5, individuals try to operate in ways that remain faithful to their own value and belief systems. Managers cannot simply impose their ideas and will on others, however forcefully and determinedly they might try to do so. Each person or group will tend to hold onto the reality of organizational life as they perceive and experience it through their everyday relationships with others. Local interpretations of the organization's history and the extrapolation of its lessons into the future will also heavily condition these views of reality. This does not mean that managers are impotent when it comes to cultural change. Far from it. But they do need to rethink what this means in rela-tion to the notion of organizations as dynamic networks of self-organizing conversations. In particular, they need to understand what it means to "think culturally" as they go about their everyday leadership tasks.

## Thinking culturally

If the cultural patterns within an organization are jointly created by everyone in it; if culture doesn't exist as an object that can be designed and built by management in the conventional sense; and if a so-called "strong culture" is not all its cracked up to be, the obvious question is, *Where does all of this leave the leadership role in relation to cultural change*?

## Moments of leadership truth

In the previous chapter, we explored the Leadership Communication Grid, which extends the view of leadership communication beyond its traditional confines of the "box" labeled "formal" and "structured" (quadrant C1). As we've discussed, cultural patterns are formed, embedded and potentially changed through people's everyday interactions. Perceptions, interpretations and evaluations are made of what's going on in the organization; and these are shared in diverse conversations with others across the business. These conversations spawn other conversations. And so on. The behaviors of those in leadership positions throughout the organization, as perceived and interpreted by others, ordinarily provide the most influential input into this sensemaking and use-making process. This is the case *whether they intend them to or not*. This core aspect of leadership communication is represented in quadrant C4 of the Leadership Communication Grid.

Whenever someone in a leadership position interacts with one or more members of their staff, this represents a "moment of leadership truth." That is, it serves as a symbol of what is important, what the organization stands for, what sort of behavior is valued and so on. It is therefore critical for leaders to recognize the symbolic power that their words and actions carry within this continuous sensemaking process. Everything that they say and do during their everyday interactions with staff, and the way that they say and do it, is significant. Meaning making occurs whether managers actively engage with it or not. So, paradoxically, silence and inaction can have an equally potent effect. The Leadership Communication Grid therefore serves to remind managers that they need to recognize their position as cultural role models whenever they interact, formally and informally, with their staff (*or decide not to*). That is, they need to think how their words and actions (including silence and inaction) are likely to be perceived, interpreted and made sense of by others.

The symbols that a leader's everyday behaviors provide, and the sensemaking conversations that these fuel, are much more powerful influencers of cultural patterns than are many of the formal "culture-change initiatives" and structural aspects of organization. For example, a new statement of vision and values, the introduction of new structures and processes, the application of new competency frameworks, the use of team-building events, and so on may all help to generate or sustain the momentum of change. However, it is people's perceptions, interpretations and evaluations of leaders' everyday behaviors, and the sharing of these in informal conversations, which will primarily shape the nature, direction and speed of change "on the ground." *The locally constructed meaning of formal initiatives and events will always take precedence*, if this differs from that intended. For example, consider what is likely to happen if formal statements express the desire for a more collaborative approach to working across the organization whilst, *at the same time*, managers are seen to impose their will unilaterally, through the ways in which they restructure and re-people the organization. It is these latter perceptions that will channel people's thinking and behavior, rather than the formally stated value of team working and collaboration.

## Leaders as cultural symbols

As we illustrated in Figure 2.2, people engage continuously in conversations with others across the organization. They do this to make sense of what is going on and to decide what to do in the light of the sense that they have made. Through this process of perception, interpretation, evaluation and sharing, various stories enter the organization's mythology and folklore. And these stories become embellished, distorted or abandoned over time, as they are shared between organizational members. Patterns of taken-for-granted assumptions become embedded (and potentially changed) through this everyday conversational process. As we have seen, existing assumptions tend to channel sensemaking conversations down paths that are consistent with currently dominant patterns of perception and interpretation. So this process is mutually reinforcing. This ordinarily makes cultural change (i.e. pattern shifting) difficult to achieve. Despite this, the same conversational process holds the possibility for change to occur. This can happen if interpretations suggest that different dynamics are in play than those anticipated; and if new sense begins to be made of emerging events. Figure 4.2 illustrates the contribution that leaders' everyday words and actions (including their silence and inaction) make to this ongoing sensemaking activity. Because of these dynamics, people in formal leadership positions serve as powerful cultural symbols for others in their organizations. In particular, they represent the meanings that other employees associate with the organization. *But their symbolic power, and the meanings that these symbols are given, depends upon the interpretations that other members of the organization give to them.* Some of the specific leadership behaviors that typically "send messages" to staff (through communication mode C4) are listed in Table 4.1.

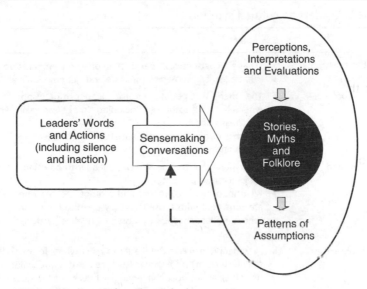

**Figure 4.2** Leaders as cultural symbols

## Changing the conversations

A fundamental change-leadership task is for leaders (throughout an organization) to stimulate, support and enable this patterning process to develop, in ways that bring about beneficial changes in organizational performance and capability. From an *informal coalitions* viewpoint, this requires them to *think culturally* as they engage with others in the organization; and, through this, help to shift the everyday patterns of conversation that take place.

To do this, leaders first need to raise their own awareness of the ways in which existing assumptions are channeling people's perceptions and interpretations of what is going on and how they should behave. In particular, they need to try to detect how their own words and actions are being interpreted and acted upon. With this greater understanding, they can then try to adapt what they say and do to take account of this. They can also participate in the sensemaking processes through which these interpretations are being made. In this way they may be able to help people to reframe their understanding, so that they come to make different sense than they might otherwise have done. That is to say, their specific focus in seeking to bring about organizational change should be on helping to change the everyday, sensemaking conversations that people have – both with themselves (thinking) and, most importantly, with each other.

**Table 4.1** Leaders as cultural symbols

| Behavior | Examples |
| --- | --- |
| Focus of interest and attention | • What a leader notices, spends time on and comments upon.<br>• What a leader chooses to measure and get emotional about. |
| Resource allocation | • The criteria that people *perceive* a leader to be using when allocating resources (including time) – especially when the "heat's on."<br>• Whether or not these criteria match up to the leader's *stated* values and priorities. |
| Recruitment and progression | • The criteria that people *perceive* a leader to be using, when they recruit or promote people.<br>• Whether or not they recruit and promote people whose values are consistent with those that they claim to believe in.<br>• Whether a leader tends to ignore or sideline particular types of people. |
| Incidents and crises | • How people *perceive* the leader to react when, for example, they face an external threat (such as a fast approaching deadline); an internal challenge (such as someone questioning a decision); or if a mistake happens (such as looking for someone to blame). |
| Rewards and status | • The kinds of behavior that a leader is seen to reward and punish (both formally and informally).<br>• The nature of the rewards and punishments. |
| Team working and collaboration | • How a leader is seen to interact with, and talk about, their own peers and other functions.<br>• How they are seen to deal with the tensions between independence (individuality and individual performance) and interdependence (team working and collaboration). |
| Change management | • *How* a leader sets about managing and changing the organization.<br>• Whether or not the way in which a leader approaches change in practice is consistent with their expressed values, and with any that have been stated explicitly as part of the change strategy. |
| Symbolism of structures, processes, etc. | • How people perceive and interpret the nature of the structures, systems, processes, procedures and rules and so on that leaders introduce (e.g. control systems that imply low expectations of people's willingness and ability to contribute may generate response patterns of alienation and disaffection).<br>• How people perceive and interpret more informal or ad hoc incidents and events that leaders initiate or subscribe to (e.g. privileged parking arrangements, rule-bending justified by status, etc.) |
| Stories, language and imagery | • The sort of language that a leader habitually uses (such as positive or negative, elevating or demeaning, empowering or controlling, collective or individual).<br>• The metaphors that a leader predominantly uses (such as machine-like language, sporting analogies, military metaphors, organic references, etc.). |

- The congruence of particular language, metaphors and everyday phrases with what a leader claims to be trying to achieve.
- The consistency between what a leader says in private and what they say in public – where the two don't match, the former will have the greater impact.

Resonance *v* Dissonance

- Whether or not what the leader is saying and doing connects emotionally with staff – that is, resonates with them – rather than causing dissonance and negative reaction.
- Whether or not the leader accurately captures and "matches" the mood of staff.

---

In practical terms, therefore, "thinking culturally" for leaders means three things. First, it means trying to detect the existing assumptions that are influencing the ways in which staff perceive and interpret their day-to-day words and behaviors. They might do this by asking themselves such questions as:

- What impact do my words and actions (including silence and inaction) appear to be having on the way that reality is being constructed in ("my" part of) the organization?
- How do my words and actions appear to be being perceived, interpreted and evaluated?
- What broad patterns of assumptions might be channelling these responses?

Secondly, they need to use these insights and inferences to anticipate how their staff might respond to specific actions that they wish to take. They can then use this heightened awareness to inform the ways in which they set about the task. Where necessary, they might also ask themselves what, authentically, they could say and do differently that might be perceived and interpreted in more organizationally beneficial ways. Thirdly, through their everyday conversations and interactions, they need to find out how their words and actions are *actually* being interpreted and acted upon by staff. They will then be better placed to foster more mutually beneficial outcomes. Where necessary, this means asking themselves how they might better engage with the ongoing meaning-making process, to help people make different, more useful sense of their words and behaviors. In this way, leaders can gain a new level of understanding about how their words and actions are perceived locally; and then work to increase the impact that these have on the nature, pace and outcomes of organizational change.

## Fostering an enabling environment

Many leaders attempt to address their felt need for cultural change by defining and disseminating a set of desired "organizational values." In the past, I have orchestrated many efforts aimed at achieving this; and these exercises can have some merit. However, as I've tried to suggest here, cultural patterns cannot be imposed from above. These are *co*-created through the dynamic network of conversational processes that involves everyone in the organization. And, many attempts at inculcating a new set of values fail because the rhetoric doesn't fit with people's conception of everyday organizational reality. For example, the values might champion participation but be imposed from above; managers might not practice what they preach; the values might be introduced as part of a "cultural change program" rather than as an integral part of the ongoing management of the business; and so on.

Paradoxically, these outwardly failed attempts at instilling a set of organizational values from above *do* help to define and embed the "culture" of the organization; although this is perhaps not always in the ways that their initiators intended! For instance, the above examples might contribute to a construction of a reality that includes the following assumptions. Participation is really about compliance. It's ok to say one thing and do another. And this "values stuff" is nothing to do with the normal work of getting the job done; so, if I have to choose between the two, I'd better make sure I do the job!

If leaders really want to influence the judgments that their staff make and the actions they take, the real lesson of what we've been saying is that they need to look at their own behavior first. So, it's perfectly valid for them to set down the values that they judge to be important to organizational success. But they need to communicate these through their own actions first, rather than through the formal communication programs that are usually adopted as part of a top–down *education and training* approach to change.

## Leaders are part of the culture too!

One final thing for leaders to remember is that they themselves are part of the culture. That is, they too are inextricably involved in the ongoing process of shared meaning making that constitutes "culture" from an *informal coalitions* perspective. Leaders are therefore being influenced *by* existing cultural patterns, even while they are trying to be influencers *of* those patterns.

## In summary

If leaders want to take culture seriously, they need to recognize that:

- An organization is a network of ongoing, self-organizing conversations, through which meaning is created, embedded and, potentially, changed. "Culture" is another name for this *active process* of shared meaning making.
- As a result, culture is not something that can be measured on a scale because it exists solely within and between the heads of people as they interact with each other. Surface-level surveys might give the impression of understanding "the culture;" but these tend to be superficial and misleading, especially if too much reverence is paid to the analytical process rather than to the conversations that flow from it.
- Decisions and actions cannot be taken (or left "untaken") in any aspect of organizational performance without these having cultural implications. Everything that leaders do, and the way that they do it, has symbolic significance.
- Leaders constantly communicate their beliefs, values and assumptions to staff – consciously and unconsciously – through their day-to-day actions *and* inaction. These everyday interactions *unavoidably* influence the ways in which staff experience the organization and make sense of it. The choice that leaders have is whether or not they wish to participate in this *joint* meaning-making process in a deliberate and informed way. By doing so they may be able to help staff make different, more useful sense of what's going on and to act on this understanding in more value-adding ways.
- Leaders can never *control* the cultural patterns that emerge. These arise spontaneously and in a self-organizing way, which is not amenable to direct control by any single individual or group. Even when they introduce new ways of working or define a set of core values and beliefs for people to adopt, this is only one ingredient of the cultural mix. How staff perceive, interpret and react to a manager's words and actions, individually and collectively *at the local level*, will have the most telling effect on the cultural patterns that emerge. The *informal coalitions* perspective recognizes, though, that leaders (or others for

that matter) can work to shift these patterns deliberately, through the ways in which they engage with the meaning-making process.

- If leaders choose to engage with the process, they can do so in a number of ways. These include becoming aware of the symbolic consequences of their own actions, attempting to foster desired values through the environment that they create, and taking part in various acts of meaning making (articulating key themes, sharing sensemaking stories with staff, helping staff to extract meaning from everyday events, etc.).

- Leaders' *observed* resource decisions signal those outcomes and actions that are *acceptable to the leader* and therefore presumed to be desired by the organization. These might include such things as what is "core business" and what is peripheral; what level of risk is acceptable; or what criteria to use in making choices and deciding priorities. Which initiatives and constraints should be taken account of and which ignored, or which activities are valued and which seen as marginal are amongst many other interpretations that might emerge in the wake of seemingly innocuous actions taken by those in leadership positions.

- Many factors that are more usually associated with cultural change (such as formal statements of values, organizational restructuring, etc.) also provide potential symbols that people might use as part of the sensemaking process. However, these will only "work" as potential influencers of cultural patterning if they are congruent with the symbols drawn from observation of managers' everyday words and actions. If they are not, staff will tend to ignore them and interpret events in line with the latter.

- Leaders who are aware of their powerful symbolic role have a much better chance of using themselves effectively to shift cultural patterns than do those who are unaware of these dynamics. As a major focus for their staff's attention, leaders help to create change when the interpretations that others give to their words and actions shift the patterns of underlying assumptions in new ways. Where leaders remain unaware of their symbolic power, their everyday words and actions can easily undermine their formally stated intentions.

## And finally ...

The ways in which people perceive, interpret and react to a leader's words and actions, at any moment in time, provide a true reflection of *who the leader is* and *what they stand for, at that time* and *in the context of that relationship.* As an analogy, all of the things leading up to the hitting of a golf ball are encapsulated in the instant that the club hits the ball. Wherever the ball goes from that point onward is the only place that it could have gone. Similarly, all of the things leading up to a leader's interaction with his or her staff are encapsulated in the moment of the interaction. Whatever staff perceive and interpret to be the meaning of the interaction *is the only meaning that could have emerged.* These are *moments of leadership truth.*

# CHAPTER 5

# Acting politically

> It's almost as if people treat organizational politics as a low-grade
> virus infection, hoping that if they ignore it and think positively
> it will go away.
>
> – Samuel Culbert

## Introduction

Of the six guiding principles that provide an *informal coalitions* agenda
for leading change, "acting politically" is the one that is likely to cause
managers the most discomfort. By convention, political behavior is not
what one would expect to see championed as a vital component of
effective leadership. Typically, organizational politics are thought of
in terms of conflicting agendas, self-serving behaviors and "spin." In
contrast, models and stories of high-performance leadership are usually
constructed in terms of co-operative mindsets, organization-enhancing
behaviors and open, honest communication.

The initial paragraphs below summarize some of the central elements
of this more conventional view of organizational politics, as a backcloth
to what follows. However, the *informal coalitions* view of organizational
dynamics, as set out in Chapters 1 and 2, unapologetically places power
and politics alongside conversation and thinking culturally as the central
pillars of effective, *transforming* leadership.

## Politics as "playing dirty"

Stone (1997: 1) is quite clear about both the pervasiveness of organizational politics and its negative effect on organizational processes and
performance:

> The term "company politics" refers to all the game-playing, snide,
> "them and us" aggressive, sabotaging, negative, blaming, "win–lose",

withholding, non-cooperative behaviour that goes on in hundreds of interactions everyday in your organisation.

This view of politics, which sees it as an illegitimate distortion of the formal structures and functions of organization, is widely held. Whenever I have asked managers what words and phrases come to mind when they think of organizational politics, they have been quick and eager to offer their opinions. Over the years, I have compiled the following list from their responses:

- Manipulation
- "I'll scratch your back . . ."
- Looking out for No. 1
- Game playing
- Destructiveness
- Covert deals in smoke-filled rooms
- Backstabbing
- One-upmanship
- Turf battles
- Power plays
- A . . . licking
- Hidden agendas
- Machiavellian
- Valuing appearance above substance
- "I'm all right, Jack"
- Narcissism.

Mintzberg (1989: 238) also talks about organizational politics primarily in negative terms:

> . . . political activity is usually divisive and conflictive, pitting individuals or groups against the more legitimate systems of influence and, when those systems are weak, against each other.

In reflecting this view of political behavior as dysfunctional, Simmons (1998) argues that there is a hidden force in all of us that limits our desire to give 100 percent wholesale co-operation. She calls this drive toward un-cooperative behavior a "territorial impulse;" and goes on to identify ten "territorial games" that this impulse spawns. Simmons maintains that these territorial games undermine productivity, waste

resources, sap people's energy and stir up negative feelings. To overcome this, she advocates increased self-awareness of one's own game
playing; surfacing others' game-playing behavior on a "no blame" basis
(arguing that it arises from an in-built survival drive); and using dialogue
to explore the behaviors and transform them into more constructive ways
forward.

Simmons' prescriptions make good common sense. And simply by
categorizing the various game-playing behaviors, these can be made more
accessible to exploration and challenge. However, as she herself recognizes, reasonable solutions do not appear reasonable to people embroiled
in the heat of active game playing. Trying to deal with these *a*-rational
dynamics through a rational approach, aimed at preventing emotions from
getting in the way of reasoned argument, may blind people to what is
really going on and create a false sense of security. Rather than seeking to
reframe the perceived weaknesses or dysfunctional behaviors and redir-
ecting the energy in organizationally enhancing ways, the focus is on
eliminating them altogether. A central proposition of this book is that the
political dynamics that we ordinarily view as negative and dysfunctional
are *structurally inevitable*; and that these can be used constructively, to
enhance the performance and capability of the organization. This is especially the case if, as Janov (1994) argues, we see power as "relationship
with" rather than "power over" other people.

Mintzberg (1989) presents his own catalog of 13 political games. As
with Simmons's list, all of them are recognizable to anyone who has spent
any time at all within organizations. Taken at face value, these provide
a bleak picture of organizations and of the motivations of people who
work in them. It's perhaps not surprising then that organizational politics
has retained its label of illegitimacy within mainstream management
thinking.


## The conventional response

The conventional response to issues of power and politics in organizational change has generally followed one of four routes. The first approach
has been to omit these altogether from the biographical accounts of
change, and from the writers' stories and consultants' models that translate these into "best practice" for others to follow. A quick scan of the
index pages of business biographies will rarely reveal the words power
or politics. Our thirst for "white knight"-type characters, neatly packaged
plots and easy-to-follow prescriptions perhaps makes this sanitized form

of organizational storytelling inevitable within this slice of the market. However, failure to address the messier aspects of the process make these texts less useful as tools for developing practical insights into leadership and organizational dynamics than they might otherwise be.

A second approach has been to deny that power and politics have any legitimate part to play in the dynamics of organizational change and performance at all, beyond the notion of resistance. This view also sees resistance as something that can then be anticipated, analyzed and dealt with rationally, as part of the "people management" stream of a change program or through established performance-management processes. In doing so, it conveniently confines the consideration of political behavior to the actions of those outside the leadership group, who visibly oppose the formally initiated changes and established policies. In this way, it avoids any suggestion that power and politics have any relevance to the "higher ground" occupied by those initiating and leading the change efforts or managing the organization's ongoing performance.

A third view accepts that power and politics do indeed exist and exert their influence on the behavior of leaders as well as others in the organization. At the same time, it sees these as illegitimate aspects of the leadership role, which need to be discouraged. As such, the exercise of power and the use of political strategies tend to be ignored by those designing and orchestrating the change process, developing leadership capabilities or managing organizational performance from this perspective. Instead, they tend to favor explanations and approaches that are founded on the use of wholly rational concepts, tools and techniques.

A final and related perspective sees the exercise of power and the use of politics as symptoms of organizational dysfunction. It is then argued that the successful implementation of the change program, and adoption of the new processes and behaviors that this seeks to introduce, will overcome these unwanted effects. This is a version of the "do it better and get it right" response to the anxiety of not being "in control," which we discussed in Chapter 2.

The quote by Culbert that opened this chapter neatly sums up the way that approaches such as these seek to disregard, deny, dismiss or downgrade the impact of political dynamics on organizational change and performance. Thankfully though, despite the fact that the negative game-playing identified by Stone, Simmons, Mintzberg and others is very familiar to anyone who has worked inside organizations, it is rarely all-consuming. Most organizations continue to function in spite of these dynamics. Even more importantly, the *informal coalitions* view of organizational dynamics argues that those organizations that succeed do so not only in spite of political behavior but also *because of it*.

## Informal coalitions view of organizational politics

In the remainder of this chapter, we will concentrate on the *informal coalitions* perspective on organizational politics, and look at what this has to say in relation to the change-leadership agenda. This view sees political behavior as central to everyday leadership and organizational dynamics, not something separate from them. Also, whilst recognizing that this has the potential to degenerate into the negative, self-serving and organizationally dysfunctional effects that were cataloged at the start of this chapter, *informal coalitions* sees these same dynamics as the essence of effective, transforming leadership.

## Overview

To explain this, we will first look at a number of statements that outline the case for seeing organizational politics as a central dynamic of organizational change and performance. These will provide us with the skeleton of the argument, which we can then flesh out with more detailed discussions. The bare bones of the case are as follows:

- First, as a result of *natural* organizational and psychosocial dynamics, organizations are made up of shifting coalitions of diverse – and potentially competing – interest groups.
- Each of these groups has its own perspective on what is required to meet the organization's current challenges and emerging issues.
- Because resources are limited, choices and trade-offs need to be made between competing demands and possible ways forward.
- The need for choices and trade-offs, coupled with differing interests and perspectives, means that tension and conflict are inevitable.
- Organizational politics are concerned with the ways in which these differences and conflicts are played out.
- The differences that arise can rarely be wholly resolved through formal statements and processes. However well-structured, these can never be definitive. They always have to be interpreted and enacted locally; and there is therefore always scope for this to be done in interest-skewed ways (whether intentionally or otherwise).

- In any event, even if policies and processes could be stated unam-
  biguously and interpreted in the way intended, some of the resulting
  political activity would be directed toward *changing* these formally
  established ends and/or means, not simply accommodating them. This,
  as suggested in Chapter 2, is not only the way in which formal changes
  are resisted *but also how they originate in the first place.*
- The scale and scope of the political dynamics that are experienced will
  be magnified the greater the level of uncertainty and change that exists,
  and the further away from agreement that people find themselves.
  The need for effective political leadership will also intensify in these
  circumstances.
- Finally, formal leaders and leadership groups are also party to these
  dynamics. In this, as in other aspects of organizational dynamics,
  leaders are active participants not objective observers of other people's
  actions.

## The seeds of political behavior

In positioning "acting politically" as a central element of effective, transforming leadership, there are a number of important aspects of organizational dynamics that need to be considered. These are:

- the in-built structural dynamics of organizations;
- the impact of personal mindsets on organizational interactions and
  outcomes; and
- the link between politics and meaning making in organizations.

These are discussed in turn below.

### In-built structural dynamics

There are two fundamental *and opposing* requirements of all organizational designs. First, there is a need to *divide up* activities and allocate
responsibility for carrying these out to specialist sub-units or individuals.
Secondly, there is a need to ensure effective *co-ordination* of those tasks
to achieve the organization's overall goals. This simultaneous differenti-
ation and integration of activities accounts *both* for the functional value
of organization as a way of achieving effective performance *and, at the
same time*, for the underlying political dynamics of organizations. In
effect, you can't have one without the other. The conflict referred to in the
opening paragraphs is an *inevitable* result of the fact that organizational

units are interdependent (requiring effective integration) *and* necessarily focused on their own agendas (differentiated according to function, area of responsibility or whatever). Whether this conflict is destructive or constructive depends, first and foremost, on the various parties' awareness of these dynamics and the ways in which the differences are managed.

As an example of this, I worked with an organization that was looking to develop more collaborative working between two arms of its business. Of the organizational units involved, one was responsible for providing capital- and manpower-intensive engineering services, both for internal operating units and for external customers. The second was charged with developing external business, both for the service unit in question and the wider organization. Working relationships were frayed and deteriorating; with widespread frustration expressed on both "sides" of the conflict. A number of the in-built, structural tensions that contained the seeds of this conflict are set out in Table 5.1. These are endemic in the organizational relationship between all business development (sales and marketing) and service (production) units.

The company had previously made an attempt to resolve the situation; and their approach couldn't have been more decisive. The go-it-alone manager of the service unit had been replaced, and a clear procedure put in place to clarify roles, allocate responsibilities and co-ordinate activities. These measures had been reinforced in the minds of senior management by the cross-population of the two units as new appointments were made.

**Table 5.1** Example of in-built structural tensions

| Business development unit | Service unit |
| --- | --- |
| Company-wide development focus | Single-unit management focus |
| Emphasis on long-term customer relationships | Emphasis on short-term task achievement |
| Goals based on new business development and profit growth | Goals based on cost-effective contract completion, resource productivity and capacity optimization |
| Concerned with identifying and exploiting external market opportunities | Concerned with sustaining and developing internal technical capabilities and exploiting resource capacity |
| Looking for flexibility and responsiveness to satisfy bespoke market/customer needs and challenges | Looking to optimize performance and cost through routinization of familiar processes, standardization of work, etc. |
| Aim to exploit revenue-generating opportunities – favoring a risk orientation and novelty | Aim to plug the gaps in resource utilization – favoring a security orientation and a preference for "sticking to the knitting" |
| Believe that more can be achieved by the service provider than is practicable | Believe that less can be achieved than is possible in practice |

In particular, the new manager of the service delivery unit had previously occupied a senior position in the wider business development team. In that role, he had actively promoted the use of an integrating procedure. Similarly, senior members of the business development team had had previous experience of managing in various parts of the service delivery unit. In the event, these factors simply added to the exasperation felt by senior management at the continuing failure of the two units to work together effectively. Far from the problem having been solved by these commonsense measures, it became clear from a series of one-to-one conversations with key players that territorial behaviors were generating conflicts, distorting relationships and undermining performance. It was also evident that these dysfunctional behaviors were escalating rather than subsiding.

As is inevitable in these circumstances, the underlying political dynamics were coloring people's perceptions, attitudes and behaviors. And these were being played out in ways that made rational consideration of the issues impossible. Responses had become habitual, by channeling perceptions and interpretations down increasingly well-trodden paths. In situations such as this, perceptions tend to become further distorted by the emotions that are generated, such as fear and anger, as actions appear to impact adversely upon people's own sense of "territory" and self-worth. As was the case in the situation described here, these highly charged emotions of fear and anger are often described in organizationally more acceptable terms (Simmons, 1998). Descriptors included such words as suspicion, concern, anxiety and insecurity (fear-based cluster); and frustration, exasperation and resentment (anger-based).

Unless these emotions are surfaced and dealt with, the distorted perceptual channels become deeper still and prevent alternative responses being chosen – or even being seen at all. As a result of this, each party increasingly sees its own behaviors as unquestionably justified and condemns those of others as evidence of negative politicking. This pattern was present in the stories told by the key players in the above situation. Both "sides" viewed their own actions as entirely reasonable and defensible, in the light of the perceived needs of the business and what they saw as the uncooperative behavior of the other party. At no stage did the conflict appear to be the result of deliberate, vindictive, self-seeking behavior on either side. But the natural dynamics of action, reaction and counter-action were hardening attitudes and distorting perceptions. People were behaving in ways that appeared to be perfectly sensible to them, within their own frames of reference. As we shall see below, political behaviors – and the outcomes that these produce – are the product *both* of structurally embedded tensions such as those in the illustration above (organizational dynamics) *and* the desire that we all have to maintain and protect our personal frame of reference on the world (psychosocial dynamics). The critical thing to realize is that when *a*-rational patterns of behavior become established, these cannot be analyzed rationally by the parties involved or addressed solely through reasoned argument and formal processes. Seen through the distorted perceptions that arise from these dynamics, seemingly common-sense solutions don't make sense at all to the people on whom these are imposed.

There is a related structural aspect of organizations, which frequently leads to conflict and dysfunctional behavior. This is the mismatch that exists between the "horizontal," cross-functional flow of work processes and the "vertical" structure of measures that typifies most organizations' planning and control systems. Work is accomplished through end-to-end processes that operate across the organization; such as that from customer order, through product production and dispatch, to after-sales service. Despite this, performance targets and the management actions that flow from these often fail to address this interconnectedness. Instead, these typically focus on functionally specific activities. Where targets fail to reflect the diversity of demands on the system – or the system's capacity to deal with them – these distort behavior and undermine performance rather than improving it. This lack of joined-up thinking frequently generates inter-functional friction and masks understanding of the underlying process dynamics. This, in turn, encourages game playing to "make the numbers," rather than the creative and collaborative improvement of performance.

### Personal frame of reference

Besides the inevitable structural tensions that are embedded in all organizational designs, we each develop and try to maintain a personal frame of reference throughout our lives. This mental construct is continually formed and re-formed through our everyday interactions and experiences. In turn, this affects the way in which we continue to interact and make sense of our ongoing experiences. It enables us to navigate our way through the complexities and uncertainties of life in ways that preserve our feeling of personal meaning and self-worth. It also gives us our sense of identity, our perceived place in the world and so on.

### Making the frame "visible"
*One way* of looking at this notion of a personal frame of reference is through the framework shown in Figure 5.1, borrowed from NLP.[1] This identifies six levels within each individual's personal frame, ranging from

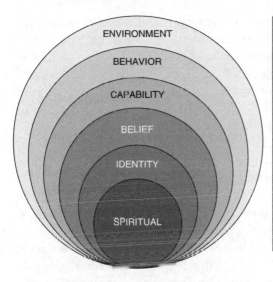

Environment: Preferred (and avoided) physical environment; working context; nature of relationships; energy levels etc.

Behavior: Habitual (and avoided) behaviors and activities, rituals and routines.

Capability: Personal strengths and weaknesses; enabling and disabling contextual factors.

Belief: Enabling (and constraining) set of personal beliefs and sensemaking frameworks.

Identity: Self-concept and self-belief, etc.

Spiritual: Connection to something "bigger"; sense of meaning; deep personal relationships; fundamental purpose in life and governing ethos.

**Figure 5.1** Personal frame of reference

surface-level, "environmental" factors to the deepest, spiritual level. As in all aspects of organization, the reality is much messier and indistinct than suggested by the diagram. However, this particular representation can be useful in helping us to recognize the sort of factors that impact upon our ways of thinking and behaving at work and beyond. It can also provide some useful insights into the ways in which we respond psychologically and emotionally to change, as we will discuss further in Chapter 6.

The surface level refers to the type of physical *environment* and organizational climate within which we prefer to work – *and* that we seek to avoid. This will include a wide range of characteristics, from the physical nature of the work environment through to the level of energy and work intensity experienced. Other aspects of organizational climate, quality and nature of working relationships might also feature here.

We are creatures of habit. In the interests of personal comfort and self-protection, we have a preference for certain routine and ritualistic ways of working, which become habitual *behaviors* over time. This draws us toward particular tasks, and to characteristic ways of approaching them; and it leads us to avoid others. Some of the thinking and behavioral preferences may be "hard wired" and others conditioned by our experience and environment (Nicholson, 2000).

Our typical behavior patterns often reflect our perceived levels of *capability*, since we seek to operate – and be seen by others to operate – competently in our various tasks and relationships (Culbert, 1996). Our capability is a function of our personal strengths and weaknesses, and the ways in which we harness and express them. Also though, our overall capability is affected by various enabling and constraining factors in our work context or other aspects of our lives. A powerful and vibrant network of relationships, for example, increases our ability to achieve things. On the other hand, formal role constraints or others' expectations of us may inhibit our ability to apply our talents to the full.

Much of what we think and do is conditioned by our personal *belief* set. We will have constructed this over time, through our experiences and our sensemaking reflections on these. The sense that we have made of past events, through our inner dialogue and interactions with others, affects the way that we view present issues, events and relationships. It also channels our thoughts about future possibilities.

At a deeper level still is our sense of who we are and what we stand for. This sense of personal *identity* is informed by – and simultaneously shapes – our beliefs, capabilities and behavior patterns. It also affects the environmental surroundings that we gravitate toward and steer clear of. For some people, their sense of who they are is intimately interwoven with their work role and/or other of their life roles (e.g. parent, local councillor, voluntary group leader). In other words, they see it primarily in terms of what they *do*. For others, identity may be bound up with their way of *being* (e.g. what they see as their bedrock "operating principles" and core values). Other aspects of identity may reflect such things as membership of particular groups, nationality, geographical location, the upholding of particular traditions and so on.

Finally, the framework acknowledges the *spiritual* dimension of our being. This sits uncomfortably with some people in the context of work life, which they tend to view in instrumental terms. This in itself is perhaps a sad commentary on the spiritually bereft and soul-destroying aspects of some workplaces. Nevertheless, whether we regard it as spiritual or not, we each desire a sense of meaning in our lives. Or we search to find a connection to something greater than ourselves. This sense of purpose and underlying ethos can be a real driving force behind our actions. Equally, where these are absent, a resulting feeling of emptiness or, in the extreme, "lack of a will to live" can be equally powerful. For some people this need for spiritual fulfillment (however they define it) may be satisfied outside the office walls and factory gates. One of the challenges for leaders is to help people to gain a sense of meaning and spiritual realization through the contributions that they make at work and the relationships that they experience (characterized, perhaps, as a sense of "team spirit"). Paradoxically, the *informal coalitions* view of organizational leadership suggests that this agenda might best be furthered by acting politically and encouraging creative self-expression, rather than by trying to create meaning for others through the imposition of a contrived set of "shared values" or top–down "Vision."

*Political implications*

In the context of organizational politics, mismatches will inevitably exist between people's personal frames of reference. The psychosocial dynamics that result from this have a key part to play in determining the way that organizations work in practice. For example, these differences are likely to cause people to compete for attention and influence on the organization's emerging agenda, so that their opinions on its objectives and work priorities will be taken into account or, better still, prevail. Clashes of personality, values, beliefs and identity also affect the ways in which individuals and groups interact with each other and make sense of emerging events. The competing agendas that emerge from this process lead people to coalesce informally (as well as formally in some cases) around different interests, either to further particular causes or to frustrate them. From an individual's point of view, this may either serve a defensive, self-protective purpose, or else represent a deliberate attempt to change the organization in some way.

As we engage with the world through our own thinking and day-to-day interactions, we try to handle all of the competing demands that arise in a way that preserves this personal frame of reference. That is, we strive to maintain our sense of integrity, self-worth and identity. This frame of reference is not static. But it does generate recognizable patterns of thinking and action over time. It shapes – and is shaped by – our everyday interactions with others. As suggested through our "plate-spinning" metaphor in Chapter 2, we each try to manage simultaneously our diverse networks of relationships, consciously and subconsciously, in ways that sustain those that we wish to (or need to) preserve. Our personal frame of reference helps us to do this – and is shaped further as a result of these continuing interactions. In particular, it offers a way of making sense of the world and of engaging with it in ways that maintain a sense of personal and interpersonal competence.

This notion of a personal frame of reference acknowledges that our view of the world is unique; and, at the same time, that it is not the world as anybody else sees it. We respond – and can only respond – to "our world" as viewed through our personal frame of reference, not directly to the world. Our perceptions and interpretations of the current state and emerging events are viewed through this frame. And this tends to reinforce our existing patterns of understanding and behavior. Also, in interacting with the world from this perspective, we are motivated to do it in ways that maintain the overall integrity of our personal framework. This means that we tend to define – and try to shape – the challenges that we face in ways that suit our view of the world *and the self-centered interests that this reflects*. In this sense at least, we are all inherently resistors of change.

A personal experience from some years ago will serve to illustrate this dynamic in practice. A colleague manager was seconded for several weeks onto a company-wide process review team. During this period, I took over his work agenda and managed his team alongside my own. This manager had a well-won reputation for his analytical skills, which he applied successfully to the company's strategic planning challenges. As part of this, he spent a significant amount of his time using spreadsheets to analyze market conditions and to explore strategic options. The unspoken expectation was that I would continue this approach during his absence. From my perspective, though, this in-depth relationship with spreadsheets and numerical analysis was far removed from my preferred way of working. This particular style of managing the task and engaging the team did not fit in with my personal frame of reference, and its underlying motive of doing *personally* meaningful work and sustaining a *personal* sense of competence. I therefore mentally constructed the role in a completely different way. Initially, one of my new direct reports expressed concern about the loss of influence that he felt the team might have with the Executive. In response, I arranged for him and other of his colleagues to sit down directly with the relevant directors in a number of face-to-face sessions. This gave them direct access to the thinking of top management. Coupled with my request for them to apply their own analytical expertise to the emerging challenges, the team's influence on the unfolding agenda remained undiminished – and their sense of ownership of the emerging strategy grew as well. As a result of this approach, I navigated this period as the company's stand-in business planning manager without the need to manipulate a single Excel program in anger!

From one perspective, this might be viewed as an example of effective, empowering leadership. And, hopefully, it was. However, as successful as this approach might have been as a leadership strategy, it was motivated in part by my own self-interests. In particular, it met my need to avoid situations in which any relative lack of competency might have been exposed, in favor of one that embraced my particular strengths and interests. If I had been challenged at the time, my "defense" would undoubtedly have been couched in terms of a desire to exploit the team's talents to the full; to expose them to the thinking of senior management; and, through this, to broaden their appreciation of the strategic context within which they were working. All of these would have been true. At the same time, I was fully at home in the style of leadership that this represented. That is, it sprang from my personal frame of reference and the particular mindset and work preferences that this embodied.

My argument here is that the strategy that I adopted – largely subconsciously at the time – to deal with a potential threat to my personal frame of reference represents the normal way that people operate in organizations (and social situations in general). It was not the exception. We all do it, to the extent that we are able. And we all do it *all of the time* – either to avoid perceived threats to our personal frames or to exploit opportunities to strengthen them. This self-serving behavior is political! The important question to consider though is whether or not it also serves the legitimate needs of others in the organization – and of the organization as a whole.

*Politics and meaning making*

How people frame issues in their own minds is critical to the way in which they view other people's actions and act themselves in the moment. Their actions (alone and in combination with the intended and incidental actions of others) determine how change unfolds and performance develops. In turn, the outcomes that emerge provide inputs to these same sensemaking and evaluation processes. These then give rise to further in-the-moment actions. As we have seen from earlier discussions, this ongoing, self-organizing process is at the heart of organizational change and performance. It involves people making sense together of what certain events and observations mean, how these should be viewed and what consequences this particular framing of events has for the actions that they and others should take. In relation to this current discussion, it is important to recognize that this process is also political in nature.

The frame that is "put around" an issue, activity or outcome through this process determines the particular meaning that it has in that situation and at that time. Crucially, frames give meaning to events that otherwise would not exist. This is critical to organizational dynamics and individual behavior, because the particular frame through which an issue, activity or event is viewed determines such things as:

- whether or not it is seen as sufficiently urgent and/or important to merit people's time and attention;
- what response is appropriate and organizationally acceptable;
- whether a particular outcome is considered a success or a failure;

- whether – if this is viewed as a failure – it is seen as providing a chance to learn and improve, or else as a reason to look for someone to blame;
- whether or not a particular contribution is thought to be valuable and worthy of recognition;
- . . . and so on.

According to established thinking, it is management's job to determine the meaning of particular issues, events and changes. That is, it is their responsibility (and their formal managerial right) to decide which interpretation of events, amongst a range of potential interpretations, is the "right" one and which aren't. They do this by communicating about issues and events in ways that aim to:

- validate particular interpretations of emerging events and management actions rather than others;
- set the context for other people's actions;
- ensure that some ideas and proposals are actioned and others rejected; and
- decide whether outcomes should be seen as successes or failures, and whether these should therefore be rewarded or criticized.

The tools that managers conventionally use to achieve these aims include such things as formal strategies, policies, and procedures; codes of practice; formally negotiated agreements; formal presentations and briefings; formal feedback and appraisal sessions and so on. These undoubtedly make a significant contribution to the sensemaking and use-making processes. However, we have seen that the ultimate meanings that people take from formal pronouncements and emerging events are *co-created* through the informal conversations that they have about them with other individuals and groups. It is through these local conversations and interactions that the particular way of framing a situation "in the moment" is constructed, modified, embraced or overturned in favor of another. Where these conversations lead people to coalesce around the meaning advanced by management, this view of events and its implications for ongoing action will be reinforced. Where this is not the case, however, the dynamics of *informal coalitions* suggests that activities will be carried out to frustrate the formally stated intentions. Dependent upon the relative power dynamics at work at the time, this resistance might also trigger shadow-side actions designed to overturn the formal strategies, structures or policies. As we recognized in Chapter 1, these dynamics operate at all levels of the organization.

As people engage in this process, they will each be motivated in part by the desire to maintain the integrity of their own frame of reference. To do this, they each need other people to make sense of current situations and emerging events in ways that "fit in" with it. That is, they each need other people to perceive and interpret organizational situations and events in ways that achieve two things. First, they need events to be framed in ways that leave their own personal frame of reference in tact – or which strengthen it further. Secondly, they need other people to value the particular contributions that they make to the world (as judged through *their* respective frames of reference). Influencing the ways in which issues are framed is therefore a key aspect of the political process. And it is the essence of acting politically from an *informal coalitions* perspective.

## The political process

In Chapter 2, we discussed how organizational outcomes emerge from the dynamic network of conversations that make up everyday organizational activity. These include the tangible outcomes (such as strategies, structures, and systems, etc.). But they also embrace the organization's informal and less tangible characteristics, such as its shadow-side activities and the patterns of underlying, cultural assumptions that tend to channel people's ongoing thinking and behavior. The incidence and nature of these interactions are affected by the patterns of cultural assumptions that already exist. As a result, the process tends to reinforce existing patterns of thinking and acting. This is why organizations often get stuck in ritualistic patterns of behavior and "set play" interactions. And it is why organizational change is so challenging.

This basic conversational process was illustrated in Figure 2.2. Figure 5.2 builds on this earlier figure, to illustrate important political dimensions of the process. It also shows the outcomes in terms of the underlying political dynamics that might emerge.

Decisions, actions, new coalitions and underlying assumptions arise from the dynamic network of conversations and interactions through which differences are addressed and accommodations made – or not! For the most part, this process is informal, unstructured and piecemeal. Outcomes emerge from an ongoing and disparate series of interactions, including incidental remarks and observations, rather than from one-off, staged events. Some of the interests around which individuals and groups align arise from the

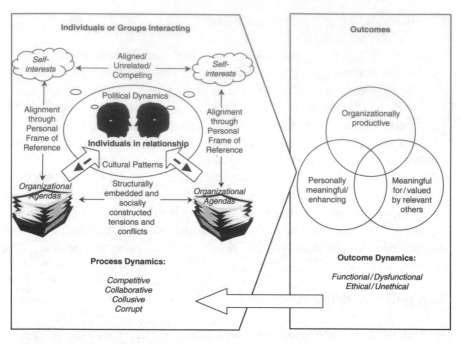

**Figure 5.2** The political process

formal, "legitimate" aims and structures of the organization. These will flow from formal statements and structured work processes. Others derive from cross-functional issues and interest-group agendas. Personal concerns, relationships and ambitions add another layer of complexity.

When individuals interact within an organization, the quality and outcomes of their relationship are affected both by their personal perceptions of the organizational agendas that they are each trying to satisfy and their own self-interests. In particular, the specific mindset that they each bring to bear on the relationship is determined by their personal frame of reference. Through this they each seek to achieve alignment between their personal self-interests and the demands of the organization, *as they see them.* An individual's personal frame of reference affects the way that they perceive unfolding events and work agendas. It therefore follows that they will tend to interpret these demands in ways that are consistent with that frame. The personal example that I outlined earlier, where I took temporary charge of a colleague's team and work agenda, reflects this dynamic in action. Each individual's frame of reference serves this purpose *simultaneously* for all of his or her important relationships. In this sense, all of those people who are important to them – by necessity or desire – are subconsciously "present" in each meaningful interaction that they have. As I suggested through the plate-spinning analogy, not all of these relationships will be "spinning perfectly" all of the time. Trade-offs will need to be made from time to time to suit specific circumstances; and pragmatic choices will be called for that will cause some relationships to flourish and others to "teeter on the brink." Nevertheless, an individual's judgments at such times will still be guided by the desire to maintain their personal frame of reference in as acceptable a state as possible.

## Process dynamics

In any particular interaction, the self-interests of participants might be aligned with each other, totally unrelated or in conflict. Similarly, tensions may arise from any structurally embedded conflicts inherent in the various organizational agendas involved; or from the ways in which these have been constructed in people's minds. As discussed earlier, the resulting interaction involves a number of simultaneous conversations. Besides participants' overt conversation with each other, they are each also engaged in a conversation with themself (i.e. thinking), which is shaped by (and further shapes) their personal frame of reference. At the same time, the background "cultural conversation" affects the way that the overt conversation itself, and the interaction as a whole, develops. It does this by tending to channel perceptions, interpretations and behaviors imperceptibly down well-trodden paths. These reflect the particular set of taken-for-granted assumptions that are shared by participants. This pattern of cultural assumptions includes those relating to the underlying political dynamics that influence everyday activity in that part of the organization. This means that, paradoxically, the integrating tendency of the cultural dynamics of organization (the shared sense-making process that embeds the patterns) will also embrace the splitting-apart tendency of its characteristic political dynamics (difference and contention).

As a result of this dynamic mix of factors, the conversation may be conducted largely "above board," whether co-operatively or competitively. Alternatively, much of what goes on may take place in the shadows of the interaction, with important elements of it remaining unspoken. Within this, participants may operate independently, or else collude to further their own self-interests and/or those of their parts of the organization at others' expense. Where this takes place with deliberate intent to achieve personal gain ahead of organizational benefit, there is a risk that corrupt practices will discolor interactions.

## Outcome dynamics

Finally, Figure 5.2 suggests that the outcomes arising from this process, *as seen from each participant's perspective* reflect the extent to which the result:

- is seen as organizationally productive;
- is in line with the individual's own frame of reference; and
- takes account of the personal interests and agendas of other key players.

In acting politically as a leader, there are always three constituencies involved. These are the organization as an entity (its purpose, ethos and strategy); the leader himself or herself (their personal frame of reference and perceived work agenda that flows from this); relevant others involved in the interaction (their own personal frames of reference and self-aligned agendas). Successful political behavior, as embodied in the *informal coalitions* leadership agenda, requires the needs of all three constituencies to be pursued.

## Functional politics and the use of power

Politics, then, is a natural dynamic of organizations, whether managers choose to engage with it or not. It is the process through which differences in self-interest and organizational agendas are played out. From an *informal coalitions* perspective, organizational vitality and success depend on effective political processes. These provide energy, enable differences to be dealt with effectively and organizationally beneficial results to be achieved in a complex and uncertain environment. However, the *informal coalitions* view also recognizes that these same processes can easily degenerate into destructive conflict and lead to organizationally dysfunctional effects, if they become overly defensive, parochially focused or corrupt.

Where these differences are dealt with in self-serving and manipulative ways, which ride roughshod over other people's interests and the well-being of the organization, the negative political game playing most readily identified with organizational politics comes to the fore.

However, where these same dynamics are approached from a politically aware, ethical and organizationally enhancing standpoint, acting politically provides one of the keys for transforming ordinary performance into *extra*-ordinary performance. Functional politics is therefore about managing differences in ways that are *both* organizationally enhancing *and* which serve the legitimate interests of organizational members – *including their own*. In practical terms, this means using *power* to modify the knowledge, attitudes and behaviors of key stakeholders in relation to important issues and events. As with talk and politics, though, power is an aspect of organizational dynamics that sits uncomfortably with most managers.

## The nature of power

I often ask groups of managers how important they feel it is for them to have power in their organizations. This usually evokes a typical pattern of response, in which one or two of them tentatively acknowledge their desire for power; but the majority "sit on their hands." The ensuing discussion soon exposes the fact that they all want to *influence* activities and outcomes. But most of them associate power with command-and-control practices (power *over* people) and unsavory attempts to "climb the greasy pole" (power as "dog eat dog" self-advancement).

To help them break out of this pattern, I suggest that they might think of influence as the *process* of modifying people's knowledge, attitudes and behaviors to achieve desired outcomes. Power is then the mixture of personal, situational and operating factors that *enable them to do it*. This allows them to view power more constructively and expansively, by seeing it as an *essential condition* for achieving improved organizational performance. Nothing at all is achieved in organizations without the use of power, whether this is formally delegated power (authority) or its many other forms that we will discuss below. Leaders who opt out of the organizational challenges that exercising their power brings, whether "on principle" or for other reasons, simply leave the way open for other, potentially less principled people to exploit the gap. In any event, they cannot avoid the impact of power on their everyday interactions and organizational outcomes. They will either be exercising power or being subject to it. In most organizationally productive situations, they will be doing both.

## The basis of power in organizations

If leaders are going to use power successfully, to influence outcomes in ethical and organizationally enhancing ways, they first need to understand the basis of their own power. They also need to develop an awareness of the power that others are able to draw upon in any particular situation. To help with this, it can be useful to think of four interrelated aspects of power that impact upon the dynamics of organizational change and performance. I have called these instrumental power, inner power, relational power, and embedded power.

### Instrumental power

Instrumental power refers to those attributes of an individual's capability and behavior that can be directly used to modify the knowledge, attitudes and behaviors of others. These are the most visible aspects of power; and they would typically include such things as:

- a person's formal position and authority (position power), which conveys the right to decide and act within defined limits and to command others to carry out organizationally legitimate activities;
- the control of limited resources and access to information that are valued by others (resource power);
- an individual's personal knowledge and expertise (expert power), which is relevant to the task in hand;
- the network of relationships that an individual has with other key people in the organization (network power), which enables the individual to leverage the position power, resource power or expert power of others to bring about the desired changes in third parties;
- physical or psychological dominance (coercive power), through which one individual or group can force another to comply with their own wishes;
- the impact of role modeling on other people's behaviors and the emergence of meaning (symbolic power), which we have discussed extensively in Chapters 3 and 4;
- the ability to establish empathy and rapport when interacting with others (communication power), which generates richer, more powerful conversations.

Coercive power has no part to play in the ethical, organizationally enhancing way of "acting politically" that we are focusing on here. It would be naïve, though, not to recognize the impact that this abuse of power can have on the dynamics of some organizations. In some instances, this manifests itself in blatant (or covert) bullying by those who are in a position to dominate other people psychologically or, less commonly perhaps, physically. In other cases, the use of fear and dependency as a means of controlling others' behavior and seeking compliance might be more subtly applied, such as during periods of organizational restructuring when jobs might be at risk. Kohn (1993), in a book of the same title, goes further still, by suggesting that people can be "punished by rewards." He argues that, where managers can withhold rewards from people who don't comply with their wishes, those rewards that are contingent upon meeting manager-determined outcomes ("carrots") are really cleverly disguised sticks!

The above power bases might either be expressed in ways that support the organization's formally adopted ends and means; or else be marshaled in opposition to them. From a conventional viewpoint, an oppositional stance might be termed "negative power." Handy (1993: 131), for example, describes this as ". . . the capacity to stop things happening, to delay them, to distort or disrupt them." From this perspective, these power bases have the potential to fuel the full range of dysfunctional political behaviors that were referred to in the opening paragraphs of this chapter. However, as argued in Chapter 2, *all* significant change originates from the informal coalescing of people around viewpoints and ideas that oppose the currently accepted wisdom or formally recognized policies and practices. If the proponents of these viewpoints can mobilize sufficient power through this means, they can then propel the proposed changes into the formal arenas and processes of the organization. These may then become the new legitimacy. This reflects the essential dynamics of *informal coalitions*, which form either to promote a particular cause or to oppose it. Actively building coalitions of support for organizationally beneficial changes is what the call to "act politically" is all about. The process is the same whether the power that this requires is applied in line with the organization's formal, "legitimate" power structures, or in opposition to them.

### Inner power

An individual's internal power bases enable them to apply the more overt forms of power, outlined above, with the most potency. This is important from the perspective of both the leader's own ability to influence others, and the performance of those being influenced. Using the levels in the personal frame of reference as a guide, these inner sources of power can usefully be thought of as being belief-based, identity-based and spiritually based.

A person's beliefs about how the world works, and the values that they use to screen emerging events, incidents and the behaviors of others, have a significant impact on how they make sense of what's happening at any particular time. These also affect how they *feel* about what's going on, and what they decide to do about it. These beliefs, and the self- and other-talk that flows from them, can either empower people to use their time and talents to the full or else limit their capacity to do so. At a deeper level still is the power that comes from an individual's sense of who they are – their identity. Where they have a positive self-concept and self-belief, this can enable them to use their instrumental power bases more self-confidently, authentically and authoritatively than they might otherwise do. It also allows their underlying character to show through in their relationships with others. An individual's spiritual power comes from their sense of purpose in life and their personal ethos. It gives personal meaning to what they do; and it provides a feeling of contributing to the greater good, which goes beyond the mere delivery of today's tasks.

Taken together, these three sources of inner power – values and beliefs, identity and spirituality – provide a powerful platform from which leaders can "act politically" in the way advocated here. These tend to reinforce each other, making their effect on perceived capabilities, attitudes and behaviors even stronger. Inner power magnifies the effect of the instrumental power bases set out earlier, stimulates people's engagement with the political process, anchors it in a higher purpose and increases their resilience to change. These areas provide the focus for much of the modern-day coaching effort and self-help literature that are directed at improving people's capability and performance; so it is not necessary to explore these issues further here. It is important to reiterate, though, that attention to these sources of inner power not only helps to magnify (or unblock) a leader's own ability to influence others' knowledge, attitudes and behaviors; but it also provides a key focus for performance-enhancing discussions with others about their own impact and contribution.

### Relational power

Although we have spoken so far about power as if it were a property possessed by individuals, it can only be exercised *in relationship with other people*. This affects the discussion in a number of ways:

- First, many of the instrumental aspects of power, such as position power, and knowledge and skills (expert power) are comparative. For example, anyone is an expert who knows more than anyone else about a particular subject, or who is more skilled in a critical area than others. Similarly, middle managers have greater position power than members of the workforce at large; but they have less position power than senior managers. And so on.

- Secondly, and more importantly, the power that anyone is able to exercise in a particular situation depends on how the intended recipient perceives, interprets and evaluates it. Power is in the eye of the beholder. For example, expert power has no potency if the recipient does not consider the person who is trying to use it to be an expert. Equally, the ability to control the deployment of resources or to limit access to information will only be effective if those people value those resources or information.

- Thirdly, some of the power bases are interrelated; and using one may limit the ability to use another or affect its potency. For example, if a manager is observed to rely consistently on coercion to get others to comply with their will, it is highly unlikely that they will be able to build the trust in others that is essential to build rapport.

- Fourthly, power relationships will affect the dynamics of the conversations and interactions through which power is exercised. This is especially – though not exclusively – the case in respect of position power and coercive power. For example, in any conversation, who says what to whom and when, the topics that are discussed and those that are avoided and so on will all be affected by the relative power of those present. This will be determined "in the moment" by those taking part. And this "assessment" will be significantly affected by the taken-for-granted assumptions (background "cultural conversation") that tend to channel everyday interactions in the organization.

The ways in which people perceive and interpret the behaviors of an individual through their own and others' interactions with them will affect their own beliefs about that individual. In particular, it will affect such things as their reputation, felt trustworthiness and (*inter*-)personal charisma.

### Embedded power

Finally, power is also embedded in the structures, processes, ideology, language and other aspects of the organization that serve to define the formal rules and norms of behavior. For example, formal delegations of authority and reporting systems provide privileged access to information, limit the decision-making ability of some people in relation to that enjoyed by others, and emphasize the centrality or otherwise of certain individuals and departments. Informal custom and practice can similarly exert differential influence on people's behavior and capacity to act. Other examples of embedded power structures would be the dress codes and office arrangements that convey and sustain people's relative status; and the types of language and discussion topics that are considered acceptable in different organizational contexts. These open the doors to involvement and influence for some people and close them for others.

Moves over the past 30 years or so to make business language "gender neutral" (such as using the term "Chair" rather than "Chair*man*") reflect one attempt to break embedded power structures in the name of greater equality and diversity. This so-called "politically correct" use of language imposes its own power structure of course, by defining what is acceptable to those making the rules; and, potentially, imposing sanctions against those whose language fails to match up to the new orthodoxy. A woman colleague of mine on a committee in the 1980s refused to be harassed by what she saw as the language police. She used to argue that she wasn't a man; but that she was closer to being a man than she was to being a chair! If she were to express that view in many UK organizations today, she might well find herself at the mercy of institutionally imposed power.

"Containers" of embedded power, such as those outlined above, are themselves cultural artifacts that have emerged from previous sense-making and use-making conversations. In some instances, senior management might deliberately seek to embed certain power differentials. For example, they might classify information and restrict access to it; strictly control the level of financial delegations; adopt recruitment criteria that exclude certain groups and so on. However, the dynamics of *informal coalitions* suggests that, in such cases, competing power networks would be likely to arise informally in reaction to this.

## Options for political action

A number of distinct interventions are available to anyone wishing to mobilize their power to achieve political ends. The diagram in Figure 5.3 uses the Change Map to illustrate the broad range of political action that managers might employ. Each of the four modes of change suggests a particular set of influencing strategies and a desired outcome. These are summarized briefly below:

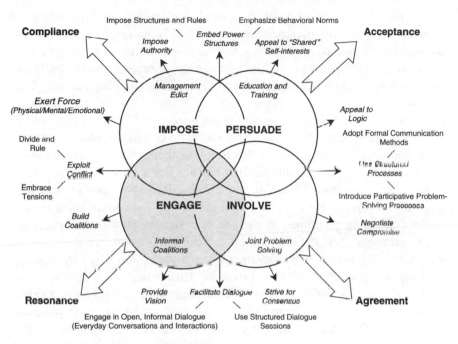

**Figure 5.3** Options for political action

- *Management edict* seeks *compliance* with the manager's will by imposing decisions on the organization. Its core strategies for achieving this are to use formal, position-based authority to shape events or, less legitimately, to exert physical or psychological force on people. Where conflicts exist, which cannot be dealt with through either of these means, the general strategy is to "divide and rule." *Management edict* can also be reinforced, and its intentions structurally embedded, by imposing structures, rules and regulations that channel and constrain people's interactions and responses.
- The political goal of *education and training* is to gain *acceptance* for a particular position through various forms of *persuasion*. This means influencing people's views through an appropriate mix of logical argument and overt appeal to the "shared" self-interest of the group (such as the organization's survival). As with *management edict*, the *education and training* approach also seeks to embed power relationships in the fabric of the organization. Here, though, the emphasis is on channeling activities and shaping outcomes through the reinforcement of organizational norms and the development of common behavioral competencies, rather than imposing structures, rules and regulations.

As we've seen in Chapter 3, formal, structured communication – aimed at "getting the message across" – is another of the instruments of choice of managers, when they operate in an *education and training mode*. At its extreme, this can degenerate – intentionally or otherwise – into indoctrination and the creativity-sapping "cloning" of behaviors.

- *Joint problem solving* sets out to reach *agreement* between competing interest groups, by selecting from a spectrum of *involvement* strategies. A common feature of these tends to be their use of formal issue-handling processes to facilitate agreement. These range from the "give and take" dynamics of negotiation and bargaining, aimed at reaching an acceptable compromise; through the search for consensus amongst the competing positions; to the use of a structured dialogue process, to encourage the joint exploration of possible ways forward.

- Finally, the *informal coalitions* approach looks for ways of making progress that *resonate* with broad constituencies of people – even though many of these people will view contentious issues from diverse perspectives. As with *joint problem solving*, one of the main political strategies that leaders can use to achieve this is to encourage, enable *and participate in* open dialogue. Here, though, this means stimulating and taking part in rich, meaningful, everyday conversations, rather than relying on structured – and necessarily intermittent – dialogue sessions. Helping people to see issues and events through different, more insightful eyes is another of the core political responses of the *informal coalitions* approach. This is achieved by providing vision *as part of managers' day-to-day interactions with their staff and other key stakeholders. Engaging* people through these means is reinforced by actively building coalitions of support for organizationally beneficial ends and means. This is the pivotal political strategy for creating and sustaining momentum behind a particular course of action (i.e. achieving change) from an *informal coalitions* perspective. An emphasis on coalition *building* also means that in-built structural tensions and conflicting perspectives are not addressed from the "divide and rule" mindset of the *management edict* approach. Instead, the aim is to embrace the paradoxes that result and work to make them livable for people.

Our main interest here is in bringing about change by acting politically from an *informal coalitions* mindset, as summarized in the last bullet point. Within this, we have already explored the power of everyday conversation in Chapter 3. In the final three chapters, we will look in turn at the political strategies of building coalitions, embracing paradox and providing vision. Before doing so, though, we need first to recognize that there are different phases of political action that need to be navigated successfully, if "acting politically" is to add most value to the change-leadership agenda.

## Phases of political action

Five phases of political action can usefully be identified in working to achieve organizational change. These are:

- Awareness
- Entry
- Engagement
- Withdrawal
- Consolidation.

Before putting more flesh on these terms, it's important to recall that, from an *informal coalitions* perspective, change is continuous. Although the conventional notion of organizational change focuses on *specific, management-initiated* programs, we have already recognized that these are seeded in, and sustained by, the everyday conversations that people have about what's going on and how they should respond. Change, as it is understood in established management practice and writing, takes place in distinct episodes between periods of relative stability (however transient these might be). As we have seen, though, these formal episodes of change emerge from the ongoing networks of conversations that constitute everyday organizational life. They are only recognized as such when the perceptions, interpretations and evaluations that flow from the various conversations gain sufficient momentum and power to penetrate the formal structures of the organization and become adopted as policy.

Since this formative process is hidden, messy and informal, the phases set out above should not be thought of as occurring in an orderly fashion. Nor is political action neatly compartmentalized between issues. Instead, leaders are faced with a patchwork of issues on which to act politically. Some of these will already exist in the formal, legitimate arena; whereas others will still be finding their way there through the shadow-side conversations. Changing the organization means interrupting the patterns of conversation that sustain the status quo; and stimulating other conversations that begin to focus upon, and develop, an alternative "map" of reality. Leaders who seek to use their power in this way do not rely on one-off interventions. Organizational outcomes ordinarily emerge from the accumulated effect of many, distinct interactions; and the progressive development of coalitions of support for new ways of thinking and acting.

## Awareness

Remaining politically aware is probably the most important aspect of acting politically. This means raising awareness on four fronts. First, it's important to be aware of the underlying political dynamics of organizations, as set out here, which validates "acting politically" as a core part of effective leadership. Secondly, effective political action is built on an awareness of our own motivations, habitual behaviors and vulnerabilities. These are distilled into our personal frame of reference that provides the perceptual filter through which we judge all significant actions and events. Thirdly, power and politics are about interaction. Awareness of the interests driving other people's behavior, the stances they are likely to take on particular issues and the tactics that they typically employ is therefore the other important ingredient of acting politically for organizational benefit. Finally, our awareness of the current situation – what's happening here and now – is critical from the point of view of deciding if, when and how we should act.

### Self-awareness

Effective and ethical political action springs from:

- a clear understanding of what we stand for – our personal purpose and ethos – and the organization-enhancing agenda that flows from this;
- awareness of, and access to, our personal sources of power;
- recognition of our personal vulnerabilities and habitual defense mechanisms;
- awareness of how we are seen by others – that is, the nature and impact of our reputation.

In our earlier discussions, we saw these factors as being embodied in the personal frames of reference that we each seek to maintain in tact, and through which we view emerging events and propositions. Acting politically therefore needs to start by uncovering the elements of this personal frame, as a basis for acting in a more informed and influential way.

*Other-awareness*

If we can identify and understand other people's interests, we are much more likely to be able to manage the political reactions that these generate. Where we don't take the trouble to do this at the outset, our ability to implement proposals will be seriously undermined.

I recall working with a group of enthusiastic and talented partners within a professional services firm. They had been identified as the company's next generation of management; and the plan was for them to operate as a form of "shadow board." During an intensive weekend workshop, they developed a challenging and creative plan for moving forward, which would see them taking collective responsibility for the day-to-day management and short-term performance of the company. This would have the added advantage of freeing the board to focus on the strategic development of the company; as plans were already afoot to grow the business substantially, both organically and by acquisition. At the end of the two days, the team presented the skeleton of their proposals to the managing partner, and to the sponsoring partner who had originally initiated the workshop. They both welcomed the ideas that were put forward; and actions were set in train to flesh out the plans before presenting these to the board. Energy levels and spirits were high at the end of the event. It was noticeable, though, that one of the more senior partners within the group was decidedly uncomfortable with what had been developed What the team didn't do was to probe that isolated reaction to anticipate some of the concerns that others in the organization might have – especially those in senior positions whose interests (personal frames of reference) might be threatened by the proposals. In the event, they were overtaken by their own enthusiasm. They were so convinced that what they were advocating made common sense, that they ignored the warning that they should take proper account of the likely perceptions of key stakeholders when finalizing their plans. Reports later suggested that they received a rude awakening when they faced the board. As a result, the implementation of the revised proposals was significantly delayed and their effectiveness undermined. This pattern is not uncommon; especially where logic-based persuasion (an *education and training* approach) is used as the sole influencing strategy.

The *informal coalitions* approach recognizes that politics enters the fray as soon as proposals are formulated. Those advocating a particular position, together with those who develop this into a specific proposal, each perceive and interpret the situation through their personal frame of reference and attempt to shape its outcome accordingly. The instant that others become aware of this, they do likewise. As we saw with the cultural dynamics of organizations in Chapter 4, politics similarly cannot be "put onto the back burner" to be dealt with at a later date.

Raising awareness of the impact that significant others might have on the political environment therefore involves "mapping the territory" within which specific events are unfolding. This provides a basis for interacting effectively with them, to shift their perceptions and influence the actions that flow from these. We will look further at this in the next chapter. For now, it is sufficient to note that this also means becoming aware of:

- the power that people have to influence activities and outcomes – for better or worse;
- their inclination to become actively involved in the issue; and
- the likelihood that their position can be changed.

It also means becoming aware of the formal and informal interrelationships of key players, the personal agendas that influence their actions, and the political tactics that they tend to use to achieve their desired outcomes.

### Situational awareness

The interactions that we have with others do not take place in a vacuum. We therefore need to remain alert to the broader political context within which current interactions are taking place. This means becoming aware of existing conversational patterns, and to the deeply embedded assumptions that sustain them. It also means remaining alert to shifting power relationships; taking account of the main risks and threats that are likely to be affecting people's responses to issues and events; and remaining sensitive to moves that others might be making.

## Entry

The entry phase is about *choosing* whether or not to intervene and, if so, in what way. Although political activity is happening all around us – in the sense we have discussed earlier – not all of it is worthy of our *deliberate* attention as part of the change-leadership agenda. Whilst, as leaders, we are "on the pitch playing," and therefore unavoidably involved in the political dynamics of our organizations, we can choose whether or not we want to become *actively* engaged in what is happening.

In organizational change, the essence of the *informal coalitions* approach is to push at half-open doors. This contrasts starkly with the universal "roll out" of initiatives across the organization. In relation to acting politically, this means picking the issues that we wish to get involved in. Sometimes, of course, we find ourselves in the middle of a political situation whether we wish to be there or not. Even then, we can choose if and how we wish to react. It is important, in the interests of political credibility, for leaders not to get drawn into fights in which they have no stake or little power to influence them. There are, though, three general situations in which effective leadership demands entry into the political arena. These are:

- to manage the ongoing, structural tensions that arise from the natural dynamics of organizations;
- to deal with any negative politicking that is undermining organizational capability and performance, or leading to other dysfunctional effects;
- to bring about organizationally beneficial changes to existing policies and ways of working.

If the judgment is to intervene, the task is then to decide how best to do this. A strategy (however rudimentary) needs to be developed, based upon the nature of the issue and complexity of relationships involved. In all cases this will include constructing a core "story" that encapsulates the main themes. This should be designed to appeal to a broad constituency of people – even though they may initially approach the issue from competing perspectives. The first requirement of this is to identify a compelling, *issue-specific* outcome. This needs to have the potential to draw together people of diverse interests into a temporary yet active coalition of support for the idea. The story should also enable potential members of the coalition to make connections with other stories that have resonance with their own constituencies, and with members of their broader relationship networks. This will enable them to maintain personal credibility; as well as increasing the likelihood of drawing other people into the coalition. Also, we earlier defined functional politics as managing differences in ways that are *both* organizationally enhancing *and* which serve the legitimate interests of organizational members. This core story should therefore address the self-interests of key players, if it is to "stick."

There are a number of critical questions to ask in relation to this, such as:

- Is this issue organizationally significant?
- Does the way forward that we propose resonate with people?

- If not, how can we create options that will address the issues and find resonance with a sufficiently large group of people to overcome inertia and establish momentum?
- How do competing agendas and alternative viewpoints play into this situation?
- What can we do to embrace these, and to build bridges to link the various agendas?

The final issue to consider during the entry phase is timing. Sometimes it's important to act politically by biding one's time before acting. At other times it's essential to press on. Timing is always critical to the success of political action – whether in terms of the ultimate outcome or the political cost of getting there. There are, though, no simple recipes for success in this. It is something that can only be judged at the time; which is why situational awareness is so important. Even though the notion of timing implies an opportunistic approach to the entry phase, effective political action requires an approach based on what might be called "planned opportunism." This means that seemingly "on the spot" interventions need to be thoroughly thought through in advance, in the way that the best comedians painstakingly rehearse their ad-libs.

## Engagement

The engagement phase is about actively building coalitions of support for ideas and changes that are organizationally beneficial and personally meaningful to people, as seeded during the entry phase.

The focus at this stage is on building momentum behind an important issue, idea or change agenda. In some instances, this means developing sufficiently powerful support for an idea to enable it to emerge from the shadow-side conversations and become a formal proposition for change. On other occasions, coalition building will be geared toward gaining buy-in for a change that has already been adopted formally. During this phase, attention will also need to be paid to the psychological and emotional impacts of change on people, if they are to engage fully with what is proposed.

There are three critical factors for leaders to focus on when acting politically during this phase of the process. These are:

- the content of their story;
- the connections that can be made between key players within the developing coalition; and
- the context within which the specific idea or change agenda is being put forward.

The outline *content* of the story was initially mapped out during the entry phase. This needs to be progressively developed; and then used to inform the everyday conversations and interactions that leaders have with their staff, or with others they are seeking to engage. It is important that, so far as is practicable, these exchanges have the sense of an intimate, one-to-one conversation. This means creating opportunities for people to explore the underlying themes in depth; and to do so in a "psychologically safe" environment. This enables people to make their own sense of what is proposed, alone and in conversation with others. When considering the timing of any intervention, we talked about the need for leaders to use a "planned opportunism" approach. Another oxymoron, flexible rigidity, captures the essence of the stance that politically astute leaders need to adopt in relation to the development of the story content. They need to be rigid in their advocacy of the essential elements of the story and, at the same time, flexible in their response to emerging issues and ideas.

Besides engaging people directly through informal, one-to-one and group conversations, leaders need to encourage and enable *connections* to be made between key people in the emerging coalition. This means asking themselves such questions as:

- Who are the natural advocates of the desired position?
- Who has credibility with whom?
- Who listens to whom?
- Who are the key influencers?
- Who are the people who act as natural connectors between different parts of the relevant informal networks?

Leaders have a powerful impact on the local *context* within which an idea or change is being advanced; and we will return to this in the next chapter. The issue to be addressed here is the extent to which the context supports the essence of the change that is being advocated. As we discussed in Chapter 4, the role modeling provided by leaders – both locally and in the wider organization – is a particularly critical aspect of the context. The *quality* of relationships forged, and the extent to which the organizational infrastructure enables people to perform in organizationally beneficial and personally competent ways, will also be critical to a successful outcome.

## Withdrawal

This phase recognizes the fact that coalitions are transient and issue specific. The critical point at this stage is the importance of withdrawing in ways that preserve (or, preferably strengthen further) the relationships that have been put in place. The completion of the coalition's purpose also provides an opportunity for reflection and learning.

One of the main purposes of communication in an *informal coalitions* mode is to strengthen *relationships*, both to improve the delivery of current performance and to facilitate future collaboration. At its best, as we saw in Chapter 3, it is about creating meaning and building trust *between* people, rather than passing messages *to* people. In the context of acting politically, it is important to ensure that the relationships that have been developed in support of a particular idea or change agenda are not destroyed when the unifying issue has been achieved and people move on.

As discussed in earlier chapters, some coalitions (or parts of coalitions) will be little more than marriages of convenience amongst individuals or groups whose broader agendas and approaches have little in common. In those relationships, the main goal might be no more than to avoid turning a current ally into a future enemy, by taking time out to acknowledge the other's contribution. However, when organizationally beneficial changes enter the formal arena, coalition building then focuses on people and groups who are more central to ongoing performance delivery. These include the leader's own work group, as well as influential external stakeholders. The decisions and actions of these groups can have a significant impact upon the means and ends of political action. In those circumstances, the quality of relationships forged during one stage of the organization's development can pave the way for ongoing change. The important thing to ensure is that these relationships are not undermined as the make-up and salience of various coalitions shifts from issue to issue.

I have witnessed several occasions on which managers have successfully galvanized support around a particular course of action only for this to be dissipated by their failure to see the changes through to completion. Often, this has arisen because managers have been promoted as a reward for meeting targets based on short-term gains (such as immediate headcount reductions) rather than sustained improvements in process performance. The effect on manager–staff relationships has invariably been damaging. Unfortunately, it is usually those managers who have followed on who have had to deal with the detrimental effects of this on performance and work climate, rather than those whose actions caused it.

The withdrawal phase also provides an opportunity for *learning*. In relation to acting politically, this primarily means the opportunity for the leader to reflect on their performance and practice during each of the phases of the political process.

## Consolidation

If leaders are to sustain the power to influence change into the future, they have to not only achieve results but also *be seen* to have achieved them. This means that they need to do two things. As a basic requirement, they need to ensure that the substance of the change agenda and the means of its delivery resonate with people's own views of what is required. This is the essence of what we have been talking about so far, in the first four phases of the process. Equally, though, they also need to orchestrate the way that other people perceive, interpret and evaluate the contribution that they themselves have made to its successful achievement. The consolidation phase is concerned primarily with this impression-management task.

Establishing and maintaining credibility *in the eyes of relevant others* is important to any individual's ability to impact upon events and outcomes. For leaders who want to make things happen, and to enhance their organization's capability and performance, being seen as credible in the role is especially critical. Staff will not respond positively to someone whom they don't see as credible. Equally though, the way in which the leader is viewed by the organization at large – and more senior management in particular – is crucial to their continuing effectiveness. Gaining a reputation for consistently helping the organization to deliver its purpose and ethos, in ways that resonate with people's own values and aspirations, is therefore an important part of "acting politically" from an *informal coalitions* perspective.

The contribution that a particular outcome makes to a leader's credibility and reputation depends primarily on how this is framed in people's minds. It is important, therefore, for leaders to pay particular attention to the ways in which the results are formally reported back into the organization; and to remain alert to the stories that circulate about the event in informal conversations. This can appear distasteful to some people, who feel that results alone should be enough. This, though, is a naïve position to take. First, people don't judge results. As we noted earlier, outcomes have no meaning until they are framed in a particular way (such as being seen as a success or a failure, for example). This meaning is socially constructed, through the conversations that people have about the event and the stories that are already circulating about it. The more powerful a story is, in terms of the sense that it makes to people and the power of its advocacy, the more likely it is to shape people's understanding. And any judgments that they then make will be based on this.

Leaders who wish to make a difference, and to have *a continuing impact on their organization's performance and development*, need to ensure that their reputation and credibility continue to rise alongside their delivery of tangible results. This, again, means that they need to *actively* engage with the sensemaking process. The aim of this here is to help to shape the stories and myths that grow up around organizational successes – and failures – of which they have been part. This is not about falsifying what happened or taking undue credit for others' work. But it is about the leader making sure that their contribution is properly represented in the stories and commentaries that emerge.

As a final comment on this, two things can be said about the stories that leaders help to construct to achieve these ends. First, credibility will be undermined if, over time, the substance of a particular change fails to live up to the rhetoric. The same dynamic is at work here as when a product is oversold and fails to perform in practice. Secondly, there is a parallel between the way in which acting politically enables outcomes to be achieved which otherwise would not have been possible, and how lateral thinking enables new ideas to be generated which logical patterns of thought would have prevented from emerging. In relation to the latter, de Bono (1990, for example) makes the crucial point that ideas created through lateral thinking techniques *always* appear obvious after the event. That is, they make logical sense in retrospect, even though it would have been impossible to have reached that point by applying logic at the outset. As he also suggests, it is this ability to make sense of the ideas retrospectively that validates them as useful. A similar argument applies to organizational changes that have been brought about by the skillful use of political action. These outcomes, and the actions that led to them, need to make sense to people in rational terms, if they are to be considered valid and praiseworthy. The stories that are told about them therefore need to appear rationally coherent, goal oriented and authoritative; especially to those whose judgments of the leader's ability are critical to the way in which their reputation is constructed within the organization and, perhaps, beyond. A key aim of acting politically during the consolidation phase is therefore to influence the sensemaking processes to achieve this. This can often be facilitated by the use of models and frameworks, which appear to bring order and structure to the mess and make it more palatable for external consumption. Pfeffer (1992) similarly argues that information and analysis are important to the appearance of rationality and objectivity whenever outcomes are brought about by political means.

## Primary strategies used during each phase

Any or all of the four political strategies identified in the *informal coalitions* segment of Figure 5.3 could feature in each of the five phases set out above. However, some strategies lend themselves more directly to particular phases than to others, as suggested in Table 5.2.

**Table 5.2** Primary strategies used when acting politically

| Phase | Awareness | Entry | Engagement | Withdrawal | Consolidation |
|-------|-----------|-------|------------|------------|---------------|
| Primary Strategy | Everyday conversations and interactions | Providing vision and embracing paradox | Building coalitions and providing vision | Everyday conversations and interactions | Everyday sensemaking conversations and interactions |
| Main Focus | Self-reflection, feedback from others, disclosure to others | Agenda setting | Results delivery | Relationship strengthening and reflective practice | Impression management |

## In summary

The conventional view of conflict in high-performing organizations is that it is both rare and illegitimate. It is seen as the result of deliberate trouble-making, which can be either eliminated through rational management strategies or else channeled away from mainstream activity and decision-making into formal disciplinary routes. In contrast, the *informal coalitions* view of organizational dynamics maintains that *inevitable* differences exist between organizational interest groups. These differences arise from the inherent structural tensions in all organizational designs, the diverse agendas of formal and informal groups, and individual idiosyncrasies. At the same time, most of the significant decisions in organizations of any size involve the acquisition, deployment or management of limited resources under complex and uncertain conditions. This requires trade-offs and choices to be made. Taken together, these factors have a critical impact upon the ways in which decisions are made and business gets done *in practice*. In particular, limited resources coupled with differing interests make conflict central to the ways in which organizations operate and in which change is effected. *How* these differences are managed is what organizational politics are all about. This insight places political activity at the center of the *informal coalitions* view of organizational dynamics. More than that, though, this view recognizes that, if properly understood and carried out with integrity, political activity can significantly enhance organizational performance and capability.

Clearly, the political dynamics that are stimulated by conflicting interests and differing views on "what's best" are not the only influence on organizational performance. These do, though, provide a powerful and all-pervasive one. The integrating tendencies of cultural dynamics that we discussed in the previous chapter, together with the other aspects of leadership performance that this book addresses, all have important parts to play in delivering results and ensuring effective change. Project management techniques and organizational development methodologies (aligned with the *education and training* and *joint problem solving* modes of change) can also facilitate the change process. However, irrespective of how well these might be performed, the need to engage constructively with the underlying political dynamics will remain paramount. The guidelines on acting politically set out in this chapter are designed to help managers navigate their way through these inevitable complexities of organizational life in ways that are both organizationally enhancing and personally fulfilling.

It is likely that everyone who has worked for any length of time inside organizations will recognize expert, value-enhancing political behavior when they see it. It is just that they are likely to describe this in other (politically) more acceptable terms – such as effective, transforming leadership, perhaps!

# CHAPTER 6

# Building coalitions

[Political savvy is] ethically building a critical mass of support for an idea you care about.

– Joel DeLuca

## Introduction

Coalition formation is a natural and dynamic process within all organizations. It occurs continuously and spontaneously, as people respond to their perceptions, interpretations and evaluations of emerging events and their everyday experiences within the organization. In the context of organizational change, coalitions form either to support a particular change or to frustrate it. The *informal coalitions* view of change calls upon managers to engage actively and imaginatively with these natural dynamics of organizations, to build coalitions of support for organizationally beneficial changes.

## The nature of coalitions

We will begin by adding a little more to our understanding of the nature of coalitions and coalitional behavior, before focusing on how we might influence their development.

First of all, participation in coalitions is voluntary. People "sign up" because they want to, not because someone else has told them to. They are driven primarily by an emotional commitment to a particular cause or attraction to a desired result, which they judge will be best served by aligning themselves with others who want the same thing. Coalitions magnify the ability of those involved to influence organizational outcomes, by harnessing the power of collective action.

Secondly, implicit in the idea of a coalition is recognition that people do not have to agree on everything or share an identical set of values to make progress. They can – and do – still come together to deliver a common change agenda. Some underpinning values and beliefs may be widely shared by coalition members of course; but frequently they will not. Often, those people who are informally coalescing around a particular theme and desired end-goal will differ greatly in their worldviews and personal values. In some instances, different sub-groups may hold views that are bitterly opposed to each other across a range of issues. Despite this, in relation to this particular objective, they set their differences aside. Coalitions may therefore have the characteristics of a "partnership of principle," a "marriage of convenience" or anything in between. And different members of a particular coalition will have different perspectives on what "membership" means to them. Sometimes, and for some people, alignment with a particular theme will be explicit and openly expressed. On other occasions, or for other people, it will be tacit and assumed.

Thirdly, the leadership of coalitions arises from people having sufficient power (in the eyes of relevant others) and a compelling enough story to cause others to perceive, interpret and value things differently, and to "sign up." Whilst a single leader of a coalition might exist, or emerge over time, leadership behavior is likely to occur at many points in a successful coalition. Various individuals may bring others with them into the fold, work to hold the coalition together or otherwise influence its emerging shape and direction.

Finally, coalitions tend to be transient and relate to specific issues, rather than being long-standing and all embracing. Because of the shifting patchwork of issues that surface at any one time, no single coalition is likely to be dominant for long periods. People who are aligned at one instant in relation to one issue may find themselves on different sides of the argument at the next. Paradoxically, therefore, coalitions embrace both the "pulling together" dynamics of *integration*, *alignment* and *common interest* in relation to a particular outcome and, at the same time, the "splitting apart" dynamics of *disintegration*, *contention* and *self-interest*.

In summary, individuals and groups hold ideas, values and beliefs that often conflict with those held by others. They nevertheless need to collaborate with each other if the organization is to succeed and their own aspirations are to be satisfied. These can rarely be reconciled into a single set of "shared values," which adequately reflects the individual identities and self-concepts of the separate members. The coalition-building element of the leadership agenda recognizes this. It looks instead to stimulate the formation of coalitions of support behind organizationally beneficial objectives and activities that resonate with a broad constituency of people.

## Building coalitions – The leadership challenge

Fueled by a rich mix of differing perceptions, varied emotions and diverse personalities, *informal coalitions* form and exert significant influence on an organization. They do this whether managers deliberately choose to get involved with the process or not. From an *informal coalitions* view of organizational change, a key aspect of the leadership task is to *work with* these natural dynamics. The aim of this is twofold: to stimulate the formation of coalitions that support proposed changes; and to address those issues and themes that are causing other coalitions to seek to block progress in the desired direction. Figure 6.1 illustrates the broad task.

The diagram shows four broad constituencies of people, labeled A, B, C and D, which might be involved in a particular situation. These people are positioned within the grid according to the *sense* that they make of what's going on, and the *use* to which they put this view of events. The critical distinctions here concern whether they view the proposed changes, on the whole, as *positive* or *negative*; and whether, in the light of that judgment, they respond *actively* or *passively* to them. As we will discuss in more depth later, the aim is to build a *sufficiently powerful*

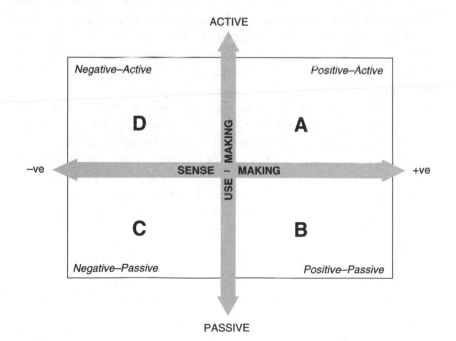

**Figure 6.1** Building coalitions

coalition of people who are both positive about the changes and *actively engaged* in making them happen (quadrant A).

## Focus of coalition building

The opening quotation suggests that the leader's aim in coalition building is to construct a critical mass of support for an idea that they care about. Within this, two types of coalition can usefully be identified, which we will call "issue coalitions" and "action coalitions." We noted in Chapter 2 that change originates through informal, shadow-side conversations in which an idea that runs counter to current practice is seeded and built upon. When this idea becomes strong enough (i.e. when a sufficiently powerful coalition of support has grown up around it), it will surface as a formal proposition within the organization's official processes. The type of coalition in this instance is what I am calling an *issue coalition*. When used as a deliberate leadership strategy, as part of the *informal coalitions* approach to change, its aim is to change the organization's *agenda and policies* for the better. It does this by building support for, and maintaining momentum behind, an issue or idea that departs from currently established policies and practices. The leader's challenge here is to influence others over whom they have no formal authority. And the immediate goal is to garner a majority of the relevant "votes" that are needed to carry the day. In some instances, these may be formal votes, as in a Board meeting. At other times, they may simply reflect the prevailing balance of power in a less formal sense.

In an *action coalition*, the focus shifts toward the leader's own staff. The challenge is then to secure their active support for a proposal that has been formally adopted as organizational policy. The aim here is to change the organization's *actions and outcomes* for the better, by stimulating as many staff as possible to become actively engaged in making the desired changes happen. Power is still a key factor in achieving success here; but the fact that the leader has formal authority (position power) inevitably changes the dynamics of the process. In some instances, position power can inhibit the process of coalition building as I'm describing it here. Its use at the wrong time, or in the wrong place, can ignite feelings of forced compliance rather than resonant co-action. Position power can be important, though, in helping to shape some of the contextual factors that enable or constrain the coalition-building process.

We will look below at the leadership tasks involved in building these issue and action coalitions.

## Issue coalitions

As suggested in Chapter 5, people who want to make a positive difference to the way in which their organizations work, and the successes
that they achieve, must act politically. That is, they must use their power
to influence processes and outcomes. And they must do this within
the complex environment of competing demands, different interests and
limited resources that characterize all organizations. They must also do it
in a way that sustains their own credibility, if they are to remain able to
influence events into the future. For people who want to lead, therefore,
acting politically is a necessity, not an option.

There will be times when leaders need to take a stand in support of
agenda-shifting issues and ideas that are important to them – and, in
their view, to the future success and well-being of the organization. In
some instances, where the logic of an argument appears irrefutable, it
might appear natural to raise the matter "cold" during an appropriate
management forum. In those circumstances, strategies of persuasion (to
gain acceptance), involvement (to reach agreement) or even imposition
(to achieve compliance) might be adopted to move things forward in
the formal arena. However, as we have seen, people view ideas and
the changes that these bring through their own personal frames of reference, not through a blank screen. Any perceived misfit between the
self-interested framing of events that this represents and the proposal on
the table will stimulate resistance. This might be expressed openly at the
meeting or through shadow-side ("coffee machine") conversations after
the event. Preferably then, those seeking to shift the organization's agenda
need first to build coalitions of support around organizationally enhancing
issues and ideas ("issue coalitions") before introducing these formally.

## Mapping the territory

In essence, before surfacing an issue as a formal proposition, there needs
to be a sufficiently powerful constituency of people in quadrant A to
ensure that it will be adopted. These are people who are positive about
the idea and willing to become actively engaged in getting it through.
In particular, this coalition needs to be organizationally more powerful
than the combined "weight" of those who are actively against the idea.
In some instances, it will need to carry enough formal voting power to
enable the proposition to be officially adopted within the organization's
mandatory procedures. The framework that we looked at in Figure 6.1

can be used, both conceptually and as a practical tool, to develop a "map" of the territory on which an issue coalition needs to be built. Where the issue is relatively straightforward, a manager might be able to develop this in their head – alone or with others. In more complex cases, it can be useful to use the framework as the basis of a written map.

In mapping the territory, a number of key questions need to be asked. These are:

- Who are the *main players*, who have the *organizational power* to make this happen or to thwart it?
- What is their basic *stance* on the issue – Are they known to be, or thought likely to be, for it or against it? And how strongly?
- How *active* are they likely to be in pursuing their point of view?
- How *open to influence* are they likely to be on the issue? And *by whom*?

The first three questions enable the people identified above to be "assigned" to one or other of the four quadrants. The fourth question introduces two additional factors. First, if the framework is being used to draw a physical map, it enables these entries to be coded according to the extent that the current stances adopted by these people are thought to be open to change. And, secondly, it aims to identify the best channels of influence for each of these people, by showing the important power relationships that exist. That is, it shows how connected they are to each other, positively or negatively, in an influencing sense. In reviewing this last question, it might be necessary to introduce some *other players* into the picture. These are people who are insufficiently powerful within the formal organization to affect the outcome directly, but who carry significant influence with others who can. As we discussed in the last chapter, this might result from such things as their acknowledged expertise in a relevant area, their informal working relationships with key players, or other personal or social factors. Also, some stakeholders external to the organization may wield substantial power informally, even though they have no "legitimate" role in organizational decision-making. This might arise from their personal links with internal decision-makers or the impact that their own decisions and actions have on organizational capability and performance.

In developing a coalition-building map of this kind, it is rarely sensible for people to work alone. A core group of like-minded people can ordinarily provide a wider and potentially more balanced perspective on the situation than a single individual can. In addition to this, DeLuca (1999) argues that working together in this way, with the avowed aim of improving the overall well-being of the organization, can also help to legitimize the task and overcome any ethical concerns that might exist. In any event, it is the conversational process through which the map is developed that is most important, not the map itself. It is certainly not any pseudo-quantitative data that might be derived from it. The process is subjective and indicative, not objective and definitive!

## Building an issue coalition

Armed with the insights provided by the mapping process, a strategy and action plan can be developed. This can then be used to build an issue coalition in support of the proposed agenda change or policy shift. *Specific actions need to be identified, according to the particular circumstances and personalities involved. However, the following generic guidance applies*

### Generic strategy for quadrant D (negative–active)

People who fall into quadrant D are those most likely to provide the main opposition to the proposal. If a physical map has been drawn, specific positions within the quadrant might indicate the degree of opposition and extent to which they are likely to get actively involved in any "No" campaign. In the case of those with the power to affect the proposal adversely – or even to stop it – it is critically important to understand as much as possible about their work agendas and personal frames of reference. The aim should be to try to develop a story that addresses as many of these concerns as possible, whilst still maintaining the potency and integrity of the coalition's objectives. The ideal goal is to turn potential opposition into active support (a move to quadrant A). However, given that this may not be possible, reducing the intensity of the opposition or the likelihood of it being actively applied (a move to quadrant C) is the next best thing.

Some people in this quadrant, who are thought likely to be strongly opposed to the proposal, may have insufficient power to influence the outcome directly. However, they might still be able to derail it through their links with others who do have the necessary power. It is equally important, therefore, to understand their agendas and to seek to develop an approach that takes account of these.

### Generic strategy quadrant C (negative–passive)

Powerful players are positioned within this quadrant if they are likely to view the proposition as negative but are nevertheless thought unlikely to oppose it actively. As such, they are less of a threat to the coalition than those in quadrant D, provided that they remain where they are. However, they should not be ignored. Their latent power means that, if their interest was to be raised and they were stimulated into action (perhaps by players in quadrant D), their opposition could prove damaging. It is equally important, therefore, to understand those aspects of their personal frames of reference and work agendas that could be affected by the proposal. The strategy should then be to ensure that the proposal is framed in a way that meets their basic needs in these areas.

*Strategy for quadrant B (positive–passive)*

The broad strategy here is to bring these people into the coalition by turning their current passivity into active participation. It is patently important to engage powerful people who are thought likely to fall within this quadrant because their actual or metaphorical "votes" may make the difference between success and failure. Here the strategy needs to address those things that might otherwise prevent them from participating actively in the coalition. For less powerful players, who have been identified in this quadrant because of their links to others, the aim should be to capitalize on those links to help deliver the objectives outlined for quadrants C and D. They may also be able to help to "activate" those powerful but latent supporters of the coalition who, like themselves, sit in quadrant B.

*Strategy for quadrant A (positive–active)*

People who fall naturally into quadrant A, or who migrate there as a result of the strategies outlined above, represent the issue coalition itself. As such, it might not be thought necessary to spend time with them. However, these people have their own work agendas and personal frames of reference too. The inference of their presence in quadrant A is that the proposal resonates with these sufficiently to win their support. This support needs to be nurtured though, not taken for granted. For example, they may feel that it is risky to be seen to take part in the "enterprise;" or their active support might be fragile for other reasons. Steps might therefore need to be taken to provide reassurance and to seek to bolster people's positions. Positive social and political relationships should also be used to consolidate this existing support; and to remain alert to how people respond to emerging events.

*Turning strategy into action*

Building coalitions is part of a political approach to leadership and organizational change. As suggested in Chapter 5, its aim is to achieve *resonance* between people's personal frames of reference and the agenda changes or policy shifts being advanced by the coalition. Coalition building is underpinned, first and foremost, by a belief in the power of everyday conversations to deliver organizational change. It is strengthened by the leadership task of providing vision *through those day-to-day conversations and interactions*; and it is sustained by a willingness to embrace the tensions and ambiguities that characterize "real world" organizations. As such, the *informal coalitions* approach to change leadership uses the *dynamics of the organization's conversational networks* to build coalitions of support for desired changes, rather than formal persuasion processes or structured bargaining techniques. This is not to say, of course, that personal advocacy of a position or informal give-and-take don't come into play as part of natural, everyday interactions. Indeed these natural dynamics of everyday conversations and relationships are central to the notion of *informal coalitions*. However, the coalition-building approach is primarily about achieving a position that resonates with the aims and aspirations of a broad constituency of people. It is not about settling for passive acceptance of a rigidly held position, or even for agreement reached by lowest-common-denominator consensus or formal negotiation.

When we talked about the engagement phase of the political process in Chapter 5, we identified three critical factors for leaders to focus on when seeking to build coalitions of support for desired changes. These are the *content* of the unfolding story; the *connections* that exist between players within the developing coalition; and the *context* within which the specific idea or change agenda is being advanced. When seeking to build an issue coalition, credibility is vitally important in all three of these areas:

- First of all, the organization-changing agenda around which the coalition is being built, and the way this is framed, needs to be seen as credible by prospective members:
  - *Does the story hold together and make sense?*
  - *Does it play into their own agendas as well as the broader one?*
  - *Does it resonate with them emotionally as well as intellectually?*
- Secondly, the source of the story needs to be credible. This is a function of the dynamics of the personal relationships that exist within the developing coalition:
  - *Do they trust the person who is trying to engage them in this?*
  - *Do they have a long-standing relationship that gives them confidence to move forward?*

> – *Do they owe this person something for past support or a past favor?*
> – *Is the person thought of highly by others that they trust?*
> – *Are they prepared to listen to what the person has to say?*

In some instances, the strength of this relationship will be sufficient to offset doubts about the credibility of the story or the wisdom of proceeding with it. In others, it will be the strength of conviction displayed by the "storyteller" that provides the sought-after degree of confidence.

- Finally, the prospect of the proposal succeeding within the specific organizational context needs to be seen as credible:
  - *Do they believe that this is doable – here, now and in the way set out?*
  - *Do they believe that the risks are acceptable?*
  - *In the circumstances, do they believe that it is wise to proceed? Or unwise not to?*

The purpose of the relevant conversations is to move prospective members of the coalition progressively through the awareness and entry phases of their own political action into active engagement. The "pushing at half-open doors" philosophy of the *informal coalitions* approach recognizes that some of the "doors" will be half open to some people but not to others. It is particularly important, therefore, that "the right people knock on the right doors" – and in the right order – if this goal is to be achieved. DeLuca (1999) talks about this as following the organization's "credibility paths." So, in building the coalition, it is critical to use a "door-knocking" plan that recognizes the personal, social and political relationships that exist. The aim is to use the credibility that positive relationships carry, to build momentum behind the story and to engage people in making it happen.

## Action coalitions

When a specific proposal for change enters the formal channels of the organization and is adopted as official policy, the coalition-building task for leaders shifts to one of galvanizing the support of their own staff for the new ways of working. In seeking to build action coalitions, leaders need to think about their teams in two ways. First, it can be useful to see them as comprising broad constituencies of people, whose general orientations toward the change can be understood and worked with. Secondly, their teams are made up of individuals. And each individual has their own way of seeing the world (personal frame of reference) and their own personal context of issues, needs and relationships that they must honor.

The former perspective allows the leader to identify and enact some generic coalition-building strategies. It also enables them to take stock of the overall progress towards this goal, as events unfold. *At the same time*, the latter perspective recognizes that change affects each individual differently. As a result, although broad patterns of the likely psychological and emotional response to change can be identified and addressed, individual factors will have a significant part to play in deciding the outcome.

## Building an action coalition

We will look first at the broad constituencies of staff that can be identified in any change situation. We will then move on to consider how the psychological and emotional dynamics of change affect the picture. From an *informal coalitions* perspective, we can again use the Building Coalitions matrix to summarize the initial challenge. This is reproduced in Figure 6.2.

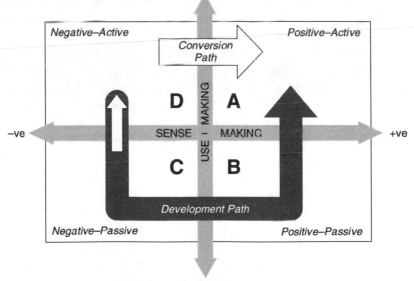

**Figure 6.2** Building an action coalition

As with issue coalitions, the broad aim is to build as large a coalition of staff as possible, who are both *positive* about the planned changes and *actively engaged* in making them happen (quadrant A). However, whereas the emphasis in building an issue coalition is on securing the *power to act*, by assembling the equivalent of 51 percent of the "votes" in quadrant A, the goal of an action coalition is, numerically at least, more ambitious.

The emphasis here is not on power as such but on *engagement*. Remember that, at this stage of the change process, the proposal has been formally adopted as organizational policy. Managers with the appropriate levels of formal authority do not need to garner the votes of their staff to put these changes into action. They already have sufficient position power to do so. But they do need them, as a minimum, to bring the changes alive "on the ground." And this requires much more than the top–down, structured "rollout" of pre-packaged initiatives that so often characterizes the implementation of change from a *management edict, education and training* or even *joint problem solving* mindset.

The *informal coalitions* approach to change, and the coalition-building strategy that flows from it, sees the change-leadership task differently. Building action coalitions is about *actively engaging* staff in bringing about the desired changes. It does this by connecting the organization's agenda to themes that *resonate* with individuals in as many ways as possible. From this perspective, engaging 51 percent of the team would fall well short of what was required for a powerful and effective response to the proposed changes.

Aspirationally, the goal might well be to achieve 100 percent engagement. However, all change shifts power relationships. It is not credible, therefore, to expect all people within an organization to fall naturally into the positive–active zone. A close approximation to this might be achieved within sub-groups of the organization, as new units are formed or the changes bring others to prominence. However, some people will inevitably view the shifts as irretrievably negative, in terms of their organizational influence or personal ambitions. Even within groups whose star is in the ascendancy, the splitting tendencies of diverse personal agendas and different mindsets are likely to cause some friction and potential fractures in the dynamics of the group. In any event, successful change will not occur if substantial numbers of people remain intellectually, emotionally or spiritually disengaged from it. Achieving a "full house" of engaged staff should therefore remain the ambition.

Whilst some people will fall into quadrant A (positive–active) from the outset, it is likely that the majority will need to be encouraged, assisted and enabled to move there from other quadrants. For example, there will be a second constituency who also view the changes as positive but who, for reasons we will explore below, fail to "pick up the baton and run with it." The diagram locates these people in quadrant B (positive–passive). Quadrant C (negative–passive) contains those people whose immediate personal reactions and/or sensemaking conversations with others have caused them to see the changes in negative terms. Despite this, they respond passively rather than working actively against them. Quadrant D (negative–active) houses those members of staff who both view the changes negatively and are unwilling to "take things lying down." In their case, they are going to do whatever they can to stop them happening or alter the planned outcomes. Some of these people – the overt "resistors of change" – will be open and vociferous in their hostility to the proposals. Others will express their opposition more covertly and/or more subtly.

The sequence D–C–B–A represents the usual "transition path" that people might be expected to take towards quadrant A, if the leader's coalition-building efforts are successful. Interestingly, though, there is also a more direct route that those people in quadrant D might follow to quadrant A. Most managers agree that those people who express their strong opposition to a particular change can, if their issues are dealt with effectively, become amongst its strongest advocates. Indeed, some people may habitually take an actively oppositional stance on issues as part of a "convince me it's right" response to proposed changes. This less common but potentially powerful "conversion path" flows directly from D to A.

The upward-facing arrow located at the start of the development path recognizes some of the more complex dynamics that might exist at this point, as a result of the natural pattern of emotional responses that is likely to occur in the wake of an imposed change. We shall explore these later in this chapter. For now, though, it is worth noting that those people in quadrant D, who are actively resisting the changes, may well have spent at least a brief spell in shock and denial immediately following the announcement of the unwelcome change. These are characteristic quadrant C–type responses.

The generic strategies relevant to each of these broad constituencies of people are set out below.

*Generic strategy for quadrant A (positive–active)*

People in quadrant A are likely to view the change as an opportunity, either to advance their careers in the organization or to carry out the type of work that appeals to them. Others may respond in this way because of their natural tendency to "go with the flow" and to embrace change as a natural aspect of organizational life. The broad approach here might be to:

- provide sufficient challenge *and continuing support*, to recognize their enthusiasm and desire for progress;
- engage them as informal "change agents," to help to bring others along and, at the same time, beware of any tendency for resentment to grow in those who see the change less favorably;
- manage their expectations;
- anticipate potential loss of enthusiasm as their initial optimism is tempered by unexpected side-effects and less favorable outcomes; and
- provide a safe space for them to raise any emerging issues and concerns that may arise, so that these can be dealt with before they escalate.

This last point is particularly important, as we shall see when we look further at the psychological and emotional impacts of change on people.

*Generic strategy for quadrant B (positive–passive)*

For people in quadrant B, the detailed meaning and benefits of the change may still be unclear. Alternatively, they may feel that they've "seen it all before" and are waiting for some tangible signs that the promised changes will actually happen. Or it may simply be that it's part of their make-up to be more cautious and less proactive. Some people here will have progressed from quadrant C. For them, it might simply be a case of tentatively "dipping their toes in the water" to find out more about the new ways of working, before committing themselves more fully. The general approach to people falling into this quadrant might be to:

- help them to frame the changes more positively, by trying to excite them with the possibilities that the changes bring for using their talents more fully, overcoming previous areas of frustration and so on;
- stimulate them to identify ways in which the changes can help to further their own purpose and ambitions;

- encourage them to get involved in specifying the desired outcomes, and facilitate opportunities for them to do so;
- enable them to shape the way that the changes take effect;
- demonstrate progress, to overcome any concerns that might exist because of the failure of past changes to be followed through;
- provide understanding and support to those who make an effort to move forward but who initially struggle to get to grips with the personal challenges arising from the new ways of working; and
- provide opportunities for them to interact with relevant staff in quadrant A, especially where strong, positive relationships already exist.

*Generic strategy for quadrant C (negative–passive)*

This quadrant might contain the bulk of the staff during the early stages of a significant change. These people are often fearful of what lies ahead; and they are gripped by some of the feelings of loss and lack of security that negatively perceived change brings into play. The leader's general approach here might be to:

- accept the reality of people's different interpretations and perceptions, and work to change their mindsets at a pace appropriate to their psychological and emotional states;
- help people to make sense of what's going on, through informal one-to-one and one-to-few conversations and interactions;
- acknowledge felt losses, recognize and accept signs of grieving, and sensitively encourage and enable movement through the relevant resistance stages;
- help people to rebuild their self-confidence – such as by providing support for them to gain new knowledge and skills;
- treat the past with respect – mark any significant endings that are brought about by the changes, and show how past successes provide a solid basis for moving forward (Bridges, 1995).

*Generic strategy for quadrant D (negative–active)*

Many people in this quadrant will feel a deep sense of hurt at a perceived loss of personal status or power. Others might appear here because the proposed changes appear to undermine in some way their deeply held values and beliefs. Some of these people will become entrenched in their stance and remain rooted in this quadrant for some time. Others may make a temporary excursion here from quadrant C, as they ride the emotional roller coaster that typically accompanies significant change

events. A further subset may include those staff whose natural position
is to use the status quo as a benchmark against which to judge all new
proposals. The aim here should be to:

- seek to understand the nature of the concerns, and respond to these
  with empathy;
- where appropriate, take account of the issues and concerns that have
  been raised, to improve the quality or effectiveness of the outcome;
- seek to create a viable role for disaffected staff, and to re-engage their
  energies in a positive way;
- acknowledge and address any psychological and emotional dimensions
  of the felt losses;
- understand the "bottom line" – how to proceed if these best endeavors
  fail to achieve a mutually constructive outcome.

## Influencing the sensemaking and use-making processes

To work towards the creation of a strong coalition of support for the
desired changes, Figure 6.2 suggests that the leader needs to influence
two things. As before, these are the *sense* that people make of what is
going on, and the *use* to which they put this in deciding how to respond.
Communication, focusing in particular on its informal and unstructured
forms (quadrants C3 and C4 of the Leadership Communication Grid), is
the key leadership tool for bringing about the desired shifts in perception
and behavior. However, the psychosocial dynamics of individuals within
an organizational context are complex. These do not lend themselves to
simple, "if you do this you'll get that" prescriptions about how to create
genuine and sustained support for a particular organizational theme or
broader change agenda. There are, though, certain aspects of the overall
process that can be expected to have a particularly influential effect
on people's perception and interpretation of events. In turn, these will
influence the way in which they decide to respond to them. Managers
need to pay special attention to these factors when working to build
coalitions of support for desired changes.

As mentioned earlier, three things in particular have a significant
impact on the sensemaking and use-making conversations that will
determine whether or not the desired changes take effect. First, the *content*
of the changes needs to make sense to people in ways that engage
them positively. Secondly, *connections* need to be forged progressively
between champions of the change and others who are more skeptical,

using the most credible paths that exist between people in the group (and, where applicable, the wider organization or beyond). Thirdly, leaders need to establish a positive, enabling *context* for the changes, which removes blockages, encourages movement and provides appropriate support.

Additionally though, unlike issue coalitions, the purpose of an action coalition is to secure participants' active and sustained engagement with the new ways of working. It is not simply to gain their transient support for a particular decision or policy shift. These features of an action coalition bring a fourth "success factor" into play. That is, the *conduct* of the change process itself. This needs to deal effectively with the underlying dynamics of change, and its psychological and emotional impacts on people.

These four factors are discussed in turn below.

## Content

It ought to be unnecessary to say that the substance of the proposed change should be organizationally beneficial. Sadly, this is not always the case. Many factors can conspire against this, such as:

- the instant gratification promised by the many fast-food "solutions" on offer;
- the desire of ambitious managers not to be left behind in the race to adopt the latest fads and fashions; and
- the felt need of newly appointed managers to "make their mark" by changing all that was there before.

These factors contribute to the high failure rate of planned change programs mentioned earlier and result in disillusioned, change-weary staff. The building of issue coalitions that we discussed earlier is designed to avoid this. It does so by seeking to move the existing organizational agenda forward in some positive way or to thwart others' attempts to take the organization down value-destroying blind alleys. Where a particular change *is* judged to be in the organization's best interests, the underlying premise of the *informal coalitions* approach is that the change also needs to resonate with staff in some way. Only then will it inspire, energize and engage them. In particular, it needs to tap into their own aspirations and work agendas, or to mesh with their personal characteristics. Preferably it will do both. The deeper the level of connection that can be made between a proposed change and people's personal frames of reference, the stronger will be their commitment to it. It will also be more likely to stick.

As we have noted, different things motivate different people within organizations. They prefer different ways of working; and they process information in different ways. This means that the ways in which the content of a specific change is communicated need to connect with people on a personal and emotional level, not simply to be intellectually intelligible. People channel incoming information through their personal frames, which embody these preferences. So both formal and informal communication needs to recognize this, if people are to "hear" what is being said and engage with it enthusiastically. Some of these contrasting perspectives are summarized in Table 6.1.[1]

In crafting the "core story" of a particular change, the aim should be to identify different aspects of it that might appeal to people with these contrasting perspectives and feelings. Formal communications should attempt to use language, metaphor and examples that embrace "both sides of the argument." This will increase the likelihood that it will tap into the diverse motivations, preferred ways of working and so on that these represent. A couple of examples from a large UK company will illustrate this:

> The aim is to introduce new processes and tools to improve our everyday operations and overall management of the business. At the same time, our existing knowledge and skills will continue to underpin our ability to deliver in line with customers' expectations.
> (Difference mixed with Sameness)

> The increasing emphasis on adding value and minimising costs will extend the scope for using individual initiative to identify options for improvement and working with others to generate new ideas. As opportunities for improvement emerge, business units will be required to work within agreed implementational plans and programmes to ensure that we extract maximum value from these across the organisation as a whole. (Options and Discretion mixed with Procedures and Order)

More importantly, leaders can use these insights to inform their everyday conversations and interactions. If they *authentically* frame the changes in ways that recognize individuals' motivational traits, work preferences and habitual ways of making sense of information, these are more likely to find resonance with staff and lead to their active engagement in making them work.

### Connections

Organizations comprise dynamic networks of conversations, through which power is exerted and influence achieved. In coalition building, the

**Table 6.1** Contrasting perspectives

| Some people | Whereas others |
|---|---|
| . . . are motivated by the chance to achieve goals; are excited by the challenges that the change bring; and prefer to focus on exploiting opportunities. | . . . want to avoid threat, potential losses, failure, and negative consequences; and prefer to focus on overcoming problems. |
| . . . are stimulated by change itself; and are keen to embrace new, unique and radical ways of moving forward. | . . . prefer to stick with the familiar; and need to see that, in moving forward, they can build on existing capabilities and past achievements. |
| . . . like to have choices; and are interested in exploring possibilities, having variety and being flexible. | . . . want clear criteria, tried and tested routines, and standards and procedures that they can follow. |
| . . . need scope for self-management; and they use their own criteria to judge success (such as their personal value set, their sense of professionalism, and self-pride in the expertise and service that they provide). | . . . need external feedback and controls; and they rely on external standards and the opinions of significant others to judge their success. |
| . . . want to focus on getting the job done: emphasizing products, processes, systems and goals; and tending to use impersonal language in their communication and relationships. | . . . want to focus on people: emphasizing feelings, emotions and relationships; and preferring to use more personal language in their communication and relationships. |
| . . . are attracted by new concepts, processes, strategies and patterns; and they value thinking about things. | . . . are attracted by clear action steps, implementation and delivery; and they value doing things. |
| . . . need to see the overall direction and longer-term implications of the proposed changes; and they tend to thrive on the complexity inherent in organizational change. | . . . want to know the detailed steps involved, and the immediate impact of these on their work; and they have a greater need for clarity and simplicity before being comfortable to move forward. |
| . . . are keen to get engaged and look ahead: they want to push forward and get on with it. | . . . are still experiencing a sense of loss and fear of the unknown; they need to see that the past is being treated with respect and to achieve satisfactory closure before turning to face the future. |

natural focus is on conversations *about* the change. The aim then is to shift these conversations from ones that convey a negative or passive stance to ones that reflect positive engagement. However, this is simply a means to the end of changed organizational capability and performance. This broader agenda requires a shift in the *patterns of everyday conversations* that people have, in carrying out their work and in relating with others. From an *informal coalitions* viewpoint, change takes place *through* these day-to-day interactions and, in particular, through the act of conversation. As the conversations change over time, so will the organization. Building action coalitions is therefore about encouraging shifts in the pattern, nature and content of conversations that people have both with themselves (how they think about things) and, more importantly, with others.

In general terms, people are especially influenced by the positions that their peer-group and people within their personal network of relationships take on particular issues. The signals that they pick up – intentionally or otherwise – from the words and actions of their line managers are also critical. We will reprise this latter point briefly below, when we look at the organizational context of the desired changes.

Not all of an individual's peers or members of their wider network will have the same influence on the way in which they think and act. Besides personal friendships, which may exert an emotional pull on some individuals, three other categories of people have a disproportionate effect upon the way in which individuals respond to organizational change. Gladwell (2000) identifies these people as:

- those who are seen as a credible, reliable and socially adept source of knowledge and advice on important issues;
- those who, individually and collectively, provide the main linkage points and connections between significant numbers of organizational members;
- those who have the personal power, advocacy skills and passion to persuade others of the worth of ideas which they themselves find attractive.

Identifying these people, and mobilizing their power to influence others, is critical to the coalition-building strategy. It is equally important that these pivotal people do not coalesce around themes that run counter to those advanced. If they do, it will be increasingly difficult for leaders to build a sufficiently strong coalition in support of the desired changes.

### Context

Context is critical. Sensemaking does not take place in a vacuum. Where the organizational context supports a particular change, it is much more likely that people will make sense of emerging events in ways that build awareness, acceptance and, ultimately, commitment to them. On the other hand, where there are mismatches between the perceived demands of the change and the quality of the supporting infrastructure, perceptions of the change are likely to be less favorable. Positive engagement will then be much more difficult to achieve. Such support might include, for example, appropriate tools and technological support; enabling management processes and systems; access to relevant information and meaningful performance feedback; the opportunity to participate fully in making the changes happen locally; and any training and development necessary to deal competently with the emerging challenges. Some people would add incentives to this list. However, the *informal coalitions* approach is about stimulating people to become engaged with the changes because these resonate with their own ambitions and sense of self-worth. They "join up" because they want to, not because there is some externally controlled, extrinsic reward for doing so.

The leader's own words and actions provide another critical dimension of the change context. The extent to which their observed behaviors and informal comments match those implied by the official change rhetoric is especially relevant. The attitudes and behaviors that leaders model through their day-to-day implementation of the change and ongoing management of the business can either enrich the context or else fuel a climate of cynicism and mistrust. As we saw in Chapter 1, *active and sustained* sponsorship of the change is a particularly powerful way of making sure that latent supporters of the coalition are not dissuaded from joining. Active sponsorship reinforces the main themes of the change and strengthens its credibility. On the other hand, its absence conveys a sense of indifference – or even thinly disguised opposition – to the changes that the leader is advocating in public.

Finally, managers need to recognize that people's own personal web of relationships sets the *overall* context within which they perceive the need for, and relevance of, proposed changes. We discussed this in terms of a plate-spinning metaphor in Chapter 2. This generates competing sets of expectations that need to be balanced continuously. Individuals resolve these competing demands through their personal frames of reference, which we initially explored in Chapter 5. For example, a required change in working practice may appear sensible in the light of market expectations. Ordinarily, this might be of minor consequence to an affected individual. However, if this were to arrive close on the heels of a number of other changes and disturbances to that person's personal circumstances, it might appear overwhelming and cause significant distress. Too often, managers think about, and express, the context for change solely in terms of the characteristics of the organization's wider business environment. Although liberally sprinkled with references to market conditions, competitor actions, shareholder expectations, cost profiles and so on, their presentation of the situation often fails to acknowledge and address its more personal dimensions. From an *informal coalitions* perspective, it is essential for leaders to take account of the impact that these more personal influencers have on individuals' responses to organizational change.

The way in which each of us views the changes that affect us, and how we respond to them, will be strongly influenced by:

- our ingrained perceptual patterns;
- our characteristic traits and preferences for particular ways of working; and
- the complex interplay of demands that are placed upon us through our unique mix of personal, social and work relationships.

These factors are embodied in our personal frame of reference. When externally imposed changes threaten to "crack" this frame, we do everything we can to preserve it intact. Our aim is to avoid the sense of personal loss that this challenge to our personal worldview, habitual behavior patterns and relationship network would bring. The deeper the potential cracks caused by the change, the greater the sense of loss and the more intense the feelings experienced. This is illustrated in Box 6.1.

---

**Box 6.1 – Intensity of loss**

If we believe that a particular change will affect only our local surroundings and immediate *environment* (such as moving to another part of the building), and we feel that this will not have any deeper impacts on our lives, our sense of loss may be slight and short-lived.

The requirement to change some of our familiar *behaviors*, to accommodate new processes and tasks perhaps, may cut a little deeper. This will especially be the case if it has knock-on effects in other aspects of our personal rituals and routines.

The "cracks" would go deeper still if the changes appeared to threaten our *capability* to perform competently. Our sense of competence at work is primarily provided by our knowledge and skills, and by our ability to influence others. The need to acquire new knowledge and skills, or the feeling that existing skills may become redundant as a result of the changes, might impact at this capability level. Also, changes in environment and/or behavior patterns may

---

affect our perceived ability to influence others. These might break up well-established informal networks, remove access to valued information and resources and so on.

In some instances, the changes may appear to run counter to some of the deeply held *values and beliefs* that motivate us to perform and guide our everyday responses to the situations we face. The greater the sense of dissonance that exists between the changes and these values, the more difficult it will be for us to embrace them.

If the changes affect our sense of *identity*, the pain will be even greater. Our sense of who we are, our self-concept and feeling of self-worth are forged and validated through the key roles and relationships in our lives. For most of us, our working life provides an important source of these identity-forming relationships. If we feel that these are threatened by changes that we cannot control, our resistance will be all the stronger.

At the deepest level of all is our *spiritual* well-being. If a change undermines the *sense of meaning* that we gain from our work or the connection that it provides to something "bigger" in our lives, we might feel a deep personal loss. For some people, their work *is* their life. To lose their job, or to be required to change in ways that require a fundamental break to be made with the past, can be traumatic. Similarly, the changes may cause deep personal relationships to be severed or badly affected, whether at work itself or outside. An example of the latter might be where family relationships are strained as a result of business relocation or a significant shift in work–life balance.

Conner (1993) suggests that people resist change to maintain the integrity of their personal frames of reference. One important thing for managers to recognize here is that any change will evoke different responses in different individuals (including themselves). For example, one person might see an enforced rearrangement of the office as little more than a minor hindrance (environmental). In contrast, a colleague might see the loss of their *perceived* privileged place in the building as a reduction in status (identity). One individual might see proposed changes in work pattern as a simple adjustment in routine (behavioral). For another, these same changes might cause a much deeper sense of hurt because of the adverse impact that this would have on a much-valued aspect of family life (spiritual).

Our earlier discussion of relationship dynamics, using the plate-spinning metaphor, recognized that we each need to "keep the plates spinning" simultaneously in all of our significant relationships. Changes that directly affect one set of relationships, such as those at work, will inevitably affect a number of other relationships. And it may be the impact on those latter relationships that cause the felt sense of loss, even if the initiating changes are themselves benign or even positive. Using a simple example, many organizations provide the use of cars to managers and other staff on a "job need" basis. As job requirements change, it might be perfectly sensible to remove this provision, if the individual's new role does not have the same travel demands. However, if they had given the impression, within their wider social circle, that the car was a symbol of their status within the company, its sudden removal might cause significant embarrassment. Negative emotions and resistant behaviors might then be inevitable. This is not a call for business needs to be subordinated to personal preferences. It is, though, a reminder to managers that change ultimately requires the active and willing engagement of staff, if it is to succeed.

## Conduct

When organizations talk about managing change well, they are usually referring to the program and project management of the physical changes that are planned to take place. Past failures to make change stick are, more often than not, put down to poor implementation (in a transactional sense) rather than to the underlying dynamics and leadership of change. And, as we saw in Chapter 2, this usually translates into a call to "do it better and get it right." Emphasis is then placed on one or more of the rational aspects of the change process. These might include:

- the planned changes to structures, systems and processes;
- the "peopling" of the new organization, including (where applicable) associated "downsizing" and outplacement procedures;
- the training and development of staff in new skills and desired behaviors;
- the formal communication of key messages to affected staff;
- and so on.

These formal, structured elements of the process are important to its success. From an *informal coalitions* perspective, though, other factors are likely to have a much more powerful impact upon an organization's long-term performance and capability. We have already seen how the informal, political and cultural dynamics of the organization shape the processes and outcomes of organizational change. To these we now need to add its psychological, emotional and spiritual dimensions. Encouraging, assisting and enabling staff to deal effectively with these aspects of the process is therefore central to the coalition-building task.

## Intellectual understanding and emotional engagement

Change is about new ideas and new ways of working. When faced with these, people respond both intellectually and emotionally. Intellectually, a new idea may make sense to them and be one that they could readily sign up to. *At the same time*, psychologically and emotionally, their response may be quite different. For example, they might judge that the personal impact of the change would adversely affect their perceived status within the organization, fracture some important relationships, or otherwise affect their ability to perform. In such cases, it is likely that they would resist the proposed change – at least initially – despite intellectually recognizing its merit. In practice, if the proposals immediately triggered a strong negative response, it is unlikely that they would recognize or acknowledge the benefits of the proposed changes from an intellectual standpoint at all. Instead later information would be channeled through different, "emotionally distorted" patterns of perception and response. In fact, it is much more likely that they would rationalize their objections in intellectual terms and deny any perceived benefits (possibly even to themselves). These feelings would be reinforced by conversations that they had with others who saw the changes in similar terms. Indeed, one likely response would be to seek out people whose views reinforced their own perceptions.

In discussing this patterning process in earlier chapters, we talked about the tendency for everyday organizational conversations to be channeled down familiar "cultural" pathways. In this way, existing patterns of meaning tend to be reinforced. At the same time, the potential exists for these patterns to change and new meaning to emerge. Where conversations are particularly emotionally charged, as at times of significant personal change, this sensemaking "landscape" biases the way in which the patterning process takes place. That is, it affects what is paid attention to, which patterns are triggered by the incoming information and so on. The downside of this for managers is that a number of familiar – and seemingly unhelpful – "resistance" patterns may be triggered by these conversations. These prevent people engaging with what managers consider to be organizationally beneficial changes. On the positive side, expressed emotion is a sign of energy (the words "emotion" and "motiv-ation" have shared roots). This energy can potentially be refocused and worked with for all-round benefit. Also, there are likely to be some people who will welcome the proposed changes, which stimulate positive emotions in them. For these people, the sensemaking patterns that these trigger will be biased toward ones that reflect opportunity and excitement, rather than threat and fear.

As Bridges (1995) points out, changes in the intellectual and phys-ical aspects of the organization (its strategies, structures and systems, for example) ordinarily take place when the plan says that they will. But people's psychological and emotional engagement with the new arrange-ments takes much longer to achieve. The latter dynamics are inherently *un*manageable in the conventional sense of the term; and these contribute to the everyday messiness and informality that provides the rationale for the *informal coalitions* perspective. The psychological and emotional phases that people typically pass through in responding to change are commonly referred to as stages in the transition process (Bridges, 1995).

## Moving through resistance to engagement

Table 6.2 illustrates some of the important ways in which these comple-mentary but distinct aspects of the change process differ from each other.

The entries in column 1 relate to the formal, structured and rational elements of the change process that we outlined earlier (such as the design and delivery of new structures, systems and processes, etc.). These more tangible, surface-level activities can be planned and managed successfully through program and project management-type disciplines and method-ologies. In addition, the visibility of column-1 activities typically places these at the center of management's monitoring and reporting procedures.

In contrast, the *informal coalitions* approach pays particular attention to the effects of column-2 attributes of the change process. These underlying dynamics of change have a significant impact on organizational outcomes. Unresolved negative emotions can seriously undermine performance in relation to a specific change; but these can't be addressed through formal planning and control procedures. What is more, failure to deal with them adequately can leave a legacy of dysfunctional effects that will continue to eat away at the organization for years to come. People who feel alienated, powerless, threatened or betrayed, for example, will always struggle to perform at their best. They are also more likely, though, to view future

**Table 6.2** Differences between surface-level changes and underlying dynamics

| Characteristics of the surface-level aspects of the change process | Characteristics of the underlying dynamics of the change process |
|---|---|
| • Intellectual and physical | • Psychological, emotional and spiritual |
| • Organizational focus | • Individual focus |
| • Context set by external, business environment | • Context set by internal, personal circumstances |
| • Rational | • A-rational |
| • Formal, structured | • Informal, unstructured |
| • Tangible | • Largely intangible |
| • Surface level, visible | • Below the surface, hidden |
| • Can be planned and programmed – pace set by business needs and common factors | • Can't be planned or programmed – pace set by individual needs and personal factors |
| • Outcomes predictable within limits | • Outcomes emergent and unpredictable (although characteristic patterns of response can be identified) |
| • Potentially controllable by management | • Uncontrollable by management |

changes with suspicion and resentment. Helping people to make the transition from this negative emotional state to one in which they feel motivated, powerful, challenged and supported is therefore central to the coalition-building task.

This emphasis on people's psychological and emotional transition through change is not intended to undermine the importance of effective program and project management to organizational success. Provided, that is, that the limitations of these are recognized and understood. Besides delivering the desired structural changes and surface-level shifts in behavior, effective management of the column-1 elements of the change process can also provide important inputs to the coalition-building task. These inputs might include, for example:

• evidence of management's commitment to the changes and to the developmental support needed to meet the emerging challenges;
• increasing management credibility, as new procedures take hold; and
• demonstrable progress toward the stated end-goal, which provides tangible reinforcement of the organization's strategic intentions.

The *informal coalitions* perspective recognizes that successful *and sustainable* change depends as much – if not more – on the self-organizing dynamics of column 2 as it does on the programmable elements of column 1. The aim is to engage with these underlying aspects of the change process in ways that enable people to embrace the future challenges quickly and productively. If they are to achieve this successfully, those leading the change need to manage their own and others' interventions in the process sensitively and with insight. As part of this, they need to facilitate the healthy expression of those emotions that arise *naturally* from people's involvement in organizational change of all kinds. The remainder of this chapter looks at how these issues affect the coalition-building task.

### Transition phases

To help us make sense of this, we will return to the framework that we used earlier. This time, though, we'll progressively introduce some additional guidance into the picture, which takes account of the psychological and emotional dynamics of change on people's willingness to move in the desired direction.

First of all, it can be useful to think of the transition process as occurring in three phases. The phases, which I've called "Holding On," "Letting Go" and "Engaging" are broadly equivalent to Bridges's "Ending," "Neutral Zone" and "Beginning" (Bridges, 1995). These are illustrated in Figure 6.3.

Where people's immediate perception and interpretation of a change (alone and in conversation with others) is negative, they try to hold on to the current state. In common management parlance, they resist the change. This is motivated by the need to retain their personal frame of reference intact and to avoid the loss of things that they consider would affect it adversely. Metaphorically, people in this state are facing backward, looking to the past and glorifying what they see there. In contrast, management wants to see people fully and positively engaged with the change, moving forward with enthusiasm and commitment.

If people are to move from one state to the other, they need to "turn around" – being prepared in their own minds to let go of the past and to face the future. Like a trapeze artist flying between swings in a circus, they can't catch hold of the new trapeze until they've let go of the old one. But letting go is risky. It means giving up something that feels familiar, comfortable and secure. It means reaching out for something else that might not be there.

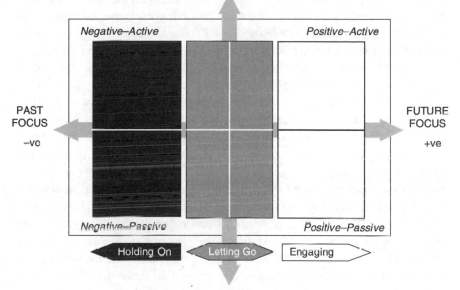

**Figure 6.3** Building action coalitions – Phases in the transition process

Even if it is there, they might not believe that it is "catchable" – at least not by them. Or not now. That is, people might feel that it requires skills and abilities that they don't possess or can't acquire. A feeling of performing capably in all of their important relationships simultaneously is critical to people's sense of self-worth and their felt place in the world. Thinking and acting in line with their personal frame of reference provides the means of achieving this. So, the greater the perceived threat that the change poses to this frame, the more difficult it will be for them to let go of the past and embrace the new challenges.

A critical issue to remember here is that people move through these phases at their own pace. The psychological and emotional journey that each individual undertakes is highly personal. And this means that, at any one time, people will be at different stages of the journey. Most particularly, it is likely that managers who initiate a specific change, or who have been closely involved in its conception, will already be in the "engaging" phase at the time that the change is formally announced. They may be there because they saw the change as positive from the outset. Alternatively, they will have progressed to that stage as a result of the backstage conversations that led to its final formulation. There will therefore inevitably be an initial mismatch of perceptions between the forward-facing initiators of the change and the bulk of those people who will be affected by it. To those on the receiving end, the announcement will often appear as an unwelcome "bolt from the blue." This can cause a significant breakdown in communication and frustration on all sides.

Leaders who adopt an *informal coalitions* stance recognize that people will *naturally* be at different stages along the path to full engagement. At various times, they've been in these different places themselves! They will therefore resist making early, universal announcements about how wonderful the new world will be. They will begin instead by engaging with people where they *are*, not where they would like them to be. People who view the changes as positive don't need the razzmatazz that often accompanies major organizational change to get them on board – they are there already. At the same time, this is the *last thing* that people in the negative camp need. All they can see at this stage is the things that they will lose as a result of the changes. *Premature* corporate events to celebrate the new world simply rub salt into the wounds of those people who are caught up in these negative emotions. This is even more the case where formal communication about the change sets out to paint a glowing picture of the future by contrasting it with a less-than-flattering description of the past. The past is where those resisting the move currently reside. And the past is where a lot of the leader's coalition-building activity will need to start. As in all aspects of the *informal coalitions* approach to change leadership, informal conversations and interactions are the manager's primary tool for achieving the shift from resistance to engagement.

*Conversations during the "holding on" phase*

Later, we will look at some of the specific emotions that people might experience at this stage, and how leaders might best respond to them. There are, though, a number of general conversational guidelines that leaders need to bear in mind, if they want to help people to begin the process of letting go of the past and moving on. These include:

- not rubbishing what's gone before;
- acknowledging where past successes provide a sound platform for moving forward;
- providing opportunities for people to celebrate the past or "put the past to bed," in a way that provides them with a sense of closure;
- enabling them to maintain a sense of continuity in the midst of change, by taking aspects of the past forward into the future;

- recognizing that many practical aspects of people's work and everyday experience will usually remain unchanged – and clarifying what these might be;
- expressing confidence in people's ability to move on successfully, as evidenced by past changes;
- identifying where the changes are themselves about holding on to things that are important to individuals, and which resonate with their own values, feelings and ambitions.

Of the above guidance, "don't rubbish the past" is perhaps the most salutary; especially for managers who are taking over the running of a business. They might be more tempted than most to "lower the baseline," so to speak, before introducing their own regime. I recall the story of one newly installed manager of a major industrial plant who called staff together at the start of his "reign." He began by removing a small pin from his pocket and declaring that all of the plant's achievements to date would fit on the end of the pin! His intention, no doubt, was to illustrate that there was much left that people could achieve. By failing to treat the past with respect, though, he alienated great swathes of the business unit's staff and made his task much harder than it needed to have been. That story bounced around the plant – and the wider organization – for years afterward.

All new beginnings are accompanied by an ending. And, according to Bridges (1995: 32), ". . . the single biggest reason organizational changes fail is that no one thought about endings or planned to manage their impact on people." Holding-on conversations recognize this and provide a platform from which, at the appropriate time, more positive, forward-looking steps can be taken.

### "Letting go" conversations

As individuals begin to let go of the past and recognize that change *is* going to happen, leaders need to shift the nature of their conversations to suit. Feelings of insecurity may be particularly acute at this stage, as people will have begun to let go of the certainties of the past but not yet turned fully to face the future and move forward with confidence. The aim here is to encourage them to move toward willing acceptance of the change, and to build a platform for their positive engagement during the final phase of the process. Whilst continuing to observe and listen for the *specific* thoughts and emotions that are accompanying and coloring individuals' responses to the changes, this means:

- empathizing with people's feelings of insecurity;
- normalizing these feelings as a natural, human response to changes that are initially viewed less than positively;
- fully acknowledging the picture of the world *as they see it* (the benefits of the status quo and the potential downsides of the proposed way forward), as a critical step in the reorientation process;
- *genuinely* taking on board any new insights that emerge from these conversations, in relation to the nature or implementation of the change;
- surfacing and dealing with the inevitable conflicts that arise, as people interact with others who are either still holding on firmly to the past or else moving on enthusiastically into the future;
- not making false promises;
- continuing the gentle pull toward the future, *without overstating the benefits*.

And, at the appropriate time, encouraging the important step toward basic acceptance, by:

- gently teasing out some of the *individual's own* dissatisfaction with the status quo and then jointly exploring some of the benefits that would accrue from moving in the direction intended;
- helping people to recognize the individual and collective resources that they already possess to cope with the challenges that lie ahead;
- underpinning this by highlighting additional resources, such as the provision of training and development, that will be made available to support them as they move forward.

People can feel lost in a mental and emotional "wilderness" at times during this "letting go" phase. This is especially the case if it becomes clear that the changes will require them to leave behind things that they have valued greatly. It is particularly important, therefore, for leaders to make themselves available for informal one-to-one and one-to-few conversations as people pass through this stage. Where these feelings are widespread, it can also be useful to supplement the day-to-day interactions with occasional, structured group sessions (mode C2 of the Communication Grid). This enables people to share their feelings, identify concerns and jointly make sense of unfolding events. Leaders should actively participate in these sessions, both as carriers of information that might help to address some of these issues and also as people who are themselves impacted upon by the emerging changes. A leader's own perceptions and feelings can provide important additional data, in their quest to understand why certain aspects of a particular change are taking hold and why others might not be. At structured, multi-party events, leaders also need to recognize that tensions might arise between people who are at different stages in their personal transitions. They need to be prepared to deal with these differences sensitively and constructively, in their role as in-line coach and boundary manager. As always, *how* a leader is seen to respond in circumstances like this will communicate a lot to people about what sort of organization they are being asked to engage with. It will also significantly influence their decision as to whether or not they wish to do so enthusiastically – or at all!

The leader's aim during this phase is twofold. First, people need to be helped toward a growing realization that change *is* going to happen. This inevitably means that some of the things that they felt they would lose will indeed not be there in the future – at least not in their previous forms. Secondly, they need to be given support as they begin to "repair the cracks" in their personal frames of reference.

As individuals move toward the end of this phase, they will also be more receptive to conversations that recognize some of the inadequacies of the past. During the "holding on" phase, even people who have complained vociferously about existing processes and practices will often resist any criticism of them. This position begins to soften as the inevitability of the change starts to dawn. As acceptance of the need to move on comes closer, conversations can usefully turn to the challenge of using change as an opportunity to overcome some of these past irritations. The very act of engaging people creatively in shaping the way forward can reinforce the shift toward acceptance and beyond. In doing this, it can be useful to adopt an appreciative stance in addressing any inadequacies that might be identified. This means recognizing the latent strengths that might reside within past practices and seeking to exploit these to meet the newly emerging challenges. This keeps the focus of the conversations on strengths and possibilities, rather than weaknesses and limitations. It can be a particularly powerful approach to build upon during the final stage of the transition process.

*Conversations for engagement*

As individuals enter this forward-looking phase, the conversations can shift much more firmly toward the future. The focus here is on the practical implications that the changes have for people and on building their commitment to them. The aim is to use people's growing acceptance of the need to change as a platform on which to build greater understanding and enthusiasm for what lies ahead. Basic acceptance falls well short of the outcome sought by the *informal coalitions* perspective. Instead, the search is for solutions that resonate with people's own aspirations and which provide the motive, means and opportunity for them to excel.

At this stage, conversations need to stimulate people to move further along the curve toward full engagement. The goal is for them to integrate the new requirements fully into their everyday behaviors, thoughts and feelings. As previously, the approach should be to encourage and enable people to move progressively through this stage, at a pace that suits them personally. This does not mean sitting back passively, and waiting for events to take their course. But it does mean continuing to pay attention to the psychological and emotional dimensions of change as the "performance wick" is turned up. Conversations during this phase might usefully be directed toward:

- ensuring that people's everyday experiences match up to the expectations that have been raised through earlier conversations – and remaining aware that people can slip backward if events disappoint them;
- encouraging movement beyond tentative acceptance of the change, towards a position in which the new perspectives and ways of working are thoroughly integrated into people's habitual ways of behaving;
- identifying opportunities for shaping or framing the emerging changes in ways that *both* further the organization's objectives *and* resonate with individuals' personal goals and aspirations;
- providing vision *through everyday conversations and interactions* (as will be discussed more fully in Chapter 8);
- reinforcing the sense of individual and collective progress, by raising awareness of personal and organizational achievements that demonstrate positive movement.

## Exploiting conversational networks

The *informal coalitions* approach recognizes the power that direct interaction between a leader and their staff can have in shaping the sensemaking and action-taking processes. At the same time, it stresses the added ability to influence events that comes from working through the organization's natural conversational networks. These form and re-form between people, as they go about their day-to-day activities. Leaders can tap into these, to gain a deeper understanding of how the changes are being received and made sense of within the wider group. And they can use the networks' natural dynamics, to stimulate and shape the formation of the desired action coalitions. Within this, the points made earlier about the importance of understanding and using the natural connections within the emerging coalition are particularly relevant. The coalition-building approach therefore exploits the self-organizing dynamics of informal conversational networks. This sets the process apart from conventional methods of dealing with change, based upon top–down instruction (*management edict*), formal persuasion (*education and training*) or structured group methods (*joint problem solving*).

## Dealing with the emotional impact of change

The final aspect of coalition building that leaders need to address is the emotional journey that people typically undertake when they experience organizational change. Where people initially perceive change as negative, they are likely to experience a wide range of unhelpful feelings. The following clusters of emotions are typical of those that might arise with varying degrees of intensity, according to personal and organizational circumstances:

- anger-based: frustration, exasperation, bitterness and resentment
- fear-based: concern, anxiety, disorientation and insecurity
- mistrust-based: unfairness, suspicion, betrayal and envy
- sadness-based: depression, guilt, desolation and rejection.

When feelings such as these are ignored or suppressed, they don't go away! Instead, they build up and become toxic, both to the individuals involved and to the organization as a whole. The immediate effect is to drain away the energy, creativity and commitment needed to make change work on the ground. Over the longer term, these remain as "unfinished business," undermining performance and frustrating future change efforts. Conditions therefore need to be created that allow these *natural* emotions to be expressed in healthy and helpful ways. The resulting feelings can then be addressed constructively; making the task of positively engaging people much more doable. To facilitate this, we need to look further into the pattern of emotions that may accompany (and therefore channel) people's responses to organizational change at various points during their personal transitions.

Figure 6.4 identifies seven behavioral responses, which leaders might detect in their staff (and themselves) at various stages during the change process. These are overlaid on the basic coalition-building matrix and described in turn below.

At one extreme, some of the people whose initial response to an imposed change is negative may move through many of these stages quickly and imperceptibly. This is particularly likely to be the case where the "cracks" that the change makes in their personal frames of reference

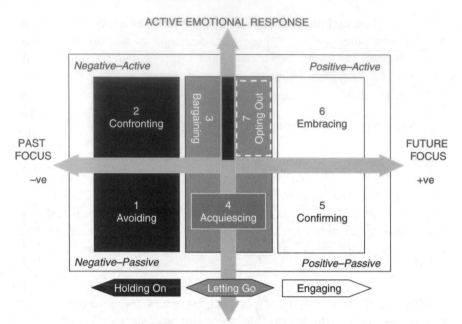

**Figure 6.4** Building action coalitions – Patterns of emotional response

are only surface deep. There will be others, though, who feel particularly hurt by the changes. They, in contrast, may spend long periods in particular emotional states and even become stuck at particular points along the path. Both of these patterns are normal – as are the multitude of other, individual-specific patterns that managers might witness.

*Avoiding*

As we know from our earlier exploration of the personal transition process, people who view a particular change as negative will initially try to hold on to the status quo. Their immediate emotional reaction is likely to be one of shock, followed by a period of denial.[2] These avoiding behaviors are very much part of the holding-on phase. These sit squarely within the negative–passive quadrant of the matrix.

*Confronting*

Typically, avoidance will be followed by an expression of anger, as individuals attempt to ward off the sense of threat that they feel to their personal frames of reference. This confrontational stance also reflects the desire to hold on to things as they are, rather than moving on. It is a much more active expression of this motivation than was evident during the period of shock and denial. Where anger manifests itself as an open sign of resistance to change, it can make for an uncomfortable time for managers. However, its visibility within the working environment at least makes it easier to address than if it were hidden. Where anger is suppressed in the formal work context, it is likely to manifest itself elsewhere. This might be in an individual's wider network of relationships (such as at home) or, perhaps, through some negative, shadow-side behaviors within the organization.

Overt expressions of anger and confrontation are found within the negative–active quadrant of the coalition-building matrix. Pent-up anger will not be immediately visible to the leader of course; so those expressing it may appear to be responding passively to the changes, whilst agitating behind the scenes to frustrate them.

### Bargaining (and opting out)

"Bargaining" is another characteristic behavior of people in the negative active quadrant of the matrix. When their anger has subsided or been subdued in some way, the next natural reaction that might occur is an attempt to negotiate an alternative way out of what remains, for them, an undesirable position to be in. Where organizations are restructured, staff numbers reduced or processes re-engineered, for example, they might put forward all manner of suggestions in an attempt to thwart, stall or modify the intended changes. "If we cut back substantially on overtime, can't we rethink the number of posts that will be lost?" Or "If we improve the way that we and the production people work together, can't we put the proposed reorganization on the back-burner?" In whatever ways the questions might be formulated, the general strategy is to try to reverse the decision, minimize its adverse effects on the individual (or wider group), or otherwise buy time in the hope that something else might turn up.

Although bargaining is still motivated primarily by a desire to hang on to things, rather than to face the future, it nevertheless represents an important first step in the process of letting go. Bargaining is about give and take. And any move in this direction is recognition by the individual – however tentative – that something will have to be given up and some movement made to accommodate the proposed changes. The purpose of a leader's conversations here will be twofold. First, they need to take the sting out of the individual's challenge and to cool their emotions.

Secondly, they need to pay attention to the substance of the individual's argument, which may have merit beyond its emotional release (Box 6.2).

---

**Box 6.2 – Rethinking resistance**

From a conventional management mindset, resistance is "bad." It gets in the way of management's intentions and slows down the change process. If the managers who are faced by this resistance already have low expectations of other people's willingness and ability to contribute, this will serve as confirmatory evidence. However, as we have seen above, resistance is a natural reaction to the impact of change on our personal frame of reference, not a sign of poor attitude or lack of team spirit and so on. In brief, resistance:

- is a way that people try to protect their self-integrity (challenges to their personal frame of reference);
- is the first phase of the process along the way to embracing the change;
- surfaces potential drawbacks in the existing proposals and/or scope for improvement that might have been overlooked; and
- points to a potential source of energy that can be worked with and redirected in organizationally constructive ways.

When managers are asked to reflect on how they would feel if no resistance was expressed to proposed changes, they usually surprise themselves by stating that they would not be at all comfortable with that reaction. They intuitively feel that resistance would still exist but that, in such circumstances, it would be happening below the surface, in the shadow side of the organization. In contrast, when resistance manifests itself in the various ways that we have discussed, and as these are dealt with effectively through the relevant conversations, this suggests that genuine change is taking place and meaningful progress is being made toward full engagement.

---

On some occasions, as a result of the "bargaining" conversations, there might be an unexpected breakthrough. In those cases, the conversations help to reframe the situation in a way that causes the individual to move directly into the positive–active quadrant. We referred to this in

Figure 6.2 as the "conversion path." This represents a discontinuous leap from Position 3 in Figure 6.4 (bargaining) directly to Position 6 (embracing). In direct contrast to this is the situation in which it becomes clear to an individual that the future as laid out before them is not one that they wish to be part of. In that case, they might choose to leave the organization – or be asked to do so. Position 7 on the matrix, labeled "opting out," represents this situation. Usually, though, the route from Position 3 (bargaining) will be to Position 4 (acquiescing).

*Acquiescing*

The cluster of behaviors that are referred to here as "acquiescing" represents the natural point of transition from a person's preoccupation with the past to a willingness to let go of this and face the future. The term embraces *both* the negatively biased notion of "giving in" *and* the more positively focused idea of "acceptance."

In its negative expression, acquiescence reflects a sense of reluctantly giving in to the inevitability of a particular change. It represents the emotional low point of the transition process, in which it becomes clear to an individual that those things that they were clinging on to will indeed be lost. For some, this can be a depressing experience. Hopefully, though, the negative feelings that accompany it will neither last too long nor become too overwhelming. Individuals in this state will "rejoin" the constituency of people who reside in the negative–passive quadrant of the coalition-building matrix – albeit in a different place emotionally. Recognizing the heterogeneous mix of people in this quadrant is therefore important, if their diverse needs are to be dealt with satisfactorily. For some of the people who have reached this acquiescing stage, their temporary excursion into the negative–active quadrant will have been brief and inconsequential. For others, they will have returned "battered and bruised" by their experience.

If individuals here can be coaxed (or coached) through any feelings of loss that they might be experiencing, the notion of acquiescing to the change can then be cast in a more positive light. Negative emotions can give way to muted acceptance of the change. Earlier, I likened the transition process to one in which a trapeze artist flies through the air from one swing to another. Continuing with this metaphor, people who have reached this point in their personal transition will have successfully made the leap to the new trapeze but will be barely holding onto it with the tips of their fingers. Despite this less-than-secure attachment to the future, reaching this point represents a very important step in the overall process.

### Confirming

Having made the transition from resistance (Positions 1–3) to acceptance (Position 4), the psychological and emotional needs change. There is now a desire to seek tangible confirmation of the "rightness" of the decision and of the seriousness with which the change rhetoric is being carried through in practice. This cluster of behaviors is referred to here as the "confirming" response (Position 5).

Confirming-behaviors include those designed to test out the new arrangements, as these are introduced. This might involve taking some tentative first steps and seeking to learn from the feedback that these provide. The desire for confirmation may also be strong in situations where scepticism is running high amongst people because of their experience of past changes that have failed to deliver. This need will also be apparent where people fail to engage fully with the changes because these lack a sense of meaning for them. As appropriate, conversations here will aim to encourage and support people's efforts to make progress; help them to gain personal meaning from the changes; and draw attention to tangible signs of progress.

### Embracing

The positive–active quadrant represents the leader's desired destination for most – if not all – of their team. The goal here is to build a constituency of people who actively and enthusiastically "embrace" the changes (Position 6). They do this because the nature and intended outcomes of these resonate with their personal aims and aspirations. When this position is reached, people will readily integrate the new ways of thinking and acting into their everyday behaviors.

At this stage, conversations can begin to challenge and stretch people much more deliberately in line with their growing confidence and competence, whilst continuing to provide support. At an appropriate time too, it can be useful to take time out to reflect on individuals' successful navigation of the change process. This can be helpful in reaffirming their ability to handle change successfully; and it can increase their resilience to continuing change.

*Positively perceived change (and opting out – again!)*

So far, we have discussed the transition process, and the emotional roller coaster that accompanies it, from the perspective of a negatively perceived change. In these circumstances, the "entry" point is via the "avoiding" behaviors at Position 1. The typical pattern of response then follows that which we have discussed in the previous paragraphs. However, as we recognized when discussing the basic coalition-building matrix in Figure 6.2, some people will perceive the change as positive from the outset. This may be because they have been involved in its initiation. Alternatively, they might view the change as a personal opportunity rather than as a threat.

In these cases, since the change is viewed positively straightaway, the "entry" point is most likely to be directly at Position 6 – embracing the change from the off. It might seem pointless then to think of this in terms of the transition process at all. However, as experience shows and research by Conner (1993) confirms, changes that are initially welcomed always carry with them unexpected negative effects that threaten to undermine the initial optimism. If people persist with the change, it is equally likely that unforeseen benefits will emerge that negate these disappointments and lead to the sought-after positive outcome. However, Conner shows that failure to anticipate and deal with the initial setbacks can cause people to "check out" from the process. Position 7 in the coalition-building matrix ("opting out") captures this condition. Conner points out that this can be expressed either publicly or privately. In organizational terms, a person opts out publicly if they leave their job altogether. Opting out in private, on the other hand, means staying at work but contributing the minimum necessary to get by.

It is critical for leaders to remain alert to these possibilities. They need to take steps to ensure that those populating the positive–active quadrant feel confident enough to raise any concerns that might arise. A lot of talent can be lost, and energy dissipated, if leaders fail to engage with this typical pattern of response to positively perceived change. Because the essence of this quadrant is positivity, it is also important to make it clear that there is no stigma involved in raising issues and identifying problems. Besides avoiding the unnecessary loss of high performers, creating a safe space for these seemingly "negative" issues to be raised can enhance learning and provide positive benefits over the longer term. At times, the most positive thing that a person can do is to express their concerns about aspects of the organization or their own engagement with it. Managers who suppress these feelings, and insist on maintaining a positive façade at all times, do themselves – and their staff – a disservice. They also undermine the longer-term ability of their organizations to learn, change and perform successfully.

## And finally ...

Remember! Coalitional activity will happen anyway. The only choice that a leader has is whether or not to engage with it purposefully and in an informed way.

# CHAPTER 7

# Embracing paradox

> Paradox . . . cannot be resolved or harmonised, only endlessly transformed.
>
> – Ralph Stacey

## Introduction

"We all believe in team working *but* . . ." was how Gareth Morgan introduced the notion of paradox in organizations, during a workshop on organizational dynamics that I attended in 1997. This provocation, and the conversations that it sparked, echoed my long-held view that an either–or mindset dominates management thinking and distorts much of its practice. Of course team working is important. An excessive emphasis on individual performance can be divisive and lead to sub-optimal performance. *At the same time, though*, an excessive emphasis on team working can be equally dysfunctional. For a start, it can lead to "group think" and the obsessive pursuit of lowest-common-denominator consensus. Failing to foster individual excellence can also undermine motivation, stifle initiative and blunt an organization's competitive edge. Managers therefore need to encourage, support and enable *both* collaborative team performance *and, at the same time*, individual excellence – even though the conditions for achieving these pull in opposite directions. The example used by Morgan reflects just one of countless situations in which managers are torn between two contending courses of action, both of which have merit but which – like team working and individuality – appear unable to co-exist. We will look at others below.

Paradox is endemic in organizations. Properly understood, it is the source of peak performance and creativity. Most managers, though, see the tensions inherent in paradox as disruptive to the normal flow of management. Attempts are usually made to design these out through so-called "rational," either–or type thinking. Indeed, conventional, "keep it simple" wisdom would see the removal of these tensions as a key purpose of management. As a result, managers often seem content to ride the organizational equivalent of the "Big Dipper." They shift their strategies and structures back and forth, for example, between centralization and decentralization, control and empowerment, diversification and divestment, growth and downsizing, team working and individuality and so on. This has become so much a taken-for-granted aspect of organizational life that the underlying assumptions on which this constant restructuring and upheaval is based are rarely, if ever, questioned. Helping organizations to escape from these well-established patterns of thinking and behavior provides a continuing, if sometimes frustrating, challenge. Crucially, when dealing with paradox, the still dominant either–or mindset wastes much of an organization's knowledge, energy and resources. It fuels the polarized position-taking that managers constantly complain about; and it can readily result in a climate of clash and confrontation – whether this is overtly expressed or remains in the shadows.

The *informal coalitions* perspective of organizational dynamics calls on leaders to develop a more enlightened view of organizational paradox. First, such a view draws on the positive aspects of contending ideas, perspectives and values (such as "non-team" working, in Morgan's example above). Secondly, it acknowledges the potentially negative aspects of what are otherwise well-intended policy shifts and seemingly common-sense actions. Embracing paradox in this way needs to become a fundamental component of organizational leadership. Otherwise, leaders' normal patterns of perception, language and behavior will hold sway, and they will remain oblivious to paradox's existence, impact and potential power. This element of the developing leadership agenda seeks to raise awareness of this role and to offer practical tools for engaging with it.

## The nature of paradox in organizations

When viewing leadership and organizational dynamics from an *informal coalitions* perspective it is important to recognize that organizational life – and life in general – is paradoxical. The essential elements of a paradox are the *simultaneous presence* of conditions that are self-contradictory and apparently mutually exclusive. In this Chapter, we will look at three of the most important ways in which paradox affects the dynamics of organizations. These are:

1  The *Leadership* Paradox, in which leaders are *both* "in control" of their organizations *and* "not in control" of them *at the same time*.
2  The *Performance* Paradoxes, which refer to the strategic tensions that must be managed continuously and dynamically, if organizations are to perform effectively in the here and now and, *at the same time*, to sustain and develop their performance into the future.
3  *Organizational* Paradoxes, which relate to the everyday tensions and contradictions that characterize life in all organizations. These also need to be managed dynamically rather than being thought of as problems to be solved in a once-and-for-all way.

The aim is to embrace the contradictions that arise and, in Morgan's terms, to make them "livable." Before addressing each of these categories in turn, though, it is important to reflect on why embracing paradox is not common management practice – and why it is important that it should be.

## Why embracing paradox is not commonplace

Why do organizations find it difficult to embrace paradox as a legitimate part of management thinking and practice? Amongst the reasons for this are the following:

- the attraction of either or thinking and the sense of being "in control" that this brings;
- the seductive nature of moving *from* something *to* something else, which promises to be better in some desired way;
- the lack of practical frameworks or tools to support the more expansive thinking that is required.

These reasons are explored briefly below.

## The attraction of either–or thinking and being in control

Either–or thinking has been part of our (essentially "Western") mindset and cultural heritage for thousands of years. It retains a powerful grip today because, amongst other things:

- it is *easier* to take an either–or decision, which appears to resolve the tension, rather than to struggle with the contradictions and ambiguities inherent in paradox;

- it is *quicker* and seemingly more in tune with the increasing pressures to make quick, "action-oriented" decisions;
- it gives the *impression of decisiveness* and *being in control* rather than risking being seen as indecisive and equivocal;
- in the UK, polarized, either–or, "black and white" thinking and action is *embedded* and reinforced by the structural and behavioral patterns that govern many of its national institutions, such as Government and Opposition, Prosecution and Defence, Management and Worker, and so on.

The penultimate point in particular recognizes the dominant managerial paradigm. Being (or appearing to be) "in control" is a powerful driving force behind many leaders' actions. The ambiguities, uncertainties and general "messiness" of being *both* "in control" *and, at the same time,* "not in control" (the Leadership Paradox) can cause anxiety, confusion and self-doubt. Appearing to "act decisively," by choosing between possible ways forward that appear to be mutually exclusive, then becomes a much more attractive option.

## The seductive nature of "from–to"

Closely aligned to either–or thinking is the tendency of many management theorists and writers to advocate moving "from" a particular state or set of characteristics "to" another, seemingly more desirable one. A prime example of this, which has exercised many managers' minds over recent years and generated considerable work for consultants, is the debate about leadership *versus* management. Bennis (1989) talks about the need for those people running organizations to move *from* being managers *to* being leaders. He then contrasts managers and leaders in an Orwellian, "four legs good, two legs bad" sort or way. As a preface to a list of "bad" (manager) and "good" (leader) traits, he writes (p. 44):

> I tend to think of the differences between leaders and managers as the differences between those who master the context and those who surrender to it.

Bennis's primary aim is to emphasize the positive aspects of the routes to improved performance that he is prescribing. Unfortunately, in framing his arguments in "from–to" terms, he both denies the potentially positive characteristics of management and, similarly, ignores the potential for those characteristics he identifies with leadership to generate negative outcomes. To take just one example from Bennis's list, he argues (p. 45) that ". . . the manager administers, the leader innovates." I would argue that leaders need to ensure *both* that their organizations are well administered *and* that they are innovative. Organizations that fail on the first count (with Enron and Barings Bank being recent, high profile examples) cannot be considered to have been well *led* simply because they had a reputation for innovation. Effective leadership demands *both* the disciplined, process-oriented and competence-based approach of a well administered organization (a focus on discipline) *and, at the same time,* the constant search to discover innovative new ways to add value (a focus on discovery). The essence of leadership, in this regard, is twofold:

- to help people to see the *inevitable and irreconcilable* tensions that this generates as symptoms of normality and vitality, rather than abnormality and incompetence; and
- to stimulate the organization to use these tensions as the source of creativity and dynamic, energizing, soul-*ful* working.

In contrast to Bennis, Quinn (1988) talks about moving *beyond* rational management, to a position that recognizes the tensions, ambiguities and *a*-rational dynamics of organizations. As he points out, the phrase "moving beyond" accepts the validity of the existing frame (as in Bennis's conception of management, for instance) but recognizes a more embracing perspective, *of which the former framework is part.* This notion of "moving beyond" more accurately captures the essence of what we are trying to achieve when we talk about embracing paradox and making it livable for people.

## Lack of appropriate concepts, tools and techniques

Finally, even if people recognize the importance of adopting other than an either–or response to a paradoxical situation, they may lack the concepts, tools and techniques to deal with the issue confidently and effectively. Thankfully, a number of practical methodologies are available that can enable managers to get to grips with the challenges that paradox brings. We will look at some of these as we progress through this chapter.

## Why embracing paradox is important

The leadership demands presented by organizational paradox are necessarily more challenging than those that managers face when opting for
a simple, either–or choice. It is therefore important to answer the question that might reasonably be raised as to why embracing paradox is an
essential part of transforming leadership. Three particular aspects of this
are set out below.

### The value of conflict and contention

In one sense, all paradoxes are about conflict. By definition, they arise
from the tension that exists when opposing and seemingly irreconcilable
positions are brought together in an attempt to co-exist. In all instances,
the conflict has an intellectual component – it reflects a clash of ideas.
But, in many cases, this conflict will be underpinned and fueled by the
emotional commitment of people to one side of the paradox or the other.
Being able to deal effectively with the paradox in these circumstances is
crucial to a sustainable outcome.

### Avoiding waste, active resistance and apathy

Effectively managing these *structurally embedded* paradoxes enables
an organization's energy, inventiveness and expertise to be harnessed
and applied constructively. The alternative is for it to be wasted in the
advocacy and defense of opposing viewpoints, turned into active resistance or simply dissipated through apathy and frustration. In Chapter 5,
we explored a brief case study that identified the tensions that existed
between a Business Development Department and Service Delivery Unit.
This illustrated how these tensions, if not managed effectively, can readily
degenerate into negative political game playing.

### The metaphorical "soul" of the organization

In viewing organizations as networks of conversations between people,
I would contend that the metaphorical "soul" of an organization resides
within the contradictions that exist within it and the ways that these are
dealt with through the everyday conversational life of its members. This

can be an uncomfortable idea for those who see organizations in purely mechanistic (structure, system and process) terms. For them, emotion and spirit (heart and soul) are relegated to the "back of the grid" or not worthy of consideration at all. Sadly though, unremittingly monotonous, soul-destroying work, and soul-*less* organizations that lack the humanizing qualities of meaning, dignity, self-worth and mutual respect appear to be all too commonplace.

The aim instead must be to create soul-*ful* organizations, which tap into people's deepest thoughts and feelings, fire their imagination and inspire their commitment. Much of what management does according to current wisdom, such as the single-minded pursuit of "maximizing shareholder value," denies the validity of other deeply held, and potentially highly motivating, values. This often rides roughshod over the desires of those who are actually charged with delivering organizational performance. "Leading with soul," on the other hand, requires managers to acknowledge, respect, *accept the challenge of, and learn from* individuals' deeply held values, aspirations and concerns. This means working with the paradoxes that these give rise to – putting shareholders (or customers) first by putting them second, so to speak. It also means allowing people to find resonance with competing values in their own ways, rather than seeking to impose the "right," one-size-fits-all solution.

## Meeting the challenge

Before introducing some practical tools for dealing with paradox, it is important to stress that the intention is not to see these as a way of resolving or eliminating paradox in some way. As suggested earlier, the *informal coalitions* perspective sees paradox as endemic. The task of management is then one of "continually rearranging" the paradoxes, as Stacey puts it in the opening quotation, not seeking to do away with them in some way or other.

One heavyweight challenge to this line of thinking is worth addressing before moving on. In their well-known text on business strategy, Hamel and Prahalad (1994: 294) recognize the futility of simply moving from one organizational philosophy to its opposite. However, they equally dismiss "... the need to manage tensions, trade-offs, paradoxes and contradictions." They argue instead for these contending perspectives to be synthesized into something new. As an example, they propose that a centralized approach should not be replaced by its antithesis, decentralization, but by what they call a "collective" approach. Similarly, they synthesize the opposites of bureaucracy and empowerment into what they claim to be the enlarged perspective of a "directed" organization. The problem with this approach, from our viewpoint, is that it represents a much more static view of organizational dynamics than that which we are considering here. Paradoxes are not only endemic; they are also dynamic. The inherent tensions that these paradoxes give rise to cannot be resolved in the once-and-for-all way that Hamel and Prahalad imply. We can illustrate this by using the two examples identified above. Managers who embrace paradox in the way we are advocating would be much more likely to describe these contrasting philosophies in terms such as "centralized decentralization" and "empowered bureaucracy," rather than in the way advocated by Hamel and Prahalad. Both of these oxymorons retain the sense of dynamism and simultaneity that are essential to an *informal coalitions* understanding of paradox.

## A practical toolkit

Against this background, the following paragraphs introduce some of the approaches that can be used to get to grips with paradox and to build paradoxical thinking into everyday sensemaking and decision taking. In all cases, the tools are included here as ways of stimulating meaningful and useful conversations about the specific issues being considered. They are not meant to provide an analytical alternative to normal sensemaking and use-making conversations.

## The leadership paradox

In Chapter 2, I introduced what might be thought of as the core paradox of organizations, when viewing these from an *informal coalitions* perspective. I called this the Leadership Paradox, in which managers are *both* "in control" of their organizations *and* "not in control" of them *at the same time*. Streatfield (2001), writing from a complexity perspective, refers to this as the "paradox of control."

On the one hand, managers have significant power and authority to decide how they wish to manage the rational aspects of organizational performance and to lead the change process. They do this by using a mix of *management edict*, *education and training* and *joint problem solving* approaches. Subject only to the need to adhere to agreed procedures, they also have the power to impose specific changes in structures, systems and processes. From this conventional perspective, managers are clearly in control. On the other hand, they are not in control – *and cannot be in control* – of the myriad of informal coalitional activity that surrounds these decisions. It is these *a*-rational dynamics that shape the longer-term effects of such decisions on organizational outcomes. For example, the formal aspects of mergers and acquisitions are usually managed thoroughly and expertly. These are typically accompanied by extensive due-diligence activities and guided by cohorts of expert advisors. However, the integration process is not confined to these visible, surface-level activities. Hidden, messy and informal processes within the participating organizations always accompany the formal activities and exchanges. And it is these underlying dynamics that will have the biggest impact on the ultimate success or failure of the enterprise.

The leadership agenda, set out in Chapters 3 through 8, is designed to enable leaders to embrace this core paradox and to manage their way through the ambiguities, tensions and unknowable outcomes that arise from it. As such, I don't intend to explore this paradox much further within the confines of this chapter. Nevertheless, recognizing and embracing this phenomenon is fundamental to an understanding of the dynamics of *informal coalitions* and of the leadership implications that flow from them.

The Leadership Paradox sets an important challenge for leaders, which many of them feel anxious about when they first come face to face with it. In a typical conversation around the dynamics of organizational change, managers will quickly and easily come to the conclusion that *informal coalitions* have a significant impact upon the process, outcomes and ultimate success of organizational change. When, though, they realize that they are not in control of these dynamics, they often feel much less comfortable with the idea. When I ask them how they feel about the fact that, as leaders, they cannot control informal coalitional activity, they usually express a range of emotions from unease to anxiety. So far, I've not encountered hostility to the idea; but the challenge that this makes to established wisdom on leadership and control means that such a reaction can't be too far away! Most of us have been brought up in an organizational world in which leadership and control are seen as inseparable. Put simply, if you're not in control, you're not leading effectively. The thought of "relinquishing" this felt sense of control is not an attractive one to many managers. However, they are not actually giving anything up at all. The original feeling of control was itself illusory.

A critical point to recognize here is that the dynamics of *informal coalitions* don't provide an alternative way of managing to command and control. They co-exist with it. The "commanders and controllers" of this world are themselves active participants in the self-organizing processes of interaction within their organizations and beyond. Their inputs to these interactions may well be conditioned by their command-and-control mindset; but the outcomes will be no less subject to the principles and processes of emergence, self-organization and co-creation than if they were unconditional disciples of *informal coalitions*. Interestingly, these managers will often see the unexpected consequences as evidence of poor implementation, rather than as the inevitable outcome of informal coalitional activity.

It is not credible for managers simply to reject the idea of not being in control. Denying the existence of these dynamics, or holding on to the "do it better and get it right" mantra of the rational school of change management that we explored in Chapter 2, will not make them go away. Instead, their aim should be to work to overcome the anxiety of being *both* in control *and* not in control *at the same time*. This means working to understand the informal coalitional interactions that are generating and sustaining these dynamics, and actively engaging with them. Streatfield (2001) argues that it is this capacity to participate creatively, *in spite of not being in control*, that constitutes effective management.

## The performance paradoxes

The Performance Paradoxes arise from the underlying, structural tensions that are embedded in all organizations and which we touched upon earlier. As illustrated in Figure 7.1, there are two fundamentally conflicting demands that impact upon all aspects of organizational performance.

The first of these is the tension that exists between the need to focus on current performance *and, at the same time*, to address future performance needs. Second is the tension that exists between the external and internal pulls on the organization. The latter reflects, for example, the need to anticipate and respond flexibly to the diverse needs of the market and wider environment (outside in) *and, at the same time*, to make full use of the organization's particular capabilities and distinct competencies (inside out).

Moving beyond these basic current–future and internal–external perspectives, each of the four quadrants of the resulting framework reflects a pull in a particular strategic direction, as shown in Figure 7.2.

*Discipline* (internal/current focus) is about adopting a disciplined, process-oriented and competence-based approach. It focuses on such

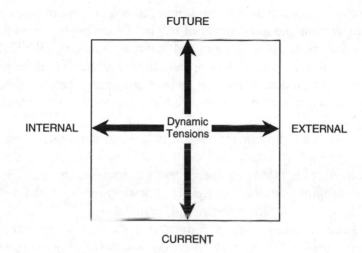

**Figure 7.1** The core performance dimensions

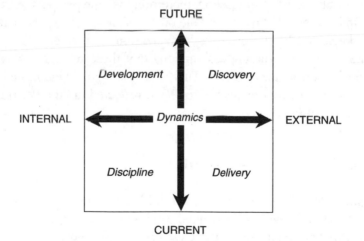

**Figure 7.2** Emphasis of each quadrant

aspects of performance as consistency, conformity, standards and constraints. *Delivery* (external/current) is about delivering commitments to customers and value to the organization. It looks to ensure goal clarity, task achievement and the delivery of results. *Discovery* (external/future) is about discovering new ways to add value, by focusing on creativity, innovation and exploration. *Development* (internal/future) is about people and organizational development. It focuses on people, their relationships and the organizational enablers that facilitate effective performance and personal well-being.

As before, opposite dimensions are in tension with each other, that is *discipline and discovery*, and *delivery and development*. Leadership is concerned with managing these strategic tensions dynamically and actively engaging with the underlying, cultural *dynamics* of the organization. The overall picture is shown in Figure 7.3.

The strategic dimensions of performance set out in the four quadrants above (discipline, delivery, discovery and development) echo those in Quinn's (1988) Competing Values Framework. This identifies four competing and contrasting, yet complementary, sets of values that are considered to shape organizational performance. Quinn has derived these from research that identified four schools of managerial thought, arrayed around his model. Within this, he sees the ability to manage the paradoxes that these give rise to as the essence of peak performance and mastery of management. He is not suggesting, therefore, that one perspective is arbitrarily and universally "right" and the others wrong. All four perspectives are important to the success of an organization over time. Quinn argues that the values, criteria and assumptions that these represent only exist as opposites in people's minds. This is the view of paradox embodied in the *informal coalitions* perspective, and reflected in "the Performance Paradoxes" outlined above.

## Beyond the balanced scorecard

Ever since Peter Drucker introduced the idea of management by objectives over 50 years ago, in his seminal work *The Practice of Management*, managers have sought to establish clear links between performance measures at successive levels of their organizations. The popular Balanced Scorecard approach, introduced in the mid-1990s (Kaplan and Norton, 1996) has continued the quest for this "Holy Grail" of effective performance management. Despite this desire to make performance management

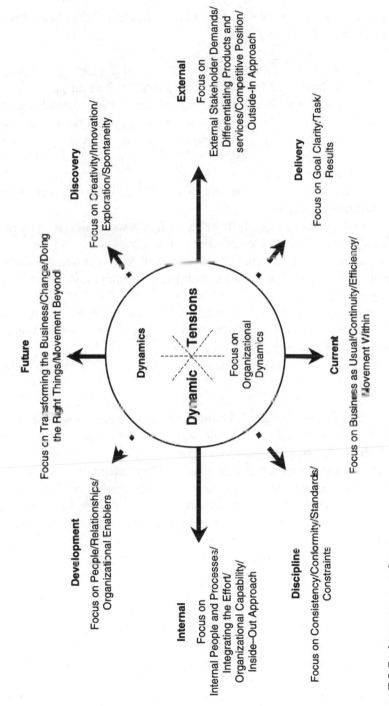

**Figure 7.3** Performance paradoxes

work, results from these conventional approaches have often been disappointing. Typical concerns include:

- the rigidity of many of the approaches and resulting lack of flexibility to deal with changing circumstances and emerging events;
- the bureaucracy associated with many of the systems, which causes managers and others to drown in a sea of paperwork, rather than allowing them to focus upon critical performance issues;
- the seemingly impossible task of establishing meaningful and useful links between individual goals and the overall performance of the organization, especially where events are changing rapidly and priorities shifting constantly;
- the tendency to focus role descriptions on inputs (activities to be carried out) rather than outputs (contributions to be made);
- the ritualistic nature of many assessment and review processes, rather than these being used to encourage and enable open dialogue between managers and staff;
- the arbitrarily selective nature of many of the frameworks, in relation to the factors that are measured – often with ease of measurability taking precedence over strategic importance;
- the low impact on actual performance that many of these approaches seem to have.

Most significantly, Kaplan and Norton identify linear, cause-and-effect links between the elements of their scorecard. This takes little or no account of the messy and paradoxical nature of organizations that the *informal coalitions* perspective exposes. They maintain instead that organizational learning improves those internal processes that deliver value to customers, and that this in turn leads to enhanced financial performance. This cause-and-effect argument fits well with established wisdom and seems like common sense. But it is a version of common sense that still sees the business world as ordered, predictable and ultimately controllable.

An *informal coalitions* view of organizational dynamics suggests that managers need to move beyond this seductive but overly simplistic view of strategic management. They need to readdress their fundamental beliefs about what it means to "manage performance" in a complex, paradoxical and constantly changing world. In doing this, emphasis should be placed firmly on performance *management* ahead of performance *measurement*. In this respect, the use of the term "scorecard," whilst popular and memorable, perhaps directs attention too much toward measurement and upward reporting, rather than to the thinking and action needed to enable staff to deliver improved performance "on the ground." It is also worth recalling that Drucker (1968: 167) described his original philosophy as one of "... management by objectives and self-control." He explained this (in paradoxical terms!) as giving "... full scope to individual strength and responsibility, and at the same time... common direction of vision and effort... " It is regrettable that the emphasis he placed on *self*-control has been lost in most of the performance-management schemes that have flowed from it.

## The performance management framework

The Performance Management Framework, shown in Figure 7.4, is designed to provide a coherent approach to managing performance under the conditions set out above. It emphasizes the need both to achieve current performance objectives and, at the same time, to address (current perceptions of) future challenges. It also looks at internal capability issues together with the crucial impact that external stakeholders have on an

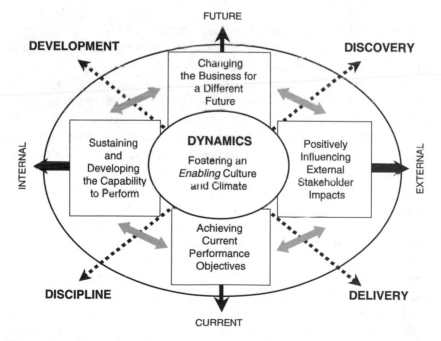

**Figure 7.4** The performance management framework

organization's performance and development. Finally, it highlights the importance to an organization's success of understanding and engaging with the underlying dynamics of organizational performance, including managing the embedded structural tensions (discipline–discovery and delivery–development). Conversations relating to each element of the framework also need to take account of the wider context of the organization and its relationships.

## The components of the framework

An organization needs to achieve its *current performance* objectives effectively, efficiently and economically. This element is typically concerned with service delivery, commercial performance and compliance. *Changing the business* for a different future is about anticipating and responding to changes in the organization's environment, identifying and realizing new opportunities, adopting new perspectives, and adapting the organization to embrace the emerging challenges. Sustaining and developing the *capability* to perform includes issues such as resourcing (people, finance, plant and equipment, tools and materials), employee capability and development, process design and improvement, technological development, the structural aspects of knowledge management and intellectual capital, systems enhancement, and relevant aspects of risk management. The crucial impact that the decisions and actions of *external stakeholders* have on an organization's ability to perform and change is dealt with through the external stakeholder dimension.

Finally, leaders within high-performing organizations use their everyday informal interactions and role-modeling behaviors to foster *cultural patterns* that enable performance to be achieved in all four of the above dimensions. Within this, they work to create a climate in which people have the motive, means and opportunity to excel. This "center box" differs from the outer four in both concept and content. It overlaps them to emphasize that decisions cannot be made (or left unmade) in any of the other areas without these having cultural implications. The framework aims to encourage managers to view the organization through a "culture and climate lens," as they shape the content of the outer four boxes and enact these through their day-to-day decisions and behaviors. The model reflects the *informal coalitions* view that cultural patterns emerge from the organization's day-to-day decision-making and actions – and, in particular, from the sense that people make of these through their everyday conversations. In turn, the cultural assumptions that become embedded through this sensemaking process have a major and continuing impact on organizational decision-making, capability and performance. So efforts in the other four boxes will inevitably be undermined if the organization fails to deal with these effectively.

*Embracing the paradoxes*

The framework is built around the performance paradoxes outlined above, which affect the underlying dynamics of all organizations. As we have seen, these paradoxes embody the tensions that arise from the interplay of:

- *current* performance ("doing things right") **and** *future* changes ("doing the right things");
- the integration, development and renewal of *internal* capabilities **and** continuing adaptation to *external* demands;
- the need to maintain process and procedural *discipline* **and** to create the freedoms necessary to promote the *discovery* of new ways to add value;
- the importance of achieving task-focused *delivery* **and** of investing in people and organizational *development*.

In addition, the framework makes explicit the tensions that exist between:

- the *alignment* of the intellectual and structural aspects of performance (the outer four boxes), and the emotional and spiritual *attunement* of the organization (the center box) – that is, metaphorically speaking, between its "mind and body" and its "heart and soul."

Overall, it calls upon decision-makers to manage, dynamically and creatively, the contradictions and inconsistencies that the structurally embedded paradoxes generate. For example, organizations too often focus on the efficient delivery of short-term results, at the expense of long-term effectiveness and viability. Or they seek to shape the perceptions of key external stakeholder groups (such as potential investors and City Analysts) about the primacy of "shareholder value" in their thinking; whilst undermining the organization's capability to sustain this performance in the long term, through numbers-driven "downsizing" and similar actions. Then again – and despite ample evidence to the contrary – managers too often seem to view "restructuring" as a cure-all. As a result, they assume that it is sufficient to redesign and re-people structures without the need to attend to the underlying dynamics and vitality of the organization.

*Linkages*

As indicated by the linkages between the four outer boxes in the framework, these need to be considered as an integrated whole, not in isolation from each other. A couple of simple examples may illustrate the point:

- Consistent achievement of current performance objectives will positively influence external stakeholders' perceptions of the business (such as those of customers, investors and regulators, etc.).
- The organization's reputation with key external stakeholders will either enable or constrain its ability to change its business in the ways it might wish to.
- Intended shifts in strategic direction (changing the business) will impact upon the capabilities that need to be developed; and, in turn, existing capabilities will either open up or constrain strategic options.
- Whilst the impact of existing capabilities on the achievement or otherwise of current performance objectives is clear to see, actual performance – good or bad – could enhance capabilities if lessons are learnt and this knowledge shared.

The components of performance identified in the outer four boxes and the cultural implications of decisions (center box) also need to be considered *as part of current decision-making*. Decisions taken to deal with "top box" issues (changing the business) will have consequences for each of the other boxes *today*; and these cannot be "frozen" for consideration and action at some future date. Similarly, "tomorrow's" current performance will largely be determined by decisions taken – or not taken – today.

*Using the performance management framework*

Against this background, the Performance Management Framework can be used to provoke and facilitate conversations designed to:

- assess the performance commitments and emerging challenges facing an organization, as the basis for developing and implementing its business strategies and development programs;
- understand the strategic focus that an organization might wish to adopt and to explore the tensions that this is likely to generate in aspects of its performance and capability;
- agree the specific contributions that teams and individuals need to make to the organization's objectives and track progress against them;

- provide a simple but comprehensive "agenda" for performance-management discussions between managers/team leaders and staff;
- highlight key strategic and organizational aspects of, for example, mergers and acquisitions; organizational turnaround; risk management; knowledge management; continuous improvement and innovation.

In the context of embracing paradox, the first two bullet points are particularly relevant. These are explored more fully below.

*Business strategy and development programs*
The Performance Management Framework is a particularly powerful tool to use in structured workshop settings (communication mode C2), to facilitate the delivery of an organization's strategic agenda. First of all, it provides a coherent structure to frame the workshop dialogue. It also generates an output on strategic business issues and the cultural aspects of these, which participants can more readily assimilate and share with others. If properly structured, the model also provides a post-workshop framework of key contributions, development objectives and enabling behavioral changes. These can then provide the basis for the ongoing management of the organization or team, and in-depth business planning.

*Strategic focus*
A further layer of understanding can be added to the strategic discussions, by getting managers to reflect upon the current balance of emphasis that they place upon the four strategic dimensions of performance – delivery, discovery, development and discipline – and how they might want these to change. What has come to be known as a "kite diagram" can quickly be drawn, to show the strategic shifts that managers believe are important, if the organization is to deliver its strategic agenda as set out in the framework as a whole. This is illustrated in Figure 7.5.

Usually, the kite diagram that reflects a management group's view of an organization's current state will show a clear emphasis on one or other of the four dimensions; with delivery often "winning out" in commercial organizations that see themselves as competing in tough, commoditized markets.

Their challenge, which will usually emerge in the shape of their "preferred future" kite, is to pay sufficient attention to the internal enablers of competitive success (development and discipline) and to the appropriate level of innovation (discovery) to sustain that success and stay ahead of the game.

When using the tool with the leadership team of a major high street retailer, they initially struggled with their own conclusion that they needed

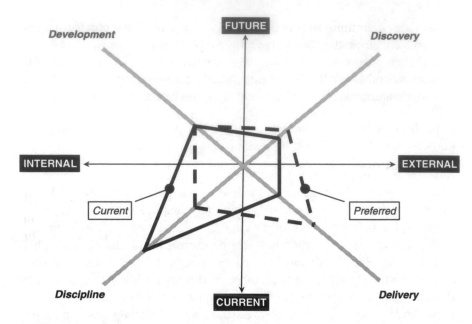

**Figure 7.5** Strategic dimensions ("kite")

to reduce their heavy emphasis on delivery. What they recognized in conversation, though, was that the *way* they were delivering results was, at times, overly aggressive. This single-minded focus on delivery was, paradoxically, undermining the organization's capacity to deliver results in the long term.

Other clients, such as those whose work demands compliance with strict standards of technical performance and rigorously safe work processes, will usually show a heavy bias toward discipline. They face a different challenge. If we are to sleep soundly in our beds at night, they need to maintain this attention to process and procedural discipline in the "mission-critical" areas of their performance. *At the same time*, this necessary aversion to risk taking can easily carry over into other areas of the business. This will often be reflected in bureaucratic procedures and lack of delegation. Where this is the case, the ensuing conversations will often highlight the need to relax this excessive focus on discipline in these subsidiary areas of their business. Reducing the organization's emphasis on discipline is then about freeing up the thinking and action needed to discover new ways to add value (discovery), to enable commercial performance targets to be achieved (delivery), or to make time and space for people's capabilities and continuing well-being to be addressed (development).

The important thing here is not to get too hung up on the precise shapes of the kites or on the "data" that underpins them. What matters most, as has been demonstrated time and again, are the conversations that the diagrams stimulate. This is the case both when drawing the kites in the first place and then in deciding what the leaders themselves might do to stimulate and support movement in the desired direction.

## Organizational paradoxes

As we saw in Chapter 2, there are many examples of paradox in the day-to-day management of organizations, which several writers comment upon. The list below identifies just a few of the everyday tensions or contradictory demands that organizations face:

- innovate – *avoid mistakes*
- increase quality – *minimize costs*
- take time out to develop yourself – *meet deadlines*
- use your initiative – *stick to the rules*
- put the team's interests first – *meet personal targets*
- look for opportunities – *avoid risks*
- play to your strengths – *demonstrate the standard competencies*
- commit to action – *keep options open*
- be yourself – *fit in.*

Employees often experience these conflicting demands in the form of "mixed messages" from management. Ordinarily, the inherent tensions and contradictions are not acknowledged at all in formal statements or presentations. These will rarely – if ever – be presented in the stark way set out above. In a desire to provide clear, unambiguous leadership, and to convey a positive, upbeat message, the *words* managers use in formal arenas will frequently place particular emphasis on the more appealing attribute within each of the above pairs. This is typically the one shown in plain text. In contrast, their *observed actions* are often more faithful to the philosophy and behaviors shown in italics. This perceived failure of managers to practice what they preach can lead to cynicism amongst staff, as they struggle to make sense of these conflicting messages. Almost invariably, as we have seen in our Chapter 4 discussions about *Thinking Culturally*, it is managers' *observed* behaviors and the things that they say informally that have the most symbolic power in the sensemaking process.

## It's difficult to "keep it simple"

Conventional management wisdom places great store in achieving clarity and "keeping it simple." However, the dynamics of organizations are demonstrably more complex than this frequently quoted recipe for success implies. The notion of *informal coalitions* challenges this simplistic view and argues that leaders need to search for the simplicity that exists *at the far side of complexity*. Schutz (1979) describes this as "profound simplicity." That is, they need to understand the complexity thoroughly before they can begin to express this in profoundly simple terms that others will understand and be able to engage with.

The challenge of embracing paradox is to think of each of the above mixed messages as paradoxical pairs of requirements, both of which need to be dealt with *at the same time*. This requires a different approach from that which managers have historically associated with decisiveness and "heroic" leadership behavior. In particular, it suggests that they need to deal openly with the inevitable tensions and ambiguities that are generated, to develop a more creative and authentic outcome than would otherwise be possible. To some managers, this approach will appear messy and indecisive. It is certainly a less comfortable way of managing than one that suppresses disagreement and denies the validity of alternative perspectives. Perhaps, though, it offers a more credible way forward, for the following reasons.

### Too much of a good thing

First, embracing paradox recognizes that any successful policy position or currently positive attribute (such as a key strength or distinctive competence) will, if relied on exclusively, inevitably become dysfunctional and destroy value. For example, Miller (1990) conducted research into the decline of previously successful organizations. He concluded that, when taken to excess, the very factors that drive success could also lead to decline. In other words, an organization's greatest asset can lead to its ultimate downfall. Miller calls this "the Icarus Paradox," after the mythical character that fell to his death when his wings made of wax (strength) melted as he flew ever closer to the sun. Figure 7.6, based on Miller's work, shows the potential cycle of decline that organizations may become drawn into, as their thinking and behaviors are channeled down increasingly narrow paths.

The need to avoid excess is also reflected in the strategic dimensions that form part of the Performance Management Framework we looked at

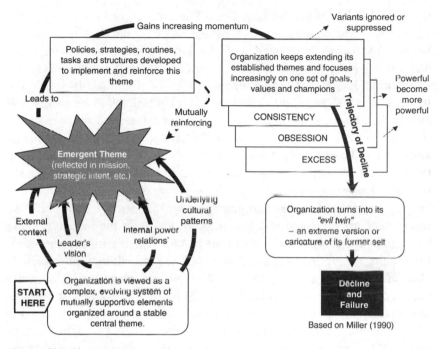

**Figure 7.6** The icarus paradox

earlier. Although delivery, discovery, development and discipline are all attributes of high-performing organizations, it is important to ensure that none of these are pursued to excess. The characteristics that reflect high performance in each of the four dimensions can easily become dysfunctional if any of them become obsessive. For example, goal clarity can turn into an obsession with numbers; innovation for innovation's sake can lead to an ungrounded, head-in-the-clouds approach to business development; collaboration can slip into lack of challenge, and group think; and organizations that believe in high standards can easily become hooked on perfectionism. Leading organizations from this perspective places a premium on the ability to manage these tensions dynamically – handling the contradictions and ambiguities that these generate and remaining alert to any signs of excess.

### Reframing negatives

Allied to this is the need for managers to recognize that seemingly weak policy stances, negative personal attributes and "deviant" behavior can generate value for organizations and individuals, if paradoxical thinking is applied to them. The conventional approach to perceived weaknesses of any kind is to try to eliminate them. Many organizations even use the euphemism "development needs" instead of "weaknesses," to avoid the perceived indignity associated with the latter term. Unfortunately, this places the developmental focus on removing perceived weaknesses rather than exploiting strengths. A similar approach is often used in relation to organizational development, which looks for problems to be solved and gaps to be closed. In contrast, a colleague and I carried out work with a client using an "appreciative inquiry" (AI) approach (see Watkins and Mohr, 2001, for example). Managers initially expressed some skepticism about AI's deliberate use of a positive frame to look at the organization and its apparent downplaying of any negative issues. Whilst accepting the idea of identifying and building upon current strengths and positive experiences, they wanted to know how to deal with the negative views and feelings that they held about important aspects of the organization's current state. Although the standard AI methodology does include ways of handling these negative perceptions, we felt it would be useful to introduce another tool (Paradoxical Thinking, below) to show how apparent negatives could be reframed and used constructively in moving the organization forward. This aspect of the work proved to be very insightful for people. In particular, it highlighted the shared mental patterns that we imperceptibly develop and habitually use as a basis for dealing with the organizational world. We saw in Chapter 4, when we looked at the patterning process involved in the formation of cultural assumptions, that these patterns channel our thinking down familiar pathways. This patterning process not only enables us to operate in culturally acceptable ways; but it also constrains our thinking and action taking. As a result, alternative perspectives are not only ignored but are frequently not seen at all.

When the paradoxical nature of organizations has been recognized, this can often be sufficient to reframe people's perceptions and shift the pattern of organizational conversations. However, there are also a number of tools that can be used to stimulate this reframing and help managers to make sense of everyday organizational paradoxes. A couple of these are described briefly below.

## Paradoxical thinking

Fletcher and Olwyler (1997) introduce a novel approach for facilitating conversations about organizational paradox, which I have found useful in a number of situations. The initial focus of their work was on the high performance of individuals; although they have developed their methodology so that it can also be applied to the performance of groups and organizations. They illustrate the role of paradoxical thinking and behavior in generating high performance through a description of high-performing athletes and other personalities who display paradoxical qualities. Using sprinting as an example, they argue that sprinters run faster if they can remain relaxed while sprinting; that is, they need to develop an ability to exert full power whilst, *at the same time*, demonstrating the apparently contradictory qualities of calmness and relaxation. They go on to make the important point that this is not a compromise position, with the sprinter being half-relaxed and half-sprinting (p. 9):

> This is not a "balance" between relaxation and sprinting. Rather it is a state of running as hard as they can and feeling relaxed, effortless, and flowing while they do.

Fletcher and Olwyler's basic strategy for dealing with paradox is to get the subject to identify what they call their "core paradox," and then to use an expanded version of this to address specific problem situations. This core paradox is an expression of the contradictory aspects of themselves or their group with which they struggle to come to terms. The aim therefore is *not* to deny or eliminate what seem, at first sight, to be negative characteristics; but rather to *reframe* them into their positive expressions. They make the point that people who are peak performers in one sphere of activity often have difficulties in other areas of their life *where these same characteristics are expressed in ways that are perceived by others as negative*. This echoes the work of Peter Drucker (1970: 74), who said that strong people always have strong weaknesses too: "Where there are peaks, there are valleys." An example that I came across when working with one management team concerned the England cricketer Geoff Boycott. Writing in the *Daily Mail* in October 1998, sports columnist Ian Wooldridge argued that Boycott's greatness as an opening batsman was a direct result of the fact that he was, by nature, self-centered and miserly in the way he went about his everyday life. When applied at the batting crease, these otherwise negative characteristics meant that Boycott rarely gave his wicket away cheaply; and this enabled him to build large scores, match after match.

In Fletcher and Olwyler's methodology, the aim is to break out of the narrow confines of the positive and negative judgments that initially accompany the contradictory qualities embodied in the core paradox. To do this, a "high performance" expression of the paradox is developed, by combining the most positive aspects of these contradictory qualities. This is then offset by what Fletcher and Olwyler describe as the "nightmare" position; which is formed by combining the extreme negative expressions of these same contradictory qualities. A judgment is then made about the extent to which current behavior, in dealing with a particular problem, approaches the characteristics of the high-performance end of the scale. Finally, appropriate action steps are put in place to move performance in the desired direction.

To illustrate the technique in practice, the following brief case study describes the use of paradoxical thinking during a strategy workshop held with a specialist commercial team within a FTSE 100 business. Despite the centrality of their knowledge to effective commercial perform-ance within the organization, the team felt that they were failing to influence the decision-making process sufficiently well and sufficiently often.

Having generated a list of positive and negative descriptors of the team – as seen by themselves and others – they settled upon "Peripheral Pivots" as their core paradox. They felt that they were too often seen as peripheral to the action – especially in relation to other parts of the wider commercial team; and yet, they felt that their contribution was pivotal to the continuing success of the organization. As we know, "pivot" is a "central" concept, whereas "peripheral" suggests the very opposite. The normal, problem solving approach would be to work on the perceived weakness, "peripheral" and seek to eliminate or reduce it – choosing "pivot" as the desired characteristic. In contrast, paradoxical thinking sees both attributes as characteristic of the group and seeks instead to express each of these in its most positive form. The group decided that the most positive expression of their core paradox (peripheral pivots) was as "standing-back facilitators." Their more reflective, less action-oriented approach enabled them to take a more considered view of unfolding events and emerging challenges than others in the wider team might be capable of. At the same time, in their high-performance mode, their inputs would facilitate a more rounded and technically sound decision than would otherwise be possible. Using the same core paradox of peripheral pivot, they recognized that each of these characteristics could be expressed and perceived equally well in negative terms. They therefore defined their "nightmare" position as oscillating between being seen as irrelevant (peripheral) or piggies-in-the-middle (pivot): formally positioned at the center of the action but bypassed by all of the other "players." This is summarized in Figure 7.7, below.

After reflecting on the implications of this discussion for key issues that they were facing at the time, the team decided that they were currently seen as being closer to the negative positions in relation to both attributes.

| High-Performance Position (extreme positive expression of both characteristics) | Standing back | Facilitators |
|---|---|---|
| Core Paradox | Peripheral (–ve) | Pivots (+ve) |
| Nightmare Position (extreme negative expression of both characteristics) | Irrelevant | Piggles-in-the-middle |

**Figure 7.7** Paradoxical thinking (example)

Armed with these insights, they were then well placed to decide upon some of the practical steps that they needed to take to move closer to their high-performance position.

The power of this tool is in its treatment of attributes that are ordinarily seen as negative (such as "peripheral"), by recognizing that these can be reframed in positive terms. Similarly, it exposes the fact that fundamentally positive characteristics of individuals, teams and organizations (as with "pivot") can, in certain circumstances, be expressed or perceived in negative ways. For example, when managers are asked to compile a list of characteristics of someone who has been described, say, as an "original thinker," the words that they use are almost entirely positive. These might include, for example, creative, innovative, expressive, opportunity generator, independently minded, intuitive and so on. Similarly, if someone is described as "inflexible," it is likely that this will invoke a list including such characteristics as narrow minded, dogmatic, obstinate, blocker, self-opinionated and so on. Our widely shared patterns of perception see "original thinker" as a positive concept and "inflexible" as negative. Given these simple triggers, our minds follow well-worn mental pathways and fill in the gaps in predictable ways. However, these same managers then surprise themselves when they are asked to identify the potentially negative attributes of an original thinker and the potential positive benefits that could flow from inflexibility. In the former case, their responses might include such characteristics as impractical, out of touch, head in the clouds, dreamer and naïve; whereas someone who was originally dismissed as inflexible might be recast as principled, determined, brave, persistent, acting with conviction and so on.

## Polarity management™

A second tool that I have found very useful in helping organizations to get to grips with organizational paradox is Johnson's notion of polarity management (Johnson, 1999). As with Fletcher and Olwyler's paradoxical thinking, this is a tool that helps people to escape from an either–or, good–bad mindset and to engage in a more expansive conversation about the paradoxical nature of the situations they find themselves in.

Problem solving techniques don't help with everyday organizational paradoxes because those techniques are designed to help people *choose between* competing options. However, as we have said earlier, these paradoxes need to be seen as tensions to be managed dynamically, rather than problems to be solved in a once-and-for-all way. For example, taking the first of the paradoxes from the earlier list, it is not possible to choose between *innovating* and *avoiding mistakes*; organizations need both of these to be pursued *at the same time*. Avoiding mistakes is important, for example, from a service delivery, quality and cost point of view. At the same time, innovation is necessary (whether in processes or products) to stay ahead of the game; even though being innovative means trying new things out and, inevitably, making mistakes along the way!

Polarity management provides a way of confronting these organizational issues that cannot be dealt with in a simple, either–or way. The approach can be used:

- when faced with a known paradoxical situation, to identify and address the competing tensions that exist between the two sides of the paradox;
- to move beyond the polarized position-taking that arises when people hold strong views on either side of an organizational paradox;
- to defuse opposition to a proposed change by recognizing (and seeking to retain) the positive attributes of the existing situation whilst acknowledging (and seeking to minimize) the perceived drawbacks of the proposed way forward.

The technique is illustrated in Figure 7.8. This demonstrates its use in relation to another of the classical paradoxes that leaders face in designing and managing their organizations. That is, the desire to promote individual excellence and, *at the same time*, to ensure that individuals collaborate effectively and put the needs of the team first.

| | Emphasize Individuality | Emphasize Team Working |
|---|---|---|
| +ve | ☐ Self-responsibility<br>☐ Personal drive and initiative<br>☐ Maximizing individual talent<br>☐ Personal accountability<br>☐ Independence/Self-reliance<br>☐ Diversity<br>☐ Multiple perspectives | ☐ Synergies<br>☐ Common direction<br>☐ Mutual support<br>☐ Connectedness (sense of belonging)<br>☐ Peer regulation<br>☐ Resource optimization<br>☐ Exploiting complementary skills |
| –ve | ☐ Duplication<br>☐ Selfishness<br>☐ Lack of cohesion<br>☐ Isolation<br>☐ Sub-optimization<br>☐ Destructive conflict | ☐ Groupthink<br>☐ Blunts individual initiative<br>☐ Excess conformity<br>☐ Loss of individual identity<br>☐ Brake on personal initiative<br>☐ Frustration of personal goals and aspirations |

**Figure 7.8** Polarity management

The resulting grid can be used to stimulate conversations about the tensions inherent in the particular paradox and about strategies for managing these dynamically in ways that:

- recognize and seek to exploit the positive aspects of the competing positions; and
- acknowledge and seek to minimize the potential negatives.

Often, simply raising people's awareness of the competing tensions can be sufficient to make progress. The routine use of the tool can also moderate overly simplistic views of organizational dynamics and dogmatic, "one best way" assertions. When used as a sensemaking tool, it also helps people to recognize that competing (positive and negative) attributes are likely to arise – and remain in tension – as a result of decisions made in relation to all significant aspects of organizational life.

The order in which the boxes are completed is not important. However, if a particularly strong minority view exists, it can be useful to record that first, before completing the grid with the alternative perspective. For example, imagine that there was a proposed move to ensure that the benefits of team working could be fully harnessed, in a situation that had grown to favor individual expression above team working and collaboration. Those resisting this shift would have a view that was shaped primarily by the positive aspects of individuality and the negative aspects of team working (as set out above). Johnson (1999) suggests that completing these two boxes first would acknowledge their "worldview" as valid *but incomplete*. Filling in the two remaining boxes (the downsides of individuality and the potential benefits of team working) would complete the picture and provide the basis for a much more informed conversation about the proposed shift in the way that these tensions were managed. When people's view of the world has been acknowledged, they are often more willing to explore other perspectives than they would have been if the validity of their position had been denied.

## Embracing paradox

In summary, embracing paradox means:

- thriving on the leadership challenge of being both "in control" and "not in control" at the same time;
- dynamically managing the strategic "performance paradoxes," in ways that enhance organizational capability and performance;

and, as a component of everyday leadership:

- recognizing when conversational patterns have become stuck in the rut of either–or, right–wrong thinking;
- exposing the paradoxical tensions and conflicts (in ideas, values or characteristics) and their origins (such as differences of perception, motivation, etc.) that are channeling current conversations in unhelpful ways;
- exploring these differences, using informal dialogue and joint inquiry to move through the inevitable conflicts and anxieties, rather than avoiding or inflaming them;
- using relevant tools, as appropriate, to help to reframe the contradictions and to show where synthesis of the contending viewpoints can enhance, rather than detract from, the performance of the individual, group or organization;
- through this, seeking to transform perceptions of the paradox in ways that enable the inseparability of the two positions to be seen and worked with constructively.

Leadership in the circumstances set out above is not about achieving the one-dimensional, either–or type of clarity that is often associated with so-called "decisive" leadership. The task instead, working from an *informal coalitions* view of organizational dynamics, is to help people to recognize and make sense of the tensions; and to help them to embrace the challenges that these bring. Paradoxical thinking recognizes strengths and weaknesses as two sides of the same coin. Whilst seeking to build on strength, it acknowledges that seemingly positive attributes can also manifest themselves in negative ways. It similarly recognizes that perceived weaknesses can often bring important attributes into play, *provided that* efforts are made to reframe these in positive terms and to act in ways that realize them.

# CHAPTER 8

# Providing vision

> The real voyage of discovery consists not in seeing new land-
> scapes but in having new eyes.
>
> – Marcel Proust

## Vision as a desired end-state

This chapter is deliberately entitled "providing vision" rather than
"providing *a* vision." It is also the final chapter, rather than the first.
Most, if not all, current management practice talks of vision in terms of
a desired end-state or preferred future – *a* vision, with a capital "V."
Often, this is seen as something that must be developed and communicated by the organization's top management (or CEO alone), operating
from a *management edict* and *education and training* mode. For others,
the vision of a preferred future is something to be crafted by members
of the organization as a whole (a *joint problem solving* approach). In
all cases, creating and communicating a vision for the organization is
conventionally seen as one of the first steps in the change process.

Visionary leadership is most readily associated with the first of
the above two images, in which it is seen as in the gift of a visionary
leader or leadership team. Mintzberg (1989: 121) contrasts two such
views of this approach. The first – all too familiar – analogy is of ". . . a
hypodermic needle, in which the active ingredient (vision) is loaded
into a syringe (words) which is injected into the employees to stimulate all kinds of energy." In the second, he cites a colleague's preference for an image of visionary leadership as drama. Here, vision, like
drama, becomes ". . . magical in that moment when fiction and life blend
together." The point of the latter analogy is that, in drama, this moment is
the result of endless rehearsal, combined with the performance itself and
the attendance of the audience. Rather than a clinical process, visionary
leadership is seen here as the more personal investment of a leader in his

or her relationship with their staff and a mutually beneficial future. We shall return to this latter analogy later. For now though, it is important to note that the focus of Mintzberg's discussion remains on creating *a* vision *for* the organization and then communicating it *to* staff.

This is also the approach advocated by Kotter (1995) in his well-known prescription for achieving organizational change. He similarly follows this design-build-and-communicate process. He argues that the leader needs to build a vision to guide the change effort, together with the strategies necessary to achieve it. This forms Step 3 of his eight-step methodology, with Step 4 focusing on the need to communicate the vision to the organization at large "effectively and often." Kotter discusses this process primarily in terms of the formal, structured approach to communication that we labeled as mode C1 in the Leadership Communication Grid. He acknowledges, though, that effective role modeling by those leading the change effort is also important (mode C4).

## Fatal flaw?

From an *informal coalitions* perspective, there is a fatal flaw in the conventional wisdom of seeing vision solely in end-state terms. A vision of this kind is likely to disappoint on one of two counts. At one extreme, it becomes too precisely defined and rigid. This soon falls foul of an everyday organizational world in which much of what happens takes place in the messier landscape that exists far from certainty and far from agreement. Alternatively, in recognition of the uncertainties and complexities within which all organizations operate, the vision is deliberately kept imprecise. This then risks the charge of being operationally inadequate, or of meaning all things to all people.

Here we have another of the paradoxes that characterize organizational life. To make progress, we need to commit resources to particular actions. To do this effectively and efficiently, we need to know precisely what we're trying to achieve. *At the same time*, we need to remain flexible and responsive to emerging events. This means that we don't want to commit resources prematurely to actions that might subsequently prove to be deficient and limit our scope for movement. Commitment calls for clear guidance and detailed roadmaps. Flexibility and responsiveness require a fuzzier and more emergent image of success.

It is therefore extremely difficult to craft and communicate a vision in terms that remain meaningful and compelling in the longer term. This challenge is further compounded where – as with most of us – managers find themselves falling short of the idealized image that others have of leaders as far-sighted, all-seeing visionaries. And none of what we have said so far takes account of the cynicism with which staff often greet a leader's attempt to convey their vision to the organization. This is especially the case where the sentiments it contains bear little resemblance to people's everyday organizational experience.

## The link with planning and goal setting

Eccles and Nohria (1992: 58) offer an important perspective on the notions of forward planning and goal setting that are associated with this end-state view of visioning:

> Rather than expecting our leaders to be clairvoyant about the future [by establishing missions, visions, plans and goals prior to action] we should expect them to be robust actors – actors who are thoughtful historians of the past and creative participators in the present.

They acknowledge that planning and goal setting serve a number of useful functions for leaders, including:

* convincing the outside world of their effective stewardship of the organization;
* helping staff to gain a sense of mastery over their work; and
* enabling people to get to grips with the complex, uncertain and rapidly changing environment.

Importantly, though, they stress that this rhetoric of rationality should not interfere with the way that managers really act. They assert that goals are created by actions that individuals continually reinterpret. That is, goals emerge from individual action ". . . and, in particular, from individual action that mobilizes collective action" (p. 57).

This notion of individual action that mobilizes collective action sits at the heart of the *informal coalitions* approach to change and organizational dynamics. It also accords with Stacey's (2003) view that a central leadership role is to notice, and help to shift, the themes that are organizing conversations in ways that improve, through active participation, the quality of conversational life.

None of this is meant to suggest that leaders should work without ambition, intention and ideals. Nor does it mean that they should keep their ambitions for the organization or team to themselves. Far from it. But, it does mean that vision is as much about *in*sight as far sight. If a leader's individual actions are to mobilize the collective action of others in the organization, these actions need to resonate with people's personal feelings and ambitions. And, for this to happen, individuals need to be able to make credible connections between their personal hopes and experiences, and the organization's stated intentions. This means helping people to explore new "ways of seeing" their everyday organizational world. They will then be better placed to gain new insights, make the necessary connections and actively engage with the emerging challenges.

## Vision as everyday engagement

### All the world's a stage

When Mintzberg (1989) talks about visionary leadership as drama (above), he frames this as a performance *by* the leader. In this role, he or she communicates his or her vision *to* an attentive audience. Although this one-way process is out of kilter with the *informal coalitions* view of visionary leadership, the qualities of the leader–staff relationship that Mintzberg describes are certainly not. His description echoes important aspects of the *informal coalitions* perspective, including:

- the idea of fiction and life blending together;
- the personal investment of a leader in their relationship with their staff;
- the search for mutually beneficial outcomes; and
- a jointly empowering connection between leader and staff.

The emphasis here is on relationship, mutuality and joint empowerment. This is entirely consistent with the *informal coalitions* approach to organizational dynamics. Furthermore, the notion of fiction and life blending together reflects a socially constructed view of reality and the co-creation of meaning.

*Informal coalitions* are built upon the socially constructed fictions and fantasies that emerge from everyday conversations and interactions. Eccles and Nohria's view of leaders as thoughtful historians of the past and creative participators in the present elegantly underlines the role of the leader in shaping the ways in which past events are construed and meaning jointly created in the present. As we saw in Chapter 6, it is through the individual action of leaders themselves – and through their stimulation of individual action in others – that collective action is mobilized and coalitions of support built around organizationally beneficial changes.

From an *informal coalitions* perspective, the meaning of "endless rehearsal" referred to by Mintzberg demands some comment. This is not about practicing for hours beforehand with the aim of becoming word perfect in the delivery of a formal script. Instead, it is about working constantly *in the moment* to "re-hear" what staff are thinking, feeling and saying in relation to the issues and events that are emerging. In particular, it is about leaders "re-hearing," how their own words and actions (including their silence and inaction) are being perceived, interpreted and acted upon by their staff. This raised level of awareness and connection will then help them to stimulate new, more congruent ways of seeing, hearing and feeling about the organization.

Leaders' everyday conversations and interactions with staff, colleagues and others provide the main means for achieving this. The visionary challenge is then to:

- detect the themes that are organizing people's responses to emerging issues and events;
- understand how these responses affect the delivery of successful organizational performance;
- actively engage with staff and others, to reinforce those themes and responses that enhance the organization's position and to reframe or re-orientate those that don't; and
- do this in ways that resonate with people's own aims and aspirations.

## Super*vision*

Seeing vision as an act of everyday engagement with staff places "hands-on" supervision back at the center of a leader's role. However, this is not about tightly overseeing the work of others, in the initiative-stifling ways that still disfigure leadership practice in many of today's organizations. Instead, it calls on leaders to provide super*vision*, by working with staff to:

- frame emerging events in more constructive ways;
- see their here-and-now activities in broader, more meaningful and more creative terms than they might otherwise have done;
- identify pathways through the challenges that they face; and
- envisage successful outcomes to their work.

## Keep chipping away

Stewart (1990: ix) reminds us that when he was asked how he had managed to sculpt his Statue of David from a solid block of marble, Michaelangelo is reputed to have said something along the lines of: "It's easy. You just chip away the bits that don't look like David."

In his mind's eye, Michaelangelo no doubt had a rough image of what he wanted the finished statue to look like. But, in getting there, he had to adapt the design to take account of challenges that arose along the way. These would have included such things as the demands of the materials he was working with; the constraints arising from decisions he had made earlier (such as bits already chipped off!); and his changing relationship to the shape emerging in front of him. Michaleangelo didn't simply have *a* vision – a fuzzy, end-state view of what David might look like – he also *exercised vision along the way*. He did this to make the best of the possibilities and potentialities available to him as the details of the work and new challenges unfolded. Organizations need their leaders (*throughout the organization*) to do the same. Providing vision includes developing and sharing compelling images of what the organization's future might look, sound and feel like. More importantly, though, it is about *exercising vision on a day-to-day basis*. In practical terms, this calls on leaders to use everyday conversations and interactions with their staff and others to help them "chip away the bits that don't look like David." This means enabling them to:

- gain *perspective* – so that they can make sense of the emerging challenges that the organization is facing and see these in new light;
- realize their *purpose* – so that they can relate their contributions to the organization's wider objectives *and* to their own aspirations;
- understand the nature of customer demands on their work *processes*, and increase their capacity for self-managing these demands for business benefit;
- identify and explore new *possibilities* – encouraging them to challenge assumptions and constraints, and to exploit the value-adding opportunities that emerge;
- understand and capitalize upon their personal *potential* to make a difference to the organization's performance and capability, by building upon their own and others' strengths; and
- ignite and channel their *passion* about what is important to *them*, and about what they and the organization as a whole are jointly engaged in.

These six components of *everyday* visionary leadership – or super*vision* – are explored in turn below. As with other elements of the *informal coalitions* agenda for leading change, the primary leadership tools for providing vision are informal conversation and everyday role-modeling interactions.

## Gaining perspective

Vision is, first and foremost, about *perspective*. And gaining perspective is about seeing the world – as reflected in our everyday experiences – in new, more helpful and more meaningful ways. As Bellman (1996: 11) points out:

> When we see the world differently, we have to honour this new perspective. Our actions will be altered by what we now see; we will use our old skills in new ways.

The visionary or transforming leadership task here is threefold. First, there is a need to help people to frame their everyday organizational experience of emerging events in ways that make different, more value-enhancing sense *than they might otherwise have made*. This is about leaders taking time out with staff and others to take stock of:

- how things are at present;
- how these are changing; and
- what needs to be done to continue to make progress in ways that both benefit the organization *and* which resonate with people's own perceptions and aspirations.

Secondly, in our discussion of the coalition-building task, we also talked about leaders helping people, metaphorically, to "turn around" from the sense of loss that they might be suffering as a result of an enforced change ("Holding On"). The desired outcome of this is to enable them to face the future with confidence ("Letting Go" and "Engaging"). Facilitating this change in perspective, through relevant conversations and other support, is another key aspect of visionary, transforming leadership.

Thirdly, helping people to gain perspective is about enabling them to see things *in relation to* other things, and, through this, to judge their relative importance. It is concerned with priorities. This enables them to make choices about where to focus their attention and energy, in both the short and the long term.

Without perspective, things have no meaning. Putting things into perspective is a central aspect of people's everyday sensemaking. Changing these perspectives opens up the possibility of people making different sense of the world than they might otherwise have made. That is, it is visionary and change making.

## Framing

Framing is the fundamental communication skill that leaders use to help others to gain perspective. Through effective framing of issues and events, leaders influence outcomes by getting people to recognize and act upon one particular view of reality in preference to another. In this way, the dominant frame sets the context for everyday decision-making and action. It also enables the results of these actions to be interpreted, validated and evaluated – that is, to be put into perspective.

By way of illustration, one particularly graphic – and tragic – example of this was the death of 96 supporters of Liverpool Football Club at an FA Cup Semi-Final match at Hillsborough, Sheffield in 1989. At that time, the standing areas in all British football grounds were separated from the pitch by tall, metal fences. These had been built to prevent people invading the pitch, in response to many years of hooliganism. Hillsborough's standing areas were fenced-in in this way; with further fences separating different sections of the terracing, to segregate rival supporters. On that particular April afternoon, one section of the ground became dangerously overcrowded. Anxious fans, hurrying to gain access to the ground as the time for kick-off approached, were funneled into an already over-full section of terracing behind one of the goals. As a result of the physical pressure caused by the late-coming supporters, those standing at the front became crushed against the fencing and underfoot. Fighting for breath, and desperate to escape, many of them attempted unsuccessfully to climb the fences to gain access to the pitch. And horrified supporters, in nearby sections of the ground, pleaded with police to open the escape gates. For many minutes though, the gates remained closed. When one of the gates sprang open due to the pressure behind it, allowing some spectators to spill onto the pitch, the police pushed these supporters back onto the terraces and locked the gate behind them!

Why was this? What was it that caused ordinary, professional police officers to react in this way? The answer lies in the frame through which they were viewing what was unfolding in front of them. For years before this event, as noted above, British football had suffered from incidents of hooliganism at many of its stadiums. In this environment, the primary role of the police had been seen as one of combating this antisocial behavior and maintaining order. The frame that had been "put around" large crowds of football supporters caused them to be seen, first and foremost, as potential hooligans. And hooligans need to be restrained and suppressed. Viewed through this well-established frame, the actions of the crowd behind the goal at Hillsborough would *unquestioningly* have been seen as characteristic signs of hooligan behavior.

As panicking people desperately tried to climb the fences, the police's anti-hooliganism response pattern was triggered. Their *natural* reaction to people who were climbing the perimeter fence was to push them back in! This pattern was deeply embedded and taken for granted. It made sense. And, in normal circumstances, it was a useful and effective way of keeping control of the situation. Also, the *last* thing that they would willingly have done was to open the safety gates and let more of these "hooligans" onto the pitch. Only when it became clear, some minutes later, that people were trying to escape to save their lives did the police respond in a supportive rather than restraining way. By that time, many of the supporters were dead or dying. In other words, only when the situation was *reframed*, from one of an act of hooliganism to one of an emerging human tragedy, did the police's actions change. As soon as the new frame was in place, police officers responded quickly with a whole series of contrary actions to those that had been the order of the day only minutes earlier.

Framing is powerful. Thankfully, in business, the ways in which situations are framed will rarely result in the devastating consequences that arose at Hillsborough. Nevertheless, in determining how issues and events are viewed, the predominant frame in any situation will channel people's perceptions and actions down particular paths. This will happen just as surely, and in just the same way, as the "hooligan frame" channeled the initial actions of police at that fateful FA Cup Semi-Final in 1989. For example, if managers have low expectations of people's willingness and ability to contribute, they will frame the behaviors they observe in those terms. So, outward signs of disaffection and low productivity will be seen as confirmatory evidence of this. An alternative perspective – that these behaviors might simply be the alienated reaction of staff to overly tight controls imposed by their leaders – will not even be seen by them, let alone acted upon. Framing not only explains action, it determines action. By focusing people's perceptions, interpretations and evaluations in particular ways, framing gives meaning to everyday events, experiences and outcomes that otherwise would be absent. By doing so, it directs the ways in which people act; and it determines how the outcomes of those actions will be evaluated. It is also important to recognize that, as noted by Fairhurst and Sarr (1996: 4), "Frames exert their power not only through what they highlight but also through what they leave out." Once a particular frame is in place, information that doesn't fit with it will tend to be ignored – or not seen at all.

## Surfacing and testing assumptions

Metaphor is a particularly pervasive framing device (see Morgan, 1998; Grant et al., 1998; and Clancy, 1999, for example). By actively listening for those metaphors that are habitually used by staff, leaders can tap into a rich seam of knowledge about the underlying dynamics of their organizations. For example, people might pepper their conversations with metaphors that reflect dependency, subservience or mistrust. In those circumstances, it is unlikely that they will readily and enthusiastically embrace emerging changes. Negative metaphors also provide important clues to potential areas of organizational dysfunction. In contrast, metaphors that convey a sense of powerfulness, self-worth or enthusiastic engagement, say, suggest fertile ground in which to sow the seeds of change.

The leadership task here is to tap into the conversational networks:

- to surface the metaphors in use;
- to "unpack" them, to understand what they mean to people, how these have arisen and, more importantly, why they are current; and
- if necessary, to talk with others with the aim of instilling alternative metaphors that help to frame situations and relationships in more helpful and constructive ways.

Especially where the predominant metaphors are negative, this needs to be done in a spirit of genuine inquiry and in an open, non-defensive way. This can be particularly challenging, given that staff will begin by viewing the leader's actions through their existing, negative frames. If that frame is one of mistrust, for example, the leader's intervention will *inevitably* be greeted with suspicion. There would then be a risk that the relationship might degenerate into a vicious circle of mutual mistrust, personal point scoring and alienation. Because of the role-modeling dynamic that we discussed in Chapter 4, the leader must take the initiative to prevent this happening in their relationship with their staff. Or they must work to break the cycle if it begins to take hold.

## A leader's own dominant metaphors

A leader's day-to-day interactions with their staff will either give rise to new metaphors or else reinforce those already in play. They therefore need to be aware of the metaphors that dominate their own language – and those that are used by others on their management team. These will imperceptibly structure their thinking, behaviors and interactions. And it's through these everyday interactions that the metaphors shaping organizational behavior will either become further embedded or changed. Where relationships are sufficiently open and trusting, a leader might be able to shift the patterns of conversation directly. For example, they might openly explore the ways in which events are currently being framed and expose the metaphors that are currently channeling perceptions and behaviors. Genuinely seeking feedback from staff, and volunteering their own view of the situation "warts and all" can help to expand the area of shared understanding. Where relationships are more fraught or in their infancy, however, it would be naïve to expect an uninhibited, free-flowing conversation to take place spontaneously. As always, the ways in which the leader behaves during this informal inquiry process will send powerful signals to staff about the stance that they take on particular issues and their openness to candid feedback.

Mismatches frequently occur between a leader's formally expressed positions on issues and the metaphors that they habitually use in their day-to-day interactions. For example, they might formally advocate greater self-direction and a more "organic" approach to management, whilst lacing their conversations with metaphors that reflect deep-seated, mechanistic assumptions about organizations. Thus mechanistic, machine-type metaphors have managers "pulling levers" to achieve desired (and presumed predictable) outcomes; "designing and building" organizational strategies and cultures; using "scorecards" and "dashboards" to measure and control performance; searching for the "one best way" to proceed; and so on. Mechanistic metaphors also see people as replaceable "cogs in the organizational machine." These see the behaviors of staff as being predictable and controllable, provided that leaders, in their role as controller, "push the right buttons." And they see people's outputs as being determined by the extent to which each of them "pulls their weight."

When leaders frame their thoughts and language in these ways, they should not be surprised if the responses they get show a lack of initiative, passion or commitment. If they want people's attitudes to change, they need to help them frame things differently. And that often means that they need to begin by framing things differently themselves. Only then will their everyday words and actions evoke the sort of responses in others that they desire. This is why, in Chapter 4, we identified lack of congruence between espoused goals and the metaphors that leaders use as being important symbols of what leaders *actually* believe. As an example of this, I attended a conference that was populated by HR directors from some of the UK's foremost companies. During one session, a director in the audience was strongly advocating the need for the HR function to promote a more egalitarian, less "us and them" approach to doing business. It was, she said, "Important to involve 'the troops' more in decision-making." Her (probably unconscious) choice of military-style language made it clear that, in this new, hierarchy-free world she was arguing for, she still saw herself as one of the "officers" in command and control of the lower ranks! In all cases, the issue is not whether a particular metaphor is "right," but rather how it shapes people's perceptions, interpretations and actions. In particular, the question for leaders is whether or not it helps to frame situations in useful, organizationally enhancing ways.

It is also important to remember that it is how people perceive and interpret the metaphors in use that matters, rather than what leaders *intend* to convey by them. In the early 1990s, the CEO of a large, recently privatized company wanted to move the organization away from its public-sector past. His aim was to enable it to compete effectively in a commercially competitive world. To reflect this aim, he articulated the characteristics of a new, empowered management style using metaphors from the sporting world. This statement of intent still reads well today. It skillfully contrasts the bureaucratic rigors of the past with the need for initiative and flexibility in the future. Interestingly, though, a senior woman manager of the time only recalls how the CEO's statement was couched solely in terms of masculine sporting analogies. To her, it suggested little real change in the power relationships that had governed the organization's practices in its previous guise.

## Stories

So metaphors frame issues, events and information. They shape people's perceptions and offer the possibility of them seeing things differently. And if people see things differently, they can choose to act differently. Metaphors allow complex ideas, images and situations to be discussed in ways that enable them to be made sense of more easily. The recent popularity of storytelling as a management tool attests to this point, since stories weave together and extend basic metaphors into more complex forms. This is particularly clear where the stories are allegorical. These are intended to symbolize a deeper meaning and enable people to establish broader connections with a subject than is likely to be achieved through the use of matter-of-fact description. Stories can be used to provoke new ways of thinking, feeling and acting. At times, they will transform people's understanding and tap into deeply held values that provide self-motivation to move forward. On other occasions, they might rekindle the passion for addressing present-day challenges, or simply build confidence in the "rightness" of a current course of action.

It is important, though, not to think of storytelling solely in these terms. From an *informal coalitions* perspective, all of the descriptions and prescriptions that arise at work are stories, whether crafted as such or not. Even the driest report or strategy document is a story. It is a made-up account of what has happened or what is intended to happen. So are a leader's everyday commentaries on unfolding events; or their communication of forthcoming plans and their feedback of results achieved to date. The rumors, personal interpretations of events and gossip that people share in the privacy of their offices, by the side of the coffee machine or in the bar after work are further examples of storytelling in action. Each of these is a story. That is, it is a made-up interpretation of events, flowing into and out of the networks of formal and informal conversations that constitute day-to-day organizational life.

Even if such stories fail to tick all of the purists' boxes in terms of character construction, plot and flow, the people who craft them are just as much storytellers in our terms as those who use the more obviously symbolic type of story for rhetorical effect. And each of these everyday, "matter-of-fact" stories will be framed in a particular way, using metaphor-laced language. These metaphors may not be as visible, as colorful or as obvious as those used in set-piece storytelling. Nevertheless, their effects on organizational change and performance can be equally powerful. Often, the metaphors in use will be embedded in common-or-garden language which subtly locks-in current patterns of thought and action, rather than challenging or restructuring them. A simple example might be a reference to more "bottom–up" involvement in planning and decision-making. Whilst the apparent aim might be to signal the organization's commitment to greater empowerment of staff, use of the term "bottom–up" serves to reinforce existing power relationships rather than to narrow them. This is analogous to the earlier example of the HR director's use of the word "troops" to describe other employees in her organization.

In short, metaphor is everywhere. It is reflected in – *and shapes* – the way we talk, the way we think and the way we act. If leaders are to help people to gain perspective as part of their "providing vision" agenda, they therefore need to begin by understanding the impact that metaphor has on people's ways of knowing, being and acting – *including their own.*

## Realizing purpose

Vision is about purpose and meaning. It is about our outward contribution to something greater than ourselves. It is about knowing where we are heading and why. Understanding why we are doing something gives our work meaning. If the answer to the "Why?" question resonates with us, it also motivates us to contribute our time and talents to the full. However, habitual thinking patterns often cloud the picture and reduce our ability to see and hear what is going on around us. These tend to channel and constrain our thoughts and behaviors down familiar, well-trodden paths, rather than encouraging us to change our perceptions and actions in line with the shifting organizational and personal landscape.

This patterning process is critically important to our everyday functioning because it enables us to go about our business without having to think things out from scratch every day. The downside of this otherwise essential process is that it can lead us into what Odiorne (1975) calls the Activity Trap. Our habitual activities then become ends in themselves, rather than means to an end. To escape from this, we need to establish or regain a sense of purpose. And we need to understand the ways in which our roles make value-adding contributions to both the organization and our personal ambitions.

This aspect of providing vision is therefore about helping individuals and groups to realize their purpose – that is, to make it *real and actionable* for them. This means looking at purpose from two angles. First, it is about people gaining a clearer line of sight between their own contributions and the changing performance demands on the organization as a whole. At the same time, it is also about helping them to find their *own purposes* in the challenges that they face in delivering these contributions. The routes for achieving this include:

- talking with staff about the *unique contribution* that they and their team can make to the organization's success – and how and why this might be changing;
- encouraging and helping them to reflect on their own, broader purpose and ambitions – and on how the planned changes might help to further these; and
- stimulating and encouraging these conversations to occur routinely between people in the team – and within the organization at large.

## Making contribution visible

The notion of contribution can be used to focus the initial dialogue. This involves working with staff to make meaningful and motivating sense of where they each add value to the organization. The resulting "contribution statement" provides a clearer picture of an individual's (or group's) role and the unique contribution that this makes to the organization's overall performance and capability. It provides vision by answering the question: "What specific contribution do I/we need to make which, if performed excellently, would make a significant difference to the organization's performance and/or capability?"

This conversation first needs to settle upon why the role exists at all – its purpose or raison d'être. It should then identify the performance aims for which the role is accountable. The focus of the conversation should be on outputs (contribution and results) rather than inputs (resource usage and activities carried out). This shift in emphasis enables people to escape from the activity trap of rigid job descriptions and procedural straightjackets that too often stifle initiative and limit vision. Instead, it encourages and allows them to focus on delivering value to the organization and on discovering new ways in which their contribution can add value. This conversation should therefore:

- relate to *objectives* rather than activities;
- describe contributions in terms of *achieving outcomes* rather than carrying out matter-of-fact responsibilities;

- reflect the *desired "quality"* of the required contribution (effective, efficient, timely, optimum, least-cost, commercially focused and so on);
- increase rather than limit the scope for *individual initiative*;
- focus *upward and outward* on contribution to the organization as a whole;
- encourage *personal growth and development*.

The vision-creating dimension of the conversation arises from the enhanced understanding that can emerge from it; and the stimulation that this provides for individuals to become more fully engaged in their work. It aims to raise the bar above the routine delivery of baseline activities.

## Embracing uncertainty and complexity

Organizations are messy and paradoxical. This means that, in many aspects of everyday organizational life, things will be *un*-clear, *far from* simple and straightforward, and *un*-predictable. Even in reasonably defined areas of work, uncertainties arise because of emerging and unforeseeable changes in the organization's environment. Unavoidable imprecision in objectives and priorities and incomplete knowledge about decisions being made in related areas of the business add further layers of uncertainty and ambiguity. Such conditions are rarely a sign of managerial incompetence – although there will be times when they are! In most cases, these reflect the in-built complexities of organizational life, and the self-organizing and emergent characteristics of the underlying dynamics of organizations.

The linear, rational and predictable model of organizational management suggests that these complexities are within the gift of competent managers to control. All they need to do is to "do things better and get them right" (Streatfield, 2001). Managers who are trapped in this paradigm do little to dispel the myth of omnipotence and control that this is built upon. The result for staff is frustration and loss of confidence in management. For the organization, it inevitably means continuing waste, underperformance and disappointing outcomes from formal change efforts.

From an *informal coalitions* perspective, which sees managers as being *both* in control *and* not in control *at the same time*, mess and uncertainty are inevitable. The challenge then is to cultivate a flexible and responsive mindset to deal with this. Unexpected events are viewed as the norm (that is, expected!). And these are seen as temporary setbacks *or* potential opportunities to refocus and exploit newly emerging conditions. Adopting this stance, the visionary leadership task is to help people to tolerate mess and ambiguity, and to persevere with the challenges that these present.

## Resonance

Finally, for purpose to provide vision, it needs to resonate with people's own hopes and ambitions. People therefore need to be encouraged to find ways in which specific changes can serve their own purposes as well as those of the organization. People coalesce around particular themes and ideas because they want to, not because they have to. This is the essence of informal coalitional behavior in organizations. And *working with* these dynamics is what the *informal coalitions* view of change leadership is all about.

As we saw earlier, people who coalesce around a specific viewpoint or proposition may share a common set of values but it is just as likely that they won't. What they will share, though, is a belief that "membership" of the coalition will provide the best chance of securing their personal goals. Helping individuals to make the connection between their own agenda and the steps needed to secure the desired organizational changes is therefore a central contribution that visionary leadership can make to the coalition-building task. It is the means through which individual action mobilizes collective action for organizational benefit.

## Self-managing processes

Vision is as much about process as it is about purpose. From a conventional perspective, the idea that process has anything at all to do with vision might appear odd. As we discussed in the introduction to this chapter, vision has come to be associated with the notion of far-sighted and expansive thinking about future possibilities. In contrast, process evokes images of current practice, the inner workings of the organization and "feet on the ground" practicality. As we have already seen, vision *is* partly about generating an outward-looking sense of purpose. Later, we will look at it in terms of its "possibilities" dimension. But vision is also about offering ways of seeing the core work processes of the business through different, more powerful and more *in*-sightful eyes.

Talking about work processes in the same breath as organizational change conjures up a picture of consultant-generated process analysis maps and business process reengineering projects. That is not what we are talking about here. Instead, the visionary-leadership and performance-management task is about having conversations aimed at:

- helping individuals to understand where value is added and destroyed through the processes that they are involved in;
- increasing their capacity to self-manage the demands that their external and internal customers place on these processes;
- managing the boundaries within which increasing self-management is exercised; and
- eliminating organizational or system barriers that get in the way of effective process performance.

## Understanding the process

The first of the above tasks is about helping people to understand the nature and extent of demands on the processes that they are responsible for operating. Implicit in this is also the need to understand how these are likely to develop as the wider changes take effect. This means stimulating conversations through which staff can:

- make sure that they fully understand the dynamics of the relevant processes and how their interventions affect the outcomes that are achieved;
- identify changes that are taking place in the wider organization, and explore the impact that these might have on their own processes, or on the quantity and nature of customer demands (internal as well as external);
- see what is needed, in process terms, to meet the existing and changing demands of their customers; and
- anticipate and respond effectively to legitimate customer demands, whilst seeking to reduce any that don't add value or that waste resources.

In most cases, it is likely that relevant members of staff will be the process experts, rather than the leader. The leader's role is to help them question and learn from their own practice, and to encourage them to challenge constraints constructively. This means asking questions to raise awareness and understanding, rather than always seeking to provide answers or impose solutions.

## Self-management and collaboration

Visionary leadership here is about increasing the capacity of individuals to manage more of their own processes. This means having conversations aimed at increasing their self-sufficiency, self-direction, self-control and collaboration.

*Self-sufficiency* is about individuals having the capability to deal with the diverse range of customer, plant or system demands on the processes for which they are responsible. This means that gaps in relevant process knowledge and skills need to be identified and any important shortfalls addressed. As more capabilities are integrated into the core, so the scope for further self-sufficiency increases. The aim is not to turn staff into "jacks of all trades" but to build on their own strengths and ensure that they have the capacity to stand on their own two feet, so to speak, in relation to the challenges that they face.

Individuals' capacity for *self-direction* depends upon their ability to plan and organize more of their own work. It also requires them to have the decision-making authority to respond to customer or other work demands on their own initiative. Conversations here need first to turn toward the extent of delegated authority required to facilitate this. It is also important to identify any necessary training and development in related management systems and processes, to ensure that this increased authority to act can be exercised competently. The aim is to give people responsibility in the fullest sense of the word. That is, the ability to determine their own response to situations, without having to ask permission or without being constrained by an excess of rules and regulations.

Attention needs to turn next toward individuals' capacity for *self-control*, in relation to such things as the quality, progress and cost of their work. The aim is to release people from the suffocating grip of tight supervision and enable them to regulate many of their own outputs. This means identifying any shortfalls in the level and quality of information and feedback currently made available to them. It also calls for thought to be given to the training and development needed to ensure that this information can be used effectively.

Finally, a growing capacity for self-management needs to be accompanied by the opportunity for staff to *collaborate* effectively together. This means identifying and providing increased scope for intra- and inter-team participation, to amplify overall process performance and extend organizational learning beyond the individual through free-flowing conversation. The aim of increased participation is not to make staff "feel better" – although that may well be a positive side effect. Its purpose is to tap into their creative potential to produce *better decisions*; to build the relationships and joint sensemaking that are essential for *real communication* and to establish a sense of *ownership* of systems, processes and results.

## Boundary management

Boundary management is the third element of visionary leadership around process performance. This is concerned with clarifying and managing the boundaries within which staff are able to regulate their own performance in the ways set out above. Its goal is to allow individuals to express themselves freely and creatively, in line with their developing competence and confidence. At the same time, it aims to ensure that the collective outcomes of the process continue to serve the interests of the wider organization. Conversations can usefully focus on a number of factors, including:

- the shifting organizational context (as in Perspective, above);
- the required contribution of their role (as in Purpose, above);
- ways of dealing with any interdependencies with other people's roles and responsibilities, where these impact upon the individual or team's ability to manage their process performance;
- identification of, and attention to, any relevant constraints on the scope for increasing self-management and collaboration.

The overall purpose of boundary management is to balance the growing capability of individuals to manage their own performance with the increasing level of challenge presented to them. Where mismatches occur, these are likely to create anxiety (high challenge–low capability), boredom (low challenge–high capability) or apathy (low challenge–low capability); all of which are dysfunctional for individuals and organizations alike.

## System barriers

Finally here, it is important to throw light on any of the system barriers and managerial demands that are getting in the way of high-quality process performance. In essence, this means identifying, and critically examining, any system factors that are obscuring people's vision rather than enhancing it.

A brief excursion into the world of Formula 1 motor racing may help to clarify this point. Michael Schumacher has indisputably been the best driver in Formula 1 for the past several years, with more world champion-ship titles to his name than any driver in history. If, though, he had been driving an inferior car during this period, his record would have been far less remarkable. No amount of target-based "people management" or adverse comparison with those who were winning races would have rectified the resulting performance shortfall. In Formula 1 terms, it is the overall "package" that determines the outcome. In particular, it is the quality of the racing car design and performance and the effectiveness of the supporting infrastructure (team management, pit-crew performance, race strategy, etc.) that have the biggest impact on the overall result. People management in Formula 1 is about providing the driver with the technology, information and feedback to enable them to get the best that they can out of the equipment available – given the variety of demands placed upon them during the race. And development discussions seek as much feedback from the driver about the performance and "handling" of the car as they do about the skills and practices of the driver.

In contrast, so-called "performance management" in organizations too often focuses almost exclusively on the individual, rather than on the overall system within which their performance is embedded. Heavy emphasis is usually placed on such things as numerical target setting; formal assessment of individual performance against these targets; and the comparative rating and ranking of staff for payment and/or other purposes. However, the underlying dynamics of performance mean that the results achieved by individuals are heavily influenced by the context within which they are working. This includes the effectiveness and effi-ciency of the work processes, management systems and leadership rela-tionships that they are involved in. Too often, seemingly common-sense management actions, such as rating people against their peers or imposing inspection regimes, constrain rather than enable value-adding perform-ance. Many of the factors that impact upon individual and organizational performance are intrinsic to the system. Far fewer are within the gift of the individual. It is therefore important that these system issues are adequately addressed before assessing the effect of personal attributes on performance outcomes. Only then can individual excellence become the differentiator of organizational performance.

This element of the vision-making process is therefore more likely to place the onus on managers to remove system barriers and provide an enabling infrastructure, than to emphasize shortfalls in individual performance. In many cases, this will require managers to turn the spot-light onto their own leadership performance. In others, the focus will need to shift to the surrounding management systems that they have initiated or are sustaining. The case for giving priority to these "system dynamics" surrounding everyday work is powerfully argued by Seddon (2003), as part of his head-on challenge to the "flawed logic" that he feels misdirects the design and management of many of today's organizations. Amongst the areas that are worthy of reflection and exploration here are:

- the distorting effect that many of the target-setting and reward-management practices have on individual performance;
- any failure to provide *useful* process performance feedback *directly* to relevant individuals;
- any tendency to use performance information as a "stick" with which to beat people, rather than as a tool to enable them to manage their own work processes more effectively and efficiently;
- any over-reliance on high-level business performance measures to govern decisions over day-to-day operations – these rarely provide useful inputs to the process management arena;
- the existence of unnecessary layers of authorization and inspection, which can undermine personal accountability and delay people's response to customer demands;
- the impact of the leader's own performance and interactions on individual and team performance; and
- when appraising and "managing" people's performance, the imbalance that often exists between the emphasis placed on an individual's personal attributes and perceived "application to the task," and the much more scant attention paid to deficiencies in end-to-end work processes or related management systems.

When seeking to provide vision in relation to people and process performance, therefore, leaders should pay attention to the overall "performance package," as set out above, not simply the surface-level performance of individuals. Where long-standing problems are identified, conversations should also seek to understand the assumptions that have prevented this knowledge being surfaced earlier and the problem addressed.

## Exploiting possibilities

Vision is about possibility and opportunity, rather than limitation and constraint. The *Perspective* aspect of vision was about seeing things through "new eyes," from new angles or through new frames. The *Possibilities* thread is about seeing things that others don't see, as a basis for enabling new patterns of behavior and outcomes to emerge. Whereas the *Process* strand of visioning was about feet-on-the-ground practicality, a focus on *Possibilities* is about thinking expansively and provocatively. It is about challenging existing ways of thinking and acting. Helping staff to seek out and take advantage of the possibilities that exist in everyday situations is therefore the fourth element of the visionary leadership task. This means encouraging and enabling them to expand their horizons, challenge assumptions and exploit any worthwhile opportunities that emerge.

## Challenging assumptions

What we imagine to be possible is often constrained by deeply embedded, taken-for-granted assumptions. These might relate to *what* we can and can't do, and *how* we can and can't do it. Helping people to surface and, where appropriate, challenge these assumptions is an important act of transforming leadership. Some of the most constraining assumptions can be those that an individual or group holds about their own capacity to perform. We will look further at this when we consider the *Potential* aspect of vision, below. Here, we are more concerned with those personal and cultural assumptions that govern the ways in which decisions are made, tasks carried out and people relate to each other.

The most important aspect of the leader's intervention here is to help staff become aware of those assumptions that are governing their everyday thinking and behavior. This is particularly important where these appear to be limiting current performance, blocking progress or preventing effective engagement with organizationally beneficial changes. Assumptions impact upon all aspects of organizational behavior and performance. At the operating level, these affect the ways in which basic operations are carried out. Strategically, assumptions channel the organization's reading of the external environment and internal dynamics. As a result, these shape its overarching strategies, policies and principles. In between, organizational strategies are translated into operations through integrating processes and procedures. These are also heavily influenced by managers' individual and collective assumptions about the nature and importance of such things as performance management and capability development.

As we saw in Chapter 4, assumptions serve an essential purpose. They enable people to navigate their everyday tasks and relationships successfully, and allow them to conform to relevant behavioral norms. In the process, these patterns become further embedded. This is particularly useful, in that it means that people don't have to learn their roles, responsibilities and relationships afresh each day. At the same time, assumptions work to limit movement beyond the confines of processes, practices and performance levels that already exist.

Conversations about possibilities therefore need to raise awareness of governing assumptions and, where appropriate, to stimulate staff to challenge these constructively. At the operating level, this can be especially useful in relation to the elimination of waste and the improvement of processes, as previously discussed. Taken-for-granted assumptions lead to the perpetuation of activities that no longer serve a useful purpose. They also result in the unnecessary production or over-sophistication of particular outputs (such as reports), based on long-past criteria that are no longer relevant. Needless third-party checking of activities and other redundant activities also become embedded through this process. At the strategic level, conversations might home in on some of the fundamental principles that currently shape the organization's overall approach. As we saw when considering the *Perspective* strand of visionary leadership, the existing patterns of assumptions might be most accessible through the predominant metaphors that leaders habitually use. At the intermediate levels, attention might focus on the prevailing management processes, systems and practices. As visible artifacts of the organizational culture, these often provide pointers to the underlying patterns of assumptions that channel management thinking and behavior. The nature of performance management systems and reward structures, development and succession practices, the structure and conduct of meetings, decision-making practices, formal levels of delegation and so on all provide important clues to underlying assumptions.

Raising awareness of current assumptions may be sufficient to unfreeze existing patterns and stimulate movement. In other cases, more deliberate action may be required to challenge and shift existing practices.

## Possibility space

Exploiting possibilities is not only about exposing and challenging assumptions. Conversations should also encourage and assist staff to identify and exploit the "possibility space" that exists within and around their existing roles and relationships. This is similar to de Bono's "opportunity search" (de Bono, 1978). Here though, the emphasis is on using informal, unstructured conversations to stimulate and support the process. The purpose of doing this is to extract maximum value from the assets that the role commands.

De Bono (1978) suggests that it can be useful to distinguish between three different types of assets. *Intrinsic assets* are those that are embodied in the role itself. These include the formal decision-making capacity that goes with it, and the resources, tools and equipment to which it has access. *Operating assets* arise as a result of the ways in which the role is carried out. Roles that bring people into contact with customers or other key stakeholders, for example, provide operating assets that might be capable of being exploited for additional benefit. How customer-facing staff handle these interactions will, in any event, help to paint a picture in customers' minds of what the overall organization is like. Finally, a third category of assets emerges as a result of the particular situations that organizations, teams or individuals find themselves in. These *situational assets* relate to circumstances that occur "in the moment." For example, a chance meeting or external event may create an opportunity to do something that might otherwise not have arisen. Remaining alert to these possibilities is the important challenge here.

## Stimulating creativity and innovation

Implicit in this focus on possibility is the need for more creative and innovative thinking. There are many tools and techniques available to support the actual "doing" in this area; so I don't propose to dwell on them here. From the leadership perspective, though, the challenge is to create conditions that encourage and enable individuals to see and exploit the possibilities available to them. This means both modeling the way and also helping to remove barriers that inhibit creativity and innovation.

On the first count, a manager's own behavior sends signals to staff about the extent to which creative thinking and personal initiative are valued. If, for example, they are excessively rule-bound in the way that they lead, or if they consistently reject ideas put forward by others, it is unlikely that staff will become more expansive in their thinking. In a similar vein, the way in which they react to well-intentioned mistakes is critical. If the ensuing conversations concentrate on apportioning blame, rather than on joint learning, it should come as no surprise if signs of individual initiative and new ideas plummet.

Mistakes and misunderstandings are close relatives of creativity and innovation, in that these provide unexpected outcomes (de Bono, 1990, for example; and Fonseca, 2001). So are humor and chance (de Bono, 1990). Humor can be used deliberately to break out of thinking ruts and to see things that are ordinarily hidden by conventional ways of doing things. This is not about "telling jokes" or gratuitously adding a dose of unrelated "fun" to set-piece workshops and similar events. It is, though, about such things as:

- looking at issues and challenges from unexpected angles – and encouraging others to do so;
- asking seemingly naïve questions, to cut through the layers of taken-for-granted assumptions that have come to mask critical thinking;
- demonstrating that it is ok not to know, and to laugh at oneself from time to time;
- recognizing that the use of appropriate humor can lighten the mood and become infectious;
- staying alert to the covert use of humor that often arises spontaneously in organizations (such as anonymous cartoons, catchphrases and "in jokes") that are often used by people as a felt-safe way to express their concerns and frustrations.

Some managers might baulk at the idea of appearing "foolish" in front of their staff. Clearly, managers need to act authentically; and natural humor might not be their strong suit. However, as regards being seen as a fool, they might reflect on the following quotation from I Corinthians (3:18): "If anyone among you thinks he is wise in this age, let him become a fool that he may become wise."

## Political implications

In a sense, all change is seeded by people's belief in the possibility that things can be better in some way – for the organization, for themselves or for both. And change, as we have seen, is political. It threatens existing power relationships and challenges vested interests. So even the most obviously beneficial ideas that might arise through this focus on possibilities can fall foul of political maneuvering and attempts to derail them. This is particularly the case where new ideas would impact widely upon organizational policies, processes and practices. But ideas for improvement at operating level might also generate resistance at peer-group level. If visionary leadership is going to encourage staff to look for and exploit new possibilities, therefore, it needs to be underpinned by adequate attention to the *Acting Politically* and *Building Coalitions* aspects of the change-leadership agenda.

## Unlocking potential

Vision is about identifying and exploiting potential. The word "potential" originates from the Latin word *potentia*, meaning power. It also suggests a latent, as yet untapped talent or capacity. And a focus on potential – as on possibility – also implies a positive mentality. Here then, the visionary leadership task is to help people to recognize the power that they have to make a difference; to identify and realize their own and others' unique talents; and to instil a positive approach to the challenges that change brings.

## Coaching for performance

Unlocking potential is the central aim of performance coaching, whether this is applied in the business world, in sport or in life in general. Channeling this potential for business benefit is the specific focus of coaching in an organizational context.

Gallwey (2000) uses the equation $P = p - i$ to relate performance to potential. He suggests that performance (P) is equal to potential (p) minus any interference ($i$) that gets in the way. A leader's coaching conversations with their staff are therefore directed at getting rid of any interference, so that natural potential can be realized and performance optimized. These conversations can address capability and performance on any or all of four levels, as illustrated in Table 8.1.

Such conversations may form part of specific coaching sessions and other structured one-to-one events. However, the "unlocking potential" element of providing vision also calls on managers to adopt a *coaching mindset* when engaging staff in everyday conversations.

## Positive spin

Over recent years, the concept of "spin" has been treated with derision. From our perspective, though, spinning is simply the art of communicating with people in ways that are more likely to develop shared understanding, gain sign-on and lead to desired action. To a greater or lesser extent, we all use spin in our interactions with other people. The ways in which we interact with others are motivated by our desire to appear capable and valued in all of our relationships simultaneously. And this necessarily requires us to present the same event or information

**Table 8.1** Coaching conversations

| | | |
|---|---|---|
| **Doing** | Focus | Activities, skills and knowledge. |
| | Approach | Telling and illustrating. |
| | Potential Interference | Aptitudes and innate preferences. |
| | Desired Outcomes | New knowledge, skills, tools and techniques. |
| **Achieving** | Focus | Tasks and results. |
| | Approach | Joint problem solving; observing and feeding back; building capability; unblocking progress; challenging and supporting; raising issue-awareness and responsibility; channeling efforts; addressing stakeholder relationships; planning and reviewing. |
| | Potential Interference | Innate preferences (such as absence of task focus or excessive task focus); mismatch between challenge and capability; lack of clarity in roles and relationships; lack of motivation; lack of opportunity. |
| | Desired Outcomes | Goal-oriented performance, insights into personal strengths and weaknesses (instrumental); clarity of role requirements; improved relationship dynamics. |
| **Being** | Focus | Person. |
| | Approach | Helping individuals to help themselves; tapping into inner resources; unpacking thinking and feelings; building self-awareness and self-esteem; exploring issues; challenging assumptions. |
| | Potential Interference | Negative self-talk; lack of self-confidence; mood and inner state. |
| | Desired Outcomes | Self-knowledge; self-belief; psychological skills; emotional resilience; coping skills; insights into personal strengths and weaknesses (inner). |
| **Becoming** | Focus | Personal and organizational context. |
| | Approach | Inspiring; encouraging; nurturing and caring; sharing wisdom and insights; raising political savvy; "opening doors;" acting as a sounding board; reflecting back. |
| | Potential Interference | Lack of ambition, self-motivation or engagement; character flaws. |
| | Desired Outcomes | Perspective; contextual awareness; organizational alignment; personal sense of purpose; self-fulfillment. |

differently in different settings. That is, we spin it in different ways, to suit the context.

From an *informal coalitions* perspective, helping people to put a positive spin on events, and to break out of negative, self-defeating mindsets, is an important part of a leader's task. This is not about setting out to mislead people. Nor is it about downplaying difficulties, ignoring mistakes or glossing over weaknesses. It is, though, about challenging assumptions and helping people to confront beliefs that are limiting their horizons, stifling progress and draining their energy. Framing things

positively, to offer alternative perspectives and to stimulate constructive
ways forward, is one of the ways that leaders can achieve this. Because
leaders will be enacting this primarily through informal one-to-one
and one-to-few conversations, rather than in set-piece presentations and
formal meetings, any suggestion that the story doesn't hold up is likely
to be more readily challenged. Whilst this might be less comfortable
than the relative safety offered by a set speech, it offers a much greater
chance of genuinely connecting with people. If the offered frame survives
the challenge, and provides a perspective that resonates with people's
own reading of the situation, it is likely to be much more successful in
generating commitment and stimulating active engagement.

## Adopting an appreciative frame and a solutions focus

As suggested by our discussion of positive spin, above, and as discussed
more fully in the *Perspective* strand, the way in which we frame things
and talk about them is fateful. It determines how we see the world and
how we act. In the context of providing vision through day-to-day interactions, adopting a so-called "appreciative" frame offers a congruent
way of looking at, and exploiting, organizational potential. An appreciative conversation is strength-based rather than deficit-based. It starts by
considering what an individual or organization is good at, rather than
becoming preoccupied with their perceived weaknesses and shortcom-
ings. And it seeks out examples of high-point experiences – however
infrequent and fleeting these might be – as a basis for making these the
norm rather than the exception.

I am not talking here about full-blown AI, which is an increasingly
popular approach to organizational inquiry (see Watkins and Mohr, 2001,
for example). However, stripping away the more structured aspects of
AI, an appreciative mindset can enrich everyday conversations that are
aimed at unlocking the organization's potential and expanding people's
horizons. Dependent upon the primary focus of attention, emphasis can be
placed either on examples that illustrate the organization at its best or on
personal high points that evoke energy, excitement and peak performance
in an individual. Common themes can then be identified and images of
high performance crafted around these, to provoke movement and stretch
performance toward them. The crucial point here is that these images are
grounded in stories that show them to be real possibilities, rather than
hopeful speculation.

Further benefit can be gained by combining this with elements of the complementary approach, known as Solutions Focus (see, for example, Jackson and McKergow, 2002). This too looks to find out what's working well and to do more of it. Scaling is a particularly useful technique in the Solutions Focus toolkit that can be used to surface latent strengths and positive aspects of the current situation. It can make visible the current perceptions about performance, capabilities, confidence levels and so on that arise during conversations between a manager and their staff about individual or organizational potential. As suggested by its name, scaling attempts to "score" people's perceptions of the current position on a scale of, say, 0–10. It also seeks to identify "what 10 looks like." These are the characteristics that would be apparent if the ideal state was achieved. Unlike conventional approaches, though, the ensuing conversation focuses on the positives in the current situation, rather than shortfalls against the ideal. Instead of concentrating on the gap between the current and ideal positions on the scale, the initial conversation turns to why the current "score" is "X" rather than zero. The answer to this question points to resources (achievements, capabilities, positive intentions, etc.) that can be mobilized to achieve movement towards the desired goal.

## Igniting passion

Finally, vision is about passion. It is, in Oliver Cromwell's terms, about knowing what you fight for and loving what you know.[1]

Passion, like soul and spirituality, is one of those words that many people feel uncomfortable about using in the context of organizations. And yet, the notion of vision *without* passion is unappealing and useless. I recall once reading a spoof definition of passion, which suggested that it is "the feeling you feel when you feel you are about to feel a feeling you've never felt before." This accords with the way that passion is most often conceived. It is viewed as an event, and an extraordinary one at that – ". . . the precious thing we feel only in life's climactic moments" Bell (2002: 22). But, this is not what we are talking about here. As Bell goes on to say:

> Passion is not an event but an energy; and it's an energy that exists in all of us all the time. The question is not whether we have it but whether we access it and how we channel it.

Passion, then, is not something that is only capable of being experienced by a few people – or by everyone but only on rare occasions. It exists in all of us all of the time. Too often though, our passion remains dormant. Or it only "comes out at night," so to speak, away from the workplace. When accessed and channeled in personally fulfilling ways, passion can make an organizational vision compelling. It can transform work into a soul-*ful* and spiritually uplifting experience, rather than it being seen – at its worst – as soul-*destroying* and oppressive.

So visionary leadership here is about creating an environment that awakens and draws upon people's passions. This means tapping into those things that energize and excite them. It means enticing them to bring this energy and excitement inside the factory and office walls, rather than reserving it for their social and leisure pursuits and relationships. And it means seeking to engage people emotionally and spiritually in their work, as well as physically and intellectually. Passion is about heart and soul, more than head and hands!

In the same way that energy is always present in situations and relationships – even if only as a latent potential rather than being actively expressed – so is emotion. Hopefully, our earlier discussions in this and other chapters have forcefully made the case for this. In particular, when exploring the coalition-building task in Chapter 6, we saw that people's sensemaking and use-making conversations are *always* influenced by their emotions – whether positively or negatively. These emotions channel the ways in which they perceive events, contexts and relationships. And the nature and intensity of the emotions trigger different sensemaking patterns and action responses. Equally, the ways in which people habitually think – their belief sets – trigger particular emotional responses in them and channel the ways in which they act. Emotion, cognition and action are therefore inseparably intertwined.

A passionate work environment is one that stimulates positive emotion and high energy. Even in the midst of change, where – as we have seen earlier – people may naturally experience transient states of negative emotion and low energy, it holds promise for the future. This promise lies not in management's expression of its long-term vision for the organization but in the individual's own deep-seated belief in themselves, their contribution and their relationships that everyday visionary leadership has fostered. For leaders, this means communicating in ways that resonate with people's own values and aspirations, not simply parroting the organization's "official" values and formal Vision Statement. It means honoring how individuals currently see and interpret the world – their personal frames of reference – even if part of the broader leadership agenda is to help them to change these. And it also means recognizing that this communication is much more about fostering high-quality relationships and joint sensemaking than it is about information transfer and message passing.

## Motive, means and opportunity to excel

If people's passions are to become awakened and their energies released through their work, in ways that lead to high-quality relationships and excellent performance, they need three things: the motive to excel, the means to excel and the opportunity to excel. Only then will they be in a position to commit to excellent performance.

If any one of the three factors is missing, energy will be depleted; and the quality of relationships and performance will be reduced. There may, for example, be good intentions without the means or opportunity to deliver against them. Or there may be the ability to deliver, without the opportunity or desire to do so. Then again, there may be a "golden opportunity" to make a real difference, which remains unfulfilled through lack of motivation or capability. In none of these cases, though, can there be a passion for excellence. At worst, pent-up energies may be applied negatively. And relationships may deteriorate to an extent that damages personal health as well as organizational performance.

Many of the things that we have already discussed in this and other chapters will help to foster an environment in which people have the motive, means and opportunity to excel. First, high energy and enthusiastic commitment is a natural outflow of situations in which work *content* is aligned to people's strengths and interests. We referred to this under *unlocking potential* above. Secondly, the degree of *choice* and capacity for self-management that people have in their work is an important factor in releasing their energies and achieving real engagement. We explored the importance of progressively increasing the scope for creative self-expression in the *self-managing processes* section, earlier in this chapter. Thirdly, the *context* within which people are working on a daily basis is also critical. This is essentially about the quality of relationships and work climate; and I want to return specifically to this below. A fourth factor in mobilizing people's commitment to excellence is the *congruence* – or lack of it – between management's public position on issues and values, and people's everyday experience of organizational life. We covered this aspect extensively as the main theme of Chapter 4: *Thinking Culturally*. Finally, the levels of energy released, and the degree of positive engagement that flows from this, will necessarily be affected by the ways in which people experience the tensions between *change and continuity*. As we have argued throughout this book, organizational change potentially enriches individuals' sense of self-worth, capability and performance; and, at the same time, it threatens to undermine them. It does the same for the reputation, capacity and performance of the organization as a whole. Visionary leadership demands that these tensions between change and continuity are managed insightfully and dynamically. This means staying constantly aware of the ways in which the capacity for positive outcomes to be achieved are inextricably intertwined with the potential for negative consequences to emerge.

## A context for high-energy relationships

Finally here, I want to home in on the contextual factors necessary to foster high-energy relationships and committed performance (the "context" element in the above list of energy mobilizers).

The notion of organizational context inevitably conjures up thoughts of structures, systems and processes. And these factors certainly warrant attention as part of the overall change strategy. However, although these elements of organizational infrastructure can enable – or disable – performance, they are insufficient to generate the high energy and commitment that we are equating with the notion of passion. It is easy to conceive of ways in which frustrations arising from the structures, systems and processes surrounding people's work might kill their passion. It is less easy to think of ways in which these elements of performance alone – however supportive – might generate it.

So, although these are important to overall performance, we will leave consideration of them to the *vision as process* discussion that we explored earlier. Here we need to shift our attention to the quality of relationships that exist within the organization. The factor that then becomes central is the level of trust that people experience and demonstrate in their relationships with others. Trust is the *sine qua non* of high-energy relationships. And high-energy relationships – or their absence – set the context within which passion will either flourish or wither. Trust, though, is not something that can be mandated by management. If it exists, it does so within the relationships that people have with each other. It grows, or is undermined, as a result of people's everyday experiences and the conversations that they have with others about these. The visionary leadership task is then to foster conditions in which trusting relationships emerge and flourish spontaneously.

Trust, though, has many facets. We all feel that we know whether we trust another person or not. But to say that we trust, or don't trust, someone doesn't get us very far. What is it about them, or about what they do, that causes us to take this view? If we don't trust someone, is it because we believe that they hold things back from us and don't tell us the whole truth? Or is it perhaps that we don't believe that we can rely on them to keep their promises? Or is it that we don't feel that we can depend on them to carry out a particular task competently? Or maybe it's a combination of these things. Trust is multi-dimensional. When we say we (don't) trust someone, we are likely to be basing that judgment on any or all of a number of different aspects of their observed behavior or perceived personal qualities. We might not trust someone, for example, because we believe that they are incompetent in a particular respect. If so, that is different from not trusting them because our experience suggests that they are likely to let us down by failing to deliver against their promises.

If leaders are to address the issue of trust in their own and others' behavior, it can be useful to think of it as comprising a number of separate dimensions, as summarized below:

- *character* (perceived integrity and innate trustworthiness) – *They believe that the person's intentions are well meant and that they are innately trustworthy.*
- *community* (whether the person is recognized as being "one of us," with shared perspectives, common interests and sense of identity) – *They believe that the person has the same outlook and objectives as the broader community with which they are concerned.*
- *communication* (perceived openness, honesty and straightforward-ness) – *They believe that the person is being open and honest in what they say and how they say it; and, at the same time, that they maintain confidences.*
- *credibility* (whether or not the "story" makes sense and is believable in its own right) – *They believe that the person's "story" (proposition, etc.) is credible and makes sense in its own right.*
- *competence* (perceived knowledge, skills and abilities in relevant areas) – *They believe that the person is competent to do what is needed in the particular situation.*
- *commitments* (dependability in keeping agreements and promises) – *They believe that they can depend on the person to do what they say they will do – or to explain why not.*

- *culture and climate* (whether the background cultural patterns and work climate are channeling behavior in ways that enhance or undermine trust) – *They believe that the organizational culture and climate foster (and reflect) high-energy, trusting relationships.*

Ultimately, the cultural dimension of trust flows from the accumulated impact of people's behaviors in the remaining six areas – as these are perceived, interpreted and evaluated through everyday conversations and interactions. A major influence on this, as we've stressed elsewhere, is people's observation of the behaviors of those in leadership positions. As always therefore, the leader's role-modeling of the desired behaviors is critical. The ways in which they deal with issues of trust in others has a powerful influence on the level of trust – and passion – that emerges in their organization.

## Putting it all together – Aiming for 20:20 vision

When people visit the opticians for an eye examination, they undergo a range of different tests, measurements and observations. These are designed to assess the health of their eyes, the quality of their natural vision and the nature of any corrective measures that are needed to improve their eyesight. All they want from the relationship, though, is to be able to see better than they could before. And they want to be able to do that all day and everyday. Similarly, from an *informal coalitions* perspective, helping staff to "see better" – all day and every day – is what visionary leadership is all about.

To achieve this, we have seen that leaders need to look at their staff's current vision from several angles. We have discussed these in terms of perspective, purpose, process, possibilities, potential and passion. In conversation with their staff, leaders need to help them create new ways of seeing that make sense to them; and which re-equip them to meet the everyday challenges that they are facing. That is, they need to help them achieve the organizational equivalent of 20:20 vision.

Vision is also personal. To continue the "optician" metaphor, the glasses that people wear may be perfect for their own needs; but these are unlikely to be equally useful to anyone else who might put them on. As well, each individual chooses the frames and the optional characteristics of the lenses they are wearing. The optician doesn't. They identify the options and help with the choices; but each individual decides which frames and lenses they want to look through. The frames and lenses that they wear are part of them – part of their personal frames of reference (literally!). Over the years, individuals may have changed their frames and lenses many times. But, on each occasion, it has been important to ensure that the new ones "fitted" properly – not only physically but also emotionally. So it is with organizational vision. It needs to embody their own perspectives and ambitions, as well as those of the organization. If people are willingly to change the "frames and lenses" that they look through, and if they are going to engage energetically with what they see, vision needs to connect with them personally. And this means emotionally and spiritually, as well as intellectually.

Most importantly, vision needs to be renewed daily. This does not mean through the monotonous repetition of vision statement, catchphrase or cliché, but by the leader's everyday engagement with the actions, thoughts and feelings of their staff.

# POSTSCRIPT

"You cannot dig a hole in a different place by digging the same hole deeper."

– Edward de Bono

## A new change-leadership agenda

In the preceding chapters, we have introduced and explored six aspects of a new change-leadership agenda that flow from an *informal coalitions* view of organizational dynamics. These are to reframe communication, think culturally, act politically, build coalitions, embrace paradox and provide vision. Surely, some might say, this places an unmanageable burden on leaders who are already struggling to cope with their existing demands. Well no, it doesn't! This new agenda is not about leaders doing *more* things. It is about them doing things *differently*. It is about them making different sense of what's going on, based on a new awareness of the hidden, messy and informal dynamics of organizations. And it is about them using these new insights and perspectives to think and act differently, *in doing those things that they are already committed to do*.

Leaders *already* communicate extensively. Conventionally, though, leadership communication is thought of almost exclusively in terms of formal, structured ways of getting the right facts to the right people. From this perspective, incidental talk and informal interactions are seen as the antithesis of action-oriented, result-focused leadership. However, *Reframing Communication* places informal conversation at the heart of effective, transforming leadership. In rehabilitating "talk" as a leader's primary *action* tool, it calls upon them to extend their understanding and practice of communication beyond formal, set-piece message passing. Instead, it emphasizes the power and purposefulness of using everyday, informal interactions to bring about the desired change. Here, attention shifts toward building relationships, jointly making sense of unfolding events, and stimulating people's active engagement in the organization's emerging agenda.

Leaders *already* expend much energy and expense in seeking to shape the culture and climate of their organizations. At present, though, much of their attention in this area is directed towards initiating and monitoring cultural change programs that are designed and orchestrated by others on their behalf. In contrast, *Thinking Culturally* places the cultural-change "ball" firmly in the leader's own court. In particular, it focuses on their day-to-day interactions with people, and the ways in which their everyday words and actions are perceived, interpreted and acted upon by them. Each of these interactions provides a moment of leadership truth. They powerfully symbolize what is important to the leader and, by inference, what is important to the organization. Thinking culturally also acknowledges that a leader's silence and inaction are equally powerful symbols of what they (and the organization) do and don't value.

Leaders *already* act politically. The structurally embedded tensions within all organizational designs, and the impact of different interest groups on organizational decision-making and performance, make this unavoidable. Conventionally, though, the political dimension of organizational leadership is most often denied. Or else it is seen as a necessary and temporary evil, which "doing things better and getting them right" will overcome. *Acting Politically* exposes this as a façade. It recognizes, first of all, that the underlying dynamics of organization make conflict inevitable. And conflict can only be dealt with through political action of one form or another. The *informal coalitions* perspective therefore focuses on how best to manage these differences and exploit the dynamics of conflict in ethical, organizationally enhancing ways, which also resonate with people's own interests and aspirations. Acting politically then becomes a core element of effective, transforming leadership, rather than something to be denied or apologized for.

Leaders *already* deal, on a daily basis, with the consequences of informal coalitional activity. Most of the decisions and actions that they face each day arise from the continuing impacts that informal coalitions have on organizational activities, capabilities and performance. Coalitions exert their influence whether leaders acknowledge them or not. These shift organizational agendas; enable or frustrate formally adopted changes; and influence the ways in which policies and procedures are implemented "on the ground." *Building Coalitions* challenges the widely held assumption that official statements, strategies and plans, if clearly presented and underpinned by formal authority, are sufficient to ensure the desired outcomes. It argues, in particular, that the ways in which formal declarations of intent, official statements of policy and structured change programs are carried out *always* depend on local interpretation and personal commitment. It therefore calls on leaders to recognize, and *proactively* engage with, the dynamics of coalition formation. Otherwise they can only wait to play "catch up" as the unexpected outcomes emerge.

The mindset and practices of coalition building enable leaders to stay ahead of the game – or, at least, to keep up with it. The approach can be used to build momentum behind formally adopted changes. It can also be used to "work against the grain," to shift the organization's current agenda and policies in organizationally enhancing ways.

Leaders *already* come face-to-face with organizational paradox and its consequences, as they go about their everyday activities. Conventionally, the response is to try to resolve the perceived difficulties that these bring in one of two ways. The first approach is to affirm one side of the paradox and deny or downplay the other. Whilst this can appear decisive, it often results in the all-too-familiar oscillation of structures, systems and processes. This inevitably leads to frustration, cynicism and other performance-sapping effects, as today's much heralded changes are rejected and reversed by tomorrow's latest "solution." A second response is to recognize the paradox implicitly, without acknowledging it openly or deliberately setting out to address it. This usually reveals itself in mixed messages to staff. So people might be called upon, say, to "think long term and deliver results now;" or to "stick to the plan and use their initiative." *Embracing Paradox* aims to bring paradoxes such as these out of the shadows and into the open. The leadership challenge then shifts toward one of recognizing and dealing with these apparent contradictions. It is about seeing them as "business as usual," and as tensions to be managed rather than problems to be resolved in a once-and-for-all, either–or way.

Finally, leaders *already* spend time and effort in seeking to provide vision for their organizations or teams. However, their efforts in this direction are usually limited to articulating *a* vision and transmitting it *to* staff. Whether crafted by management alone or through a more participative process, providing vision here is seen as a separate task that can be added to the leadership checklist and ticked off when complete. If staff later complain that there is a "lack of vision," this might well be put down to the failure of the formal communication system to transmit it adequately. Or else it might be blamed on the inability of staff to understand it. From this position, the problem cannot be one of a lack of vision *per se*. The organization demonstrably has one. So the issue must lie elsewhere. However, the dynamics of *informal coalitions* lead to a fundamentally different view of providing vision. From this perspective, the term "vision" is translated primarily as *new ways of seeing* things. In particular, it looks at vision as something that is most powerfully provided through a leader's ongoing interactions with their staff, rather than being encased in a conventional, end-state vision statement. Ambition and intention still have vital parts to play in providing vision in the ways described here. However, the emphasis is much more on sharing insights and offering new perspectives around the everyday events, situations and activities that are happening in the here and now. It is much less about presenting ostensibly far-sighted images of the organization's future.

## The *every*day job!

In conclusion, managers will not be able to deliver organizational change and performance more effectively in the future, if they persist in using the same basic approaches that they have always used in the past. As suggested by the opening quotation, they can't enable their organizations to break out of existing patterns of activity and performance unless they do something different. In response to this, *Informal Coalitions* argues that they need to "stop digging" in the hole marked "rational, structured and formal," and actively engage with the hidden, messy and informal dynamics of organizational life. At the same time, they should not look upon this new change-leadership agenda as an additional imposition on "the day job." It *is* the day job – the *everyday* job!

# NOTES

## Preface

1 Reported in Beer, M. and Nohria, N. (2000), *Breaking the Code of Change*. HBS Press.

## 1 Mapping the territory

1 The "burning platform" metaphor is said to have arisen from a comment made by a survivor of the *Piper Alpha* oil platform disaster in the North Sea. He was asked why he had jumped from the platform into a sea of burning oil, when to do so meant probable death. He replied that to stay on the burning platform would have meant certain death. Jumping was the lesser of two evils.

## 2 Underlying dynamics of change

1 I use the word "pattern" several times in the text. This usually brings to mind an ordered, repetitive arrangement or sequence (as in a wallpaper pattern, for example). In contrast, the patterns I am referring to here are emergent, self-organizing and complex. As suggested by de Bono (1990, for example), we are only able to function effectively because our minds create and use such patterns. Without this pattern-making ability, we would have to learn each activity from scratch every time we wanted to perform it. The downside of this is that we become locked into our established, self-reinforcing patterns of thinking and behavior. And these inhibit our creativity and innovation, lead to clash and confrontation, and limit constructive dialogue. Seeing organizations as networks of conversations means that these similarly become locked into their own patterns. This is reflected, for example, in the language and symbolism that they use; the strategies they adopt; the (cultural) assumptions that shape their behavior and so on. The overt management philosophy that an organization displays (*as perceived and interpreted through everyday organizational conversations*) represents a major pattern that channels and constrains many derivative ones.

   Many of the patterns into which organizations become locked are paradoxical, in the sense that these lead inexorably to outcomes that run counter to common sense. The "Icarus Paradox" (Miller, 1990) and "Abilene Paradox" (Harvey, 1996) provide well-known examples of these. In one sense, *all* either–or choices create patterns that are paradoxical, especially where a decision is emotionally charged. The overt pattern that arises when a particular route is chosen is always mirrored by the pattern "left behind" with the discarded or unacknow-ledged option. This latter pattern will continue to affect the outcome, whether its characteristics are dealt with overtly or, more commonly, if they are left to fester in the shadow-side of the organization.

2  See de Bono (1971, for example) for a discussion of the self-organizing, patterning nature of the brain.

3  The n-step change models are those that offer a universally applicable "how to change the organization in 'n' easy steps" recipe. These are popular amongst consultants because they are easily routinized and can be readily replicated from organization to organization. They are also attractive to many managers because they appear to offer an easy path through the complexities of organizational life. Sadly, the char-acteristics that make them tempting to organizations – such as their simplicity, universality and step-by-step methodologies – also combine to limit their effectiveness.

4  Bate uses the phrase primarily to signify the socially constructed nature of organization (and culture), which is consistent with the *informal coalitions* view of organizational dynamics. However, *Thinking Cultur-ally* within the change-leadership agenda set out here focuses primarily on the ways in which the leader frames their role-modeling relationship with staff.

5  Some managers and consultants like to distinguish between manage-ment and leadership. I prefer to see these as complementary aspects of the same leadership role – its mission-making and meaning-making dimensions. From this perspective, the challenge is for leaders to engage with staff to deliver the mission-making tasks in ways that inspire, encourage and energize them to perform *extra*ordinarily well. This means helping them to gain a sense of meaning from their work that goes beyond the mechanistic completion of pre-defined activities. The mission-making "deliverables" of effectiveness, efficiency and align-ment depend on successful performance of the conventional leadership roles outlined earlier, and the rational assumptions that underpin them. In contrast, the meaning-making deliverable of attunement requires the leader to engage actively, and in an informed way, with the *a*-rational,

messy and shadow-side dynamics of the organization. This means using everyday conversations and interactions to facilitate joint sensemaking amongst staff and to build coalitions of support for organizationally beneficial objectives.

6 The nature and importance of organizational symbols are discussed in Chapter 4.

7 The point here is that managers are embedded within this process. Their everyday words and actions – including their silence and inaction – unavoidably impact upon the dynamics of organizational performance. This does not mean to say, of course, that leaders should not attempt to "stand back" from the fray and take a broader, more considered look at what's happening. It makes clear though that this view will inevitably be colored by their own socially constructed and self-interested perceptions of organizational reality. And also that their own behavior (including the act of observation) unavoidably affects the "scene" that they are observing.

## 3   Reframing communication

1 I experienced this process during an experiential workshop that Dannemiller ran on large-group change methodologies in the late 1990s.

2 Sensemaking is not a one-way process. It takes place *between* people in the to-and-fro of free-flowing conversation.

## 5   Acting politically

1 In NLP (Neuro-Linguistic Programming), this framework is referred to as Logical Levels.

## 6   Building coalitions

1 Any of the many texts available on NLP will provide further guidance on this. See also Charvet (1995).

2 The series of emotions that are identified here, and in subsequent phases of the "emotional journey," are informed by the work of Dr Elisabeth Kübler-Ross (e.g. Kübler-Ross and Kessler, 2005). She identified how patients and their relatives characteristically responded when told that they were terminally ill; and noted how these emotions changed

over time. The insights she gained have been widely adopted by the organizational-change community, since these are seen as indicative of the typical pattern of response that is likely to result from any negatively perceived change.

## 8 Providing vision

1 "More than 300 years ago, Oliver Cromwell put his trust in the '... plain russet-coated captain that knows what he fights for and loves what he knows.'" (Marquand, 1982: 13).

Argyris, C. (1992) *On Organizational Learning*. Blackwell.

Bate, P. (1994) *Strategies for Cultural Change*. Butterworth-Heinemann Limited.

Beer, M. and Nohria, N. (2000) *Breaking the Code of Change*. HBS Press.

Bell, D. (2002) *Ethical Ambition*. Bloomsbury Publishing.

Bellman, G. (1996) *Your Signature Path*. Berrett-Koehler.

Bennis, W. (1989) *On Becoming a Leader*. Century Business.

Bridges, W. (1995) *Managing Transitions*. Nicholas Brealey.

Charvet, S. R. (1995) *Words that Change Minds*. Kendall/Hunt.

Chowdhury, S. (2000) *Management 21C*. FT Prentice Hall.

Clancy, J. (1999) *The Invisible Powers*. Lexington Books.

Conner, D. (1993) *Managing at the Speed of Change*. Villard Books.

Culbert, S. (1996) *Mind-Set Management*. Oxford.

Deal, T. and Kennedy, A. (2000) *The New Corporate Cultures*. Texere.

de Bono, E. (1971) *Lateral Thinking for Management*. McGraw-Hill.

de Bono, E. (1978) *Opportunities*. Associated Business Programmes.

de Bono, E. (1982) *De Bono's Thinking Course*. BBC.

de Bono, E. (1990) *Lateral Thinking*. Penguin.

DeLuca, J. (1999) *Political Savvy*. EBG Publications.

Downs, A. (1997) *Beyond the Looking Glass*. AMACOM.

Drucker, P. (1968) *The Practice of Management*. Pan.

Drucker, P. (1970) *The Effective Executive*. Pan.

Drucker, P. (1972) *Technology, Management and Society*. Pan.

Eccles, R. and Nohria, N. (1992) *Beyond the Hype*. HBS Press.

Egan, G. (1993) *Adding Value*. Jossey-Bass.

Egan, G. (1994) *Working the Shadow Side*. Jossey-Bass.

Ellinor, L. and Gerard, G. (1998) *Dialogue*. Wiley.

Fairhurst, G. and Sarr, R. (1996) *The Art of Framing*. Jossey-Bass.

Fletcher, J. and Olwyler, K. (1997) *Paradoxical Thinking*. Berrett-Koehler.

Fonseca, J. (2001) *Complexity and Innovation in Organizations*. Routledge.

Gallwey, T. (2000) *The Inner Game of Work*. Orion Books.

Gladwell, M. (2000) *The Tipping Point*. Abacus.

Goffee, R. and Jones, G. (1998) *The Character of a Corporation*. Harper Collins.

Grant, D., Keenoy, T. and Oswick, C. (Ed.) (1998) *Discourse and Organization*. Sage.

Grint, K. (1997) *Fuzzy Management*. Oxford University Press.

Hamel, G. and Prahalad, C. (1994) *Competing for the Future*. HBS Press.

Handy, C. (1993) *Understanding Organizations* (4Ed.). Penguin.

Harrison, R. and Stokes, H. (1992) *Diagnosing Organizational Culture*. Jossey-Bass/Pfeiffer.

Harvey, J. (1996) *The Abilene Paradox*. Jossey-Bass.

Hatch, M. J. (1997) *Organization Theory*. Oxford University Press.

Holman, D. and Thorpe, R. (2003) *Management and Language*. Sage.

Holman, P. and Devane, T. (Eds) (1999) *The Change Handbook*. Berrett-Koehler.

Jackson, P. and McKergow, M. (2002) *The Solutions Focus*. Nicholas Brealey.

Janov, J. (1994) *The Inventive Organization*. Jossey-Bass.

Johnson, B. (1999) *Polarity Management*. HRD Press.

Kaplan, R. and Norton, D. (1996) *The Balanced Scorecard*. HBS Press.

Kohn, A. (1993) *Punished by Rewards*. Houghton Mifflin.

Kotter, J. (1995) *Leading Change*. HBS Press.

Kubler-Ross, E. and Kessler, D. (2005) *On Grief and Grieving*. Simon and Schuster.

Marquand, D. (1982) *Russet-Coated Captains – The Challenge of Social Democracy*. SDP.

Martin, J. (1992) *Cultures in Organizations*. Oxford University Press.

Miller, D. (1990) *The Icarus Paradox*. Harper Business.

Mintzberg, H. (1989) *Mintzberg on Management*. Free Press.

Morgan, G. (1998) *Images of Organization* (Executive Edition). Sage.

Nicholson, N. (2000) *Managing the Human Animal*. Texere.

Odiorne, G. (1975) *Management and the Activity Trap*. Heinemann.

Pascale, R. and Athos, A. (1982) *The Art of Japanese Management*. Penguin.

Peters, T. and Waterman, R. (1982) *In Search of Excellence*. Harper and Row.

Pfeffer, J. (1992) *Managing with Power*. HBS Press.

Quinn, R. (1988) *Beyond Rational Management*. Jossey-Bass.

Schein, E. (1970) *Organizational Psychology* (2Ed.). Prentice-Hall.

Schein, E. (1993) *Organizational Culture and Leadership*. Jossey-Bass.

Schutz, W. (1979) *Profound Simplicity*. Turnstone.

Seddon, J. (2003) *Freedom from Command and Control*. Vanguard Education.

Shah, I. (1993) *The Exploits of the Incomparable Mullah Nasrudin*. Octagon Press.

Simmons, A. (1998) *Territorial Games*. AMACOM.

Sjöstrand, S.-E. et al. (Eds) (2001) *Invisible Management*. Thomson Learning.

Stacey, R. (1996) *Strategic management and Organizational Dynamics* (2Ed.) Pitman.

Stacey, R. (2000) *Strategic Management and Organizational Dynamics* (3Ed.) FT Prentice Hall.

Stacey, R. (2001) *Complex Responsive Processes in Organizations*. Routledge.

Stacey, R. (2003) *Strategic management and Organizational Dynamics* (4Ed.) FT Prentice Hall.

Stewart, V. (1990) *The David Solution*. Gower.

Stone, B. (1997) *Confronting Company Politics*. MacMillan Press.

Stone, D., Patton, B. and Heen, S. (2000) *Difficult Conversations*. Penguin.

Streatfield, P. (2001) *The Paradox of Control in Organizations*. Routledge.

Watkins, J. and Mohr, B. (2001) *Appreciative Inquiry*. Jossey-Bass Pfeiffer.

Weick, K. (1995) *Sensemaking in Organizations*. Sage.

Wooldridge, I. *Daily Mail*, 29 October, 1998.

*Note*: Page numbers of tables and diagrams are shown in bold type. Cross-references are indicated in small capitals